Hell Is a Very Small Place

VOICES FROM SOLITARY CONFINEMENT

Edited by Jean Casella, James Ridgeway,
and Sarah Shourd

Preface by Sarah Shourd

Introduction by Jean Casella and James Ridgeway

Afterword by Juan E. Méndez

THE NEW PRESS

NEW YORK
LONDON

"Writing Out of Solitude" by Shaka Senghor is excerpted from an essay that originally appeared in *Fourth City: Essays from the Prison in America*, edited by Doran Larson (Lansing: Michigan State University Press, 2014).

Portions of "Dream House" by Herman Wallace originally appeared in *The House That Herman Built*, by Jackie Sumell and Herman Wallace (Akademie Schloss Solitude: 2006). Reprinted by permission of Jackie Sumell.

Excerpt from "September 1, 1939" by W.H. Auden from *Another Time*, published by Random House. Copyright © 1940 W.H. Auden, renewed by the Estate of W.H. Auden. Used by permission of Curtis Brown, Ltd.

"Psychiatric Effects of Solitary Confinement" by Stuart Grassian is excerpted from an article published in the *Washington University Journal of Law and Policy 22* (January 2006).

"How to Create Madness in Prison" by Terry Kupers is adapted from a chapter in *Humane Prisons*, edited by David Jones (Oxford: Radcliffe Publishing, 2006).

Requests for permission to reproduce selections from this book should be mailed to: Permissions Department, The New Press, 120 Wall Street, 31st floor, New York, NY 10005.

Published in the United States by The New Press, New York, 2016
Distributed by Perseus Distribution

ISBN 978-1-62097-137-6 (hc.)
ISBN 978-1-62097-138-3 (e-book)
CIP data is available

Book design and composition by Bookbright Media
This book was set in Bembo and Avenir

Printed in the United States of America

10 9 8 7 6 5 4 3 2

For those who find the courage to break the silence

For those too shattered to do so

And especially for Billy

Contents

Preface: A Human Forever

SARAH SHOURD

AT SOME POINT YOU'RE GOING TO SNAP. THIS MIGHT BE AFTER ONE week or one year, depending on how you're wired. At first the scream ripping through your throat is a welcome release. You ball up your fists and pound on your cell door, vomiting every expletive you can think of. You damn the guards to hell along with the system and every person who ever cursed your life. A guard yells at you to *shut the fuck up*. You tell him to *fuck himself* and scream louder, choking on your own snot and angry tears. After a while you collapse, curl up on the hard floor of your cell, and enjoy a few of the best hours of sleep you've had in a very long time.

When you open your eyes again your system is immediately flooded by the same instinctual rage. You begin pounding on the steel door of your cell, but this time when you scream no one shouts back. Hours later, when the lunch cart rumbles by you find you've been skipped. You start up again—your fists raw, your knuckles chaffed and bloody. When the guards do arrive they come with tear gas, batons drawn. They come to make you choke on your screams.

Days later you've appeared to calm down. *To settle in.* Yet the scream doesn't stop. You try not to hear it as you brush your teeth, take your meds, force yourself to do push-ups, or attempt to focus on reading a magazine. As long as you're stuck in this coffin that silent scream becomes the backdrop of every moment of your waking life. It could last a month, a year, a decade, or the rest of your life, yet no one will ever hear it but you.

I spent 410 days in solitary confinement while being held as a political hostage by the Iranian government from 2009 to 2010. Upon returning to the United States I discovered that this draconian practice, antithetical to any pretense of rehabilitation, is used as a routine control mechanism in U.S. prisons, far more extensively than in any country in the world—or any country in history.

In solitary confinement, a grey, limitless ocean stretches out in front of and behind you—an emptiness and loneliness so all-encompassing it threatens to erase you. Whether you're in that world a month, a year, or a decade, you experience the slow march of death. Day by day you lose your connection to everything outside the prison walls, everything you once knew and everything you once were.

People in solitary commit suicide at a much higher rate than any other incarcerated population. Some go visibly crazy, whipping their skin raw, eating their own feces, or cutting off their genitals. Others adjust, showing no outward signs of insanity. But what if the adaptation is itself proof of how effective this form of torture can be? What if the silent scream internalizes what's being done to you, making you identify with, or even *become*, your own torturer?

As you will read in this anthology, the conditions and so-called "privileges" allotted to people in solitary confinement in the United States vary from state to state, facility to facility, and prisoner to prisoner. Some cells have small windows. Prisoners can usually communicate with each other, sometimes by shouting through a wall, and sometimes by sending clandestine notes. Many are allowed books, television, pen and paper, photographs, and limited access to a phone, email, canteen, and no-contact visitation. Though some isolation units in U.S prisons are filthy and dark, harking back to medieval dungeons, others are hyper-modern, where cell doors are opened and closed remotely by guards you may never even see.

Over time you experience a "social death." You wake up every morning to the reality that if everyone you knew hasn't already forgotten you, chances are they eventually will. Even if you do get out, you fear the "you" who has walked through the world since the day you were born might be irrevocably damaged, changed, and unrecognizable. If days, weeks, months can pass without a single person on the outside seeing or (as far as you know) even thinking about you—*who's to say you even exist?*

While held hostage in an Iranian prison, it was six months before I was allowed a phone call. At times, I was reduced to an animal existence, pacing back and forth eight or ten hours at a time, eating with my hands, crouched by the food slot in my door listening for something, *anything*, to remind me that I was still in the world of the living. Sometimes I wouldn't eat or move for days; at other times, I screamed and beat at the walls of my cell until my knuckles bled.

The misery of prisoners confined to the "hole" or "box" in U.S. prisons is often compounded by physical abuse: being beaten and raped by sadistic guards, subjected to freezing-cold temperatures, fed rotten food, and left to die without medical care. This alone would be enough to break a human being, but I would argue that the cruelty—*the torture*—of solitary confinement targets a part of us perhaps more essential than even our physical bodies: the part that makes us human.

Years later, standing knee-deep in snow in a Burger King parking lot, I watch road-weary passengers exit the bus one by one. The sun rises over the quaint town of Elmira, New York, as feathery snowflakes fall on delicate church steeples, austere iron monuments, and row upon row of brick houses. I imagine plucking the picturesque landscape off a shelf in a souvenir shop and shaking it up like a snow globe as a blizzard swells inside.

Something sags inside me when my eyes fall on a brick castle-like fortress perched on a hill in the distance. Elmira Correctional Facility, built in 1876, keeps vigilant watch over the sleeping town below. I'm here to visit a man named Billy Blake, one of the authors featured in this book, who's been in isolation for twenty-eight years.

The day I was released from Evin Prison, the most notorious political prison in Iran, I was allowed to walk without a blindfold for the first time since I'd been brought there. The first thing I noticed was a snowcapped mountain towering right behind the building where I'd been held in arbitrary, incommunicado detention. I'd heard the thunder coming off that mountain many times, collected moths and stray leaves that floated over the high walls of the prison compound and even felt its snow and rain on my face—but for the 410 days I'd spent there in solitary confinement I had no way of knowing that mountain was even there, or that I was surrounded by so much beauty.

In Elmira I load myself back onto the bus alongside a dozen other passengers—wives, mothers, and sons who, like me, have been riding all night from New York City, folded into piles of clothes and blankets to ward off the freezing cold. We continue to the top of the hill and enter Elmira Correctional Facility's visitor center. After an hour of filling out forms, drinking lukewarm coffee out of Styrofoam cups, and waiting, I'm led to the Secure Housing Unit (SHU, a term prison administrators commonly use in lieu of its far more sinister cousin, "solitary confinement") then into a small room with three metal cages lined up, each no bigger than an elevator.

I recognize Billy Blake instantly as he's led into the room, his hands and ankles shackled, a huge smile on his face. He barely sits down and never stops talking during the three-hour visit, his arms often hitting the bars on both sides of the metal cage as he gesticulates. I pass him chips and candy from the vending machine and he tells me story after incredible story from his early, youthful adventures, his excitement and intelligence in this context equally engrossing and horrifying.

On my way to and from the vending machine, I chat with the guard on duty, who recognizes me from the news. He comments that Blake's been in solitary confinement since before he was even born and shakes his head. I ask him what he thinks of this practice—does it keep society safe?

"If I told you what I think," he says, "I'd be out of a job."

I think of the people of the town of Elmira below, many of them probably still sleeping in their lines of neat brick houses. I wonder what they would think if they could sit and talk with Billy Blake, if they knew his story, or even knew he existed. How many of them bother to question this place?

All I dreamt about in solitary was seeing my friends and family again, but in the early weeks after my return to the United States in 2010 I couldn't look into another person's eyes without physical discomfort. I had scars, but no one could see them. A touch on the shoulder made me flinch and tense up; I slowly began to reconstruct walls around me.

A year laer, I'd still wake up terrified in the middle of the night, feeling *so alone*. I'd lie still for hours, wishing I could disappear. It was in that darkness—that *quiet*—that I could no longer escape what felt like a hole carved out of my soul. Five years later the uncontrollable bursts of rage are gone, the depression and insomnia are mostly gone—but I still have to work hard sometimes to fill that emptiness, to restore my faith in humanity.

In 2011 I started talking to other survivors, like Billy Blake, and that helped. I asked them questions I couldn't ask anyone else. Did you see flashing lights? Did you hear things that weren't really there? Did you talk to your body parts? Name them? Did the dust motes floating through the air in your cell look like a universe to you? Did you find hope? I began recording those conversations, writing letters to more and more prisoners and traveling to visit them in facilities across the country. I collected these stories, many of which appear in this anthology, alongside stories collected over more than five years by my colleagues Jean Casella and James Ridgeway, co-editors of Solitary Watch. I wove them into a play, *Opening the Box.*

The writers and storytellers in this book have achieved a hard-earned, twisted kind of beauty. They've chosen to plunge head-first into the existential pain of their isolation and construct a bridge with one of the few tools they have left: words. In so doing they found a way to write themselves out of isolation, however briefly, by being honest—so honest that many, many times during the editing process I've had to look away.

In the ensuing years since my imprisonment, I've sometimes felt pressure to create an inspiring story out of the worst experience of my life. But it didn't make sense—not then and not now. Solitary confinement is the deep-end of our prison system; it's designed to crush, weaken, and destroy a human being. No matter how much I danced, sang, exercised, debated politics with ghosts, raged, composed poetry, and tried desperately to love myself, solitary confinement continued to hurt me.

Almost losing everything didn't inspire me to become an activist. If I managed to hang on to my values and even deepen them—that's *despite* what I went through not *because* of it. Even if I had done something terrible to put me in prison, or if there'd been a so-called reason to isolate me, it still would have been unnecessary cruelty. There are better ways to manage a prison than crushing inmates, treating them worse than animals, and driving them insane and then releasing them back into society. Locking a person in a box is a sick and perverse thing to do. It benefits no one—not even the governments who allow it. It's torture.

Being human is relational, plain and simple. We exist in relationship to one another, to ideas, and to the world. It's the most essential thing about us as a species: how we realize our potential as individuals and create meaningful lives.

Without that, we shrink. Day by day, we slowly die.

Introduction

JEAN CASELLA AND JAMES RIDGEWAY

IMAGINE A CORRIDOR FLANKED BY CLOSED, WINDOWLESS CELLS. EACH cell may be so small that, inside, you can extend your arms and touch both walls at the same time. The cell contains a bunk, perhaps a solid block of poured concrete, with a thin plastic mattress, a stainless steel toilet, maybe a small table and stool. A few personal possessions—books, paper and pencil, family photos—may be permitted, or they may not. The door to the cell is solid steel.

Imagine you're locked in the cell, and don't know if you'll ever get out. Three times a day, a food tray slides in through a slot in the door; when that happens, you may briefly see a hand, or exchange a few words with a guard. It is your only human contact for the day. A few times a week, you are allowed an hour of solitary exercise in a fenced or walled yard about the same size as your cell. The yard is empty and the walls block your view, but if you look straight up, you can catch a glimpse of sky.

Imagine that a third to a half of the people who live in this place suffer from serious mental illness. Some entered the cells with underlying psychiatric disabilities, while others have been driven mad by the isolation. Some of them scream in desperation all day and night.

Others cut themselves, or smear their cells with feces. A number manage to commit suicide in their cells.

You may remain in this place for months, years, or even decades. UN officials and a host of human rights, civil liberties, and religious groups have denounced as torture the conditions in which you live, and yet you remain where you are.

This place is located not in some distant authoritarian nation or secret black site abroad, but here on American soil. In fact, places like it exist in every state in the union, many within sight of cities and towns. On any given day in the United States, supermax prisons and solitary confinement units hold at least eighty thousand men, women, and children in conditions of extreme isolation and sensory deprivation, without work, rehabilitative programming, or meaningful human contact of any kind.

These individuals live out of sight and, to most, out of mind. The conditions of their confinement have, with a few exceptions, been condoned by the courts and ignored by elected officials. As a result, over the past three decades, the use of solitary confinement in U.S. prisons has grown into one of the nation's most pressing domestic human rights issues—yet until recently, it has also remained one of the most invisible.

Those who endure solitary have long been buried, nameless and voiceless, in the dark heart of the American criminal justice system. Their experiences, which form the core of this book, take place within the context of the history of solitary confinement in the United States, its present-day workings, and the costs borne by both the human beings who endure it and the society that countenances its continued use.

An American Invention

Accounts of people confined alone in dungeons or towers abound in stories dating back to ancient times. But solitary confinement as a self-conscious, organized, and widespread prison practice originated in the United States, and was born soon after the nation itself.

In 1790, the Walnut Street Jail, named for the Philadelphia street on which it stood, was expanded to hold the growing prison population of a burgeoning city. The expansion included the addition of a new kind of cellblock where sixteen individuals were held in single cells, built in such a way as to prevent communication with one another. The individuals held in these cells were not put to work, but were left alone in their cells to contemplate their crimes and, if all went as planned, become "penitent"—thus the name of the new block, Penitentiary House.[1]

This innovation took place under the influence of a group calling itself the Philadelphia Society for Alleviating the Miseries of Public Prisons, which met for the first time in 1787 at the home of Benjamin Franklin. The Society was populated largely by Quakers, who believed in punishment for crimes, but also believed that all human beings were capable of redemption.[2] They saw the new regime offered at Penitentiary House as a kinder and more effective alternative to more viscerally cruel punishments such as flogging, the public humiliations of the pillory and stocks, and the misery of filthy, violent, overcrowded jails.[3]

Michel Foucault argues that the desire to treat those convicted of criminal offenses more "humanely" was rooted not only in Enlightenment ideas but also in the shifting power structures brought on by political and industrial revolutions. Early prison reforms served a pragmatic as well as a moral purpose, replacing the arbitrary and violent punishments of sovereigns with a more controlled and technocratic system of punishments befitting public power.[4]

The new approach spread quickly. At Auburn Prison in upstate New York in 1821, eighty people were placed in solitary confinement in a new wing. Alexis de Tocqueville and Gustave de Beaumont, in their 1833 treatise on U.S. penitentiaries, described the result:

> In order to reform them, [the convicts] had been submitted to complete isolation; but this absolute solitude, if nothing interrupts it, is beyond the strength of man; it destroys the criminal without intermission and without pity; it does not reform, it kills.
>
> The unfortunates on whom this experiment was made fell into a state of depression so manifest that their keepers were struck with it; their lives seemed in danger if they remained longer in this situation; five of them had already succumbed during a single year; their moral state was not less alarming; one of them had become insane; another, in a fit of despair, had embraced the opportunity, when the keeper brought him something, to precipitate himself from his cell, running the almost certain chance of a mortal fall.[5]

Tocqueville and Beaumont also noted that "this system, fatal to the health of the criminals, was likewise inefficient in producing their reform" since upon release most reoffended within a short time. Within a few years, solitary confinement was abandoned at Auburn. Instead, men were put to work together during the days.

Nevertheless, in 1829, Pennsylvania opened Eastern State Penitentiary in Philadelphia, with an eventual capacity to hold two hundred fifty men and women in solitary confinement. Like today's solitary cells, those at Eastern State had feeding slots in their doors and individual exercise yards to limit contact with both guards and other incarcerated individuals. On the rare occasions when they were moved outside, the occupants of these cells wore masks. They were allowed no reading material but the Bible, and they worked silently in their cells on such tasks as shoemaking or weaving.[6]

One of the earliest—and still one of the most eloquent—critics of solitary confinement was Charles Dickens, who visited Eastern State Penitentiary on his tour of the United States in 1842. Dickens walked the prison's hallways, which he described as shrouded in an "awful" silence, and visited with several of the "penitents," whom he called men "buried alive" and cut off from "the living world." The writer concluded:

> I believe that very few men are capable of estimating the immense amount of torture and agony which this dreadful punishment, prolonged for years, inflicts upon the sufferers; and in guessing at it myself, and in reasoning from what I have seen written upon their faces, and what to my certain knowledge they feel within, I am only the more convinced that there is a depth of terrible endurance which none but the sufferers themselves can fathom, and which no man has a right to inflict upon his fellow creature.
>
> I hold this slow and daily tampering with the mysteries of the brain to be immeasurably worse than any torture of the body; and because its ghastly signs and tokens are not so palpable to the eye and sense of touch as scars upon the flesh; because its wounds are not upon the surface, and it extorts few cries that human ears can hear; therefore the more I denounce it, as a secret punishment which slumbering humanity is not roused up to stay.[7]

As the observations made by foreign visitors were increasingly validated over time,[8] what had come to be called the Pennsylvania System was all but entirely replaced by the Auburn System of communal hard labor. While most prisons maintained some version of "the hole," where individuals were placed for short-term punishment or separation, through the late nineteenth century and most of the twentieth, long-term isolation existed only in exceptional cases. The so-called Birdman of Alcatraz, Robert Stroud, was sentenced in 1916 to life in solitary only as a condition of the commutation of his death sentence for murdering a prison guard—and at Alcatraz he occupied a relatively roomy open-fronted cell, where he reportedly played checkers with guards through the bars.[9]

A Nation on Lockdown

The heir to Alcatraz was the U.S. Penitentiary in Marion, Illinois, which opened in 1963, the same year the notorious island prison was closed. Marion was built to hold "difficult to control" men in the federal prison system, and over the next decade it evolved into the "end of the line" prison for individuals deemed dangerous or disruptive. In 1973, H-Unit at Marion was officially designated the Long-Term Control Unit, with all those held in the unit subjected to around-the-clock solitary confinement and a "behavior modification" program. In the ensuing years, the federal Bureau of Prisons floated several proposals to turn the entire prison into a control unit.[10]

On October 22, 1983, in two separate incidents, two corrections officers at Marion were killed by men held in the Control Unit. Although the perpetrators were immediately identified, the entire prison was placed on lockdown—and essentially, never taken off—and the supermax prison was born.

While the Marion lockdown may have provided the model for modern-day solitary confinement on a broad scale, a number of factors, all of them closely linked to the rise of mass incarceration, provided the impetus. These included, first and foremost, a rapid growth in incarceration rates due to increased criminalization of behavior, lengthening sentences, and the widespread elimination or diminution of parole. The United States now incarcerates approximately one in one hundred adults, a rate that significantly outpaces Russia and China and dwarfs all European nations.[11]

During the same period, beginning in the late 1970s, prisons largely abandoned any notion of rehabilitation. Meanwhile, the United States was undergoing a massive shift toward the deinstitutionalization of people with mental illness. They were supposed to receive treatment and support in the community once they left psychiatric hospitals, but such services were grossly lacking.[12]

These developments led to extreme prison overcrowding, and with it, a rise in prison violence. Because they had abandoned faith in rehabilitation, prison administrators' only remaining strategy was to crack down harder, piling punishment upon punishment, and more extreme confinement on top of confinement.

Throughout the 1980s and 1990s, the idea of units or whole prisons designed for "total control" rapidly gained traction. In 1989, California opened Pelican Bay State Prison in the remote redwood forests.[13] The now notorious 1994 Crime Bill provided $9.7 billion in funding to build new prisons, and many states used their federal grants to build control units or entire supermax prisons.[14] Ten years later, through a period of decreasing crime rates, forty-four states and the federal government had constructed supermaxes housing approximately 25,000 people in extreme isolation.[15] In 1993, Dr. Craig Haney, an expert on the psychological effects of solitary confinement, wrote:

> Because of the technological spin that they put on institutional design and procedure, the new super-maximum security prisons are unique in the modern history of American corrections. These prisons represent the application of sophisticated, modern technology dedicated entirely to the task of social control, and they isolate, regulate, and surveil more effectively than anything that has preceded them.[16]

Nearly every prison and jail in the country also developed a solitary confinement unit of some kind. In the five-year period from 1995 to 2000 alone, the number of individuals held in solitary increased by 40 percent, and by 2005—the most recent year for which figures are available—a U.S. Bureau of Justice Statistics census of state and federal prisoners found more than 81,622 people held in "restricted housing."[17] The census figures do not include individuals in solitary confinement in juvenile facilities, immigrant detention centers, or local jails; if they did, the numbers would certainly be higher, likely will exceeding one hundred thousand.

Cruel and Usual

Solitary confinement is the practice of isolating people in closed cells for twenty-two to twenty-four hours a day, virtually free of human contact, for periods of time ranging from days to decades. Solitary confinement cells generally measure from six by nine to eight by ten feet. Some have bars, but more often they have solid metal doors. Many do not have windows. Meals generally come through slots in these doors, as do any communications with prison staff. There may be showers within the cells, or inhabitants may be taken, in shackles, to shower two or three times a week. They may also be escorted to a fenced or walled yard for an hour of exercise, usually only on weekdays, or they may be released into an area adjoining their cells through a remote-controlled door. Most, although not all, will be permitted to have books as well as legal papers, and to send and receive letters. Some may be allowed visits, usually through a Plexiglas barrier. A few may have radio or television.

Few prison systems use the term "solitary confinement" to describe this kind of incarceration, instead referring to prison "segregation." Most systems make a distinction between various reasons for solitary confinement. "Disciplinary segregation" or "punitive segregation" is time spent in solitary as punishment for violating prison rules, and usually lasts from several weeks to several years. "Administrative segregation" relies on a system of classification rather than actual behavior, and often constitutes a permanent placement, extending from years to decades. "Involuntary protective custody" is especially common among children in adult prisons, LGBTQ individuals, and others deemed at risk of victimization at the hands of other prisoners, who live in indefinite isolation despite having done nothing wrong.

Cells, tiers, and prisons designed for the purpose of isolation are known by a series of euphemisms that vary from state to state, including Special Housing Units, Security Housing Units, Special Management Units, Intensive Management Units, and Behavioral Management Units. To the people who inhabit them, they are the SHU (pronounced "shoe"), the Box, the Hole, the Bing, or the Block.

Far from a measure of last resort reserved for the "worst of the worst," as many proponents claim, solitary confinement has become a control strategy of first resort in most prisons and jails. Today, incarcerated people can be placed in complete isolation for months or years not only for violent acts but for possessing contraband—including excess quantities of pencils or postage stamps—testing positive for drug use, or using profanity. In New York, about 85 percent of the thirteen thousand terms in disciplinary segregation handed down each year are for nonviolent misbehavior.[18] The system is arbitrary, largely unmonitored, and ripe for abuse; individuals have been sent to solitary for filing complaints about their treatment or for reporting rape or brutality by guards.[19]

In California, for example, the California Code of Regulations, Title 15 Section 3315, outlines two dozen "Serious Rule Violations" that can result in placement in the SHU. These include "Possession of five dollars or more without authorization," "Tattooing or possession of tattoo paraphernalia," "Participation in a strike or work stoppage," and "Self mutilation or attempted suicide for the purpose of manipulation."[20]

About half of the people held in California SHUs may have committed no offense at all; instead, they are held in solitary because of the gang "validation" process, in which anyone deemed an active gang member is sent to an initial six-year term in the SHU, which can be extended to decades.[21] Gang validation can take place based in large part on anonymous accusations. Commonly, these anonymous charges come from validated individuals in the SHU, for whom the only hope for early release has been summarized as "parole, snitch, or die."[22] People have also been suspected of gang membership simply by possessing the book *The Art of War* or making reference to prison activist George Jackson.[23]

While reliable data on the use of solitary confinement according to race is scarce, sampling indicates that African Americans are even more overrepresented in solitary confinement than they are in the prison system in general.[24] Muslims charged with terrorism-related offenses, including vague "material support" charges, are likely to land in extreme solitary confinement both pretrial and post-conviction.[25] Others with radical political beliefs—especially racial minorities such as members of the Black Panther Party or the Black Liberation Army—are often classified as safety risks and placed in administrative segregation indefinitely.[26]

Over the past thirty years, in the wake of deinstitutionalization, prisons and jails have become the nation's largest inpatient psychiatric centers. The Treatment Advocacy Center estimated that in 2012, more than 350,000 people with serious mental illness were housed in prisons and jails, while a tenth as many—about 35,000—were in state mental hospitals.[27] Many enter prison on relatively minor charges, then rack up additional charges as they act out because of untreated illness, and end up spending a lifetime cycling in and out of jail. Solitary confinement cells, in particular, are now used to warehouse thousands of people with mental illness, as well as people with developmental disabilities, physical disabilities, and substance addictions.[28] Human Rights Watch estimated, based on available state data, that one-third to one-half of those held in isolation had some form of mental illness.[29]

Children under the age of eighteen are not excluded from solitary confinement. In fact, anecdotal evidence suggests that juveniles placed in adult prisons and jails are disproportionately likely to land in disciplinary segregation because of immature misbehavior, or to be held in involuntary protective custody. A 2012 report on youth solitary published by Human Rights Watch and the American Civil Liberties Union estimated that "in 2011, more than 95,000 youth were held in prisons and jails. A significant number of these facilities use solitary confinement—for days, weeks, months, or even years—to punish, protect, house, or treat some of the young people who are held there."[30]

People who are LGBTQ also find themselves isolated "for their own protection." Yet they find anything but safety while in solitary. One investigation of transgender women held in men's prisons in New York State found that most had experienced prolonged solitary confinement, and many had been subjected to rape and other sexual abuse by prison staff while in isolation.[31]

Even migrants held in detention in Immigration and Customs Enforcement (ICE) facilities, whose only alleged crime is crossing the border, are frequently held in solitary confinement. With even less oversight than prisons and jails in general, ICE facilities, many of which are privately run, have placed individuals in solitary for reasons ranging from "failing to speak English when able," watching the Spanish channel on television, trying to translate for another detainee, complaining about the quality of the drinking water, having an extra blanket, and playing cards instead of attending church services, according to a 2012 report.[32]

A Sentence Within a Sentence

Even within the purely punitive model of incarceration, people are supposed to be sent to prison *as* punishment, not *for* punishment.

According to the law, deprivation of freedom alone is supposed to be the price society exacts for crimes committed. The additional suffering that happens inside prison—whether it is violence and brutality, rape, or solitary confinement—can therefore be seen as extrajudicial punishment. Solitary, in particular, operates as a "second sentence," or a "sentence within a sentence," doled out without benefit of due process.

The tens of thousands of Americans in solitary confinement have been sent there not by judges or juries, who by design have little to say about what happens to people once they pass through the prison gates. Instead, they are condemned to isolation based on a "classification" that is handed down by prison officials. Or they are sent to solitary following charges of misconduct that are levied, adjudicated, and enforced by prison officials.

Many prison systems have a hearing process, but such hearings are seldom more than perfunctory. Prison officials serve as prosecutors, judges, and juries, and the incarcerated are rarely permitted representation by defense attorneys. Unsurprisingly, in most prison systems, they are nearly always found guilty.[33]

Few people in American society have as much unrestrained control over the fates of other people as do prison wardens. The United States has virtually none of the checks and balances found in most European societies—no prison ombudsperson, no inspector of the prisons, no independent monitoring bodies made up of ordinary citizens with access to prisons.[34] Incarcerated people themselves have been disempowered by the Prison Litigation Reform Act (PLRA), a 1996 law limiting their ability to sue in federal courts. To mount a successful lawsuit against prison conditions, individuals must first exhaust the prison's internal grievance procedures—often at risk of retaliation by prison guards—and then must show that they suffered significant "physical injury." Despite evidence of the extensive damage it causes, long-term solitary confinement has been deemed not to meet the physical injury requirement under the PLRA.[35]

The Effects of Solitary Confinement

The complete isolation and sensory deprivation of solitary confinement has been shown to cause a panoply of psychiatric symptoms, detailed in a briefing paper from the American Civil Liberties Union's National Prison Project:

Research shows that some of the clinical impacts of isolation can be similar to those of physical torture. People subjected to solitary confinement exhibit a variety of negative physiological and psychological reactions, including hypersensitivity to stimuli; perceptual distortions and hallucinations; increased anxiety and nervousness; revenge fantasies, rage, and irrational anger; fears of persecution; lack of impulse control; severe and chronic depression; appetite loss and weight loss; heart palpitations; withdrawal; blunting of affect and apathy; talking to oneself; headaches; problems sleeping; confusing thought processes; nightmares; dizziness; self-mutilation; and lower levels of brain function, including a decline in EEG activity after only seven days in solitary confinement.[36]

The body of evidence showing that these effects are ubiquitous and lasting—even permanent—is constantly growing.[37] And it is increasingly bolstered by studies of the neuroscience of isolation's effects. What solitary confinement does to the brain was the subject of a panel at the 2014 annual meeting of the American Association for the Advancement of Science, where University of Michigan neuroscientist Huda Akil noted that the effects of lack of physical activity, of interaction with other human beings and with the natural world, of visual stimulation, and of touch have all been studied in both humans and other animals. "Each one," she said, "is by itself sufficient to change the brain, and change it dramatically, depending on whether it lasts briefly or is extended. And by extended I mean days, not decades.[38]

In dire cases, solitary confinement leads to extremes of self-mutilation, and the rates of suicide in solitary far exceed anything found in general prison populations. One study of the New York City jail population found incidences of self-harm were seven times higher among individuals held in solitary confinement. While 7 percent of the jail population was held in isolation, 53 percent of all acts of self-harm took place there, ranging from cutting to banging heads against walls to suicide attempts.[39] Others held in solitary have gone as far as self-amputations of fingers and testicles, even self-blinding.[40] Likewise, about 50 percent of incarcerated people who take their own lives do so while in isolation. The challenges of suicide in a bare cell have driven some to such acts as jumping headfirst off their bunks and biting through the veins in their wrists.[41]

Considering the damage it wreaks upon body and soul, it is hardly surprising that solitary confinement is associated with higher recidivism rates, particularly when people are released back into the community directly from solitary confinement.[42] Several of the writers included in this book describe their difficulties reintegrating into society—being in crowded places, relating to other people, or simply being touched. In several instances, release directly from solitary has been linked to extreme violence, as in the case of Evan Ebel, who killed two people in Colorado—including, with tragic irony, Corrections Director Tom Clements, who had worked to reduce the use of isolation in the state's prisons.[43]

In addition, despite claims to the contrary, solitary confinement does not reduce levels of violence in prison. A study published in 2015 found that short-term disciplinary segregation had no measurable effect on violent behavior in Texas prisons.[44] Other evidence suggests that violence levels actually drop significantly with decreases in the use of solitary confinement.[45] One study found that far more assaults on guards took place in isolation units than in the general prison population. A veteran Oregon corrections officer told a commission studying the use of prison segregation that solitary "creates an 'us versus them' mentality on both sides," while a Mississippi warden testified: "The environment . . . actually increases the levels of hostility and anger among inmates and staff alike."[46]

In addition to its public safety costs, solitary confinement carries a high price tag for taxpayers. Nationally, it has been estimated that the average cost of a year in a supermax prison is $75,000—two to three times the cost of housing someone in general population.[47] According to one calculation, in 2010–11 California spent at least $175 million in additional costs per year to house some twelve thousand individuals in isolation.[48] Solitary confinement has also been associated with significantly higher construction costs per cell. For example, Wisconsin's Boscobel supermax facility was built to house five hundred people at a cost of $47.5 million in 1990 dollars, or more than $95,000 per bed.[49]

More difficult to calculate are the human costs not only to those who suffer in solitary, but to the rest of us in free society. "What does it mean," Lisa Guenther asks in this volume, "to share the world with millions of people in cages?" How does it affect our humanity to dehumanize others to such an extent that we allow them to live in conditions unfit for any animal—and do so in the name of our own safety and well-being?

Stopping Solitary

Until quite recently, solitary confinement was the most pressing domestic human rights crisis that most Americans had never heard of. In the past several years, however, the issue has entered the consciousness of a large cross-section of Americans for the first time.

In 2008, advocates from across the country gathered to address solitary confinement at a conference hosted by the American Friends Service Committee. In 2009, the *New Yorker* published a seminal article on solitary, "Hellhole" by Atul Gawande,[50] who joined a small group of dedicated journalists in pioneering coverage of the subject.[51] Solitary Watch, which we founded the same year, had the aim of bringing the issue "out of the shadows and into the light of the public square."[52]

In 2010, the Vera Institute of Justice began its Segregation Reduction Project, working with states to decrease the numbers of people they held in solitary. The American Civil Liberties Union's National Prison Project also convened a meeting of its state affiliates and other legal advocates, and in 2011 it launched its "Stop Solitary" campaign involving education, litigation, and legislation. The National Religious Campaign Against Torture (NRCAT) likewise launched a new initiative focused on torture in U.S. prisons and jails, organizing faith-based groups across the country.

On July 1, 2011, men held in solitary confinement in Pelican Bay State Prison—some for as long as two or three decades—went on a hunger strike to protest their conditions. It was to be the first such hunger strike, with the third, held in 2013, drawing some thirty thousand participants in California prisons at its height, and lasting two months.[53] A class-action lawsuit, mounted by the Center for Constitutional Rights on behalf of men at Pelican Bay, followed and eventually led to a settlement that would release nearly two thousand from solitary.[54]

In August 2011, Juan E. Méndez, the United Nations Special Rapporteur on Torture and Other Cruel, Inhuman or Degrading Treatment or Punishment, produced a comprehensive report on the use of solitary confinement and made a series of strong recommendations that, if effected, would end virtually all prolonged solitary around the globe—"prolonged" defined as lasting beyond fifteen days.[55] (See the afterword to this book for more detail.) Méndez became a dedicated, high-profile opponent of the use of prison isolation in the United States. He made repeated requests to the U.S. government to conduct fact-finding visits to American state and federal supermax prisons, all of which were denied or ignored.

In 2012, the Senate Judiciary Subcommittee on the Constitution, Civil Rights, and Human Rights held the first-ever congressional hearing on "Reassessing Solitary Confinement: The Human Rights, Fiscal, and Public Safety Consequences," which drew written testimony from close to one hundred advocacy groups and individuals[56] and led to an internal audit of the Federal Bureau of Prisons' use of "segregated housing."[57]

By 2015, dozens of pieces of legislation had been introduced placing new limits on the use of solitary confinement and a few had been passed. Several states had instituted policy reforms leading to reductions in the numbers of individuals held in solitary confinement, particularly children and people with mental illness.[58] Movements to end solitary confinement have sprung up in many states, and personages no less than Pope Francis and Supreme Court Justice Anthony Kennedy have voiced their concerns about the practice.[59]

In July 2015, in a wide-ranging speech on criminal justice reform, President Barack Obama announced that he had directed Attorney General Loretta Lynch to "start a review of the overuse of solitary confinement across American prisons." The president continued, "Social science shows that an environment like that is often more likely to make inmates more alienated, more hostile, potentially more violent. Do we really think it makes sense to lock so many people alone in tiny cells for 23 hours a day for months, sometime for years at a time? That is not going to make us safer."

But for all this activity, the numbers of people in solitary do not appear to have dwindled by more than a few thousand, out of tens of thousands. And reforms that remove some individuals from solitary, distinguishing between those who "belong" in isolation and those who do not, risk driving some people deeper into the hole.[60]

Opponents of solitary also contend with the fact that data on the use of solitary confinement is thin. Supermax prisons and solitary units themselves are virtual domestic black sites, resolutely off limits to the public and the press. The only fully realized reports of what goes on in these places are provided by the people who inhabit them, or who have survived time in solitary. Yet theirs are often the last voices to be listened to, on the premise that people in prison cannot be trusted and their stories cannot be believed.

These are the voices that make up this book. They are not meant to serve as an exhaustive or even representative cross-section of people in solitary confinement. In fact, they could never be more than a partial sampling because a large number of people in solitary are not literate, while others suffer from mental illness so severe that it impedes their ability to communicate. These are just a few among the many voices that managed to reach out from a dark and closely guarded world. For those who have left their solitary cells behind and now live in the free world, the process of remembering and recording their experiences for this book was a painful and therefore courageous one. For those who remain buried alive, it was more courageous still because by allowing themselves to be published they risk retaliation in prison. They have taken this risk so that you, their readers, may bear witness to what Charles Dickens called their "terrible endurance," and in the hope that you too will denounce this "secret punishment" that none but those who suffer it can fathom.

---

1. Eastern State Penitentiary website, Timeline: http://www.easternstate.org/learn/timeline.

2. Kaelyn E. Considine, "'The Tragedy of the Penitentiary': The Philadelphia Society for Alleviating the Miseries of Public Prisons and the Formation of the Eastern State Penitentiary," *Concept* 32 (2009), 1–14: http://concept.journals.villanova.edu/article/viewFile/302/265.

3. On the birth of the prison reform movement, see Adam J. Hirsch, *The Rise of the Penitentiary: Prisons and Punishment in Early America* (New Haven, CT: Yale University Press, 1992) and Caleb Smith, *The Prison and the American Imagination* (New Haven, CT: Yale University Press, 2009).

4. Michel Foucault, *Discipline and Punish: The Birth of the Prison* (New York: Random House), 73–103.

5. Gustave de Beaumont and Alexis de Tocqueville, *On the Penitentiary System in the United States and Its Application in France* (1833). Quoted in Thomas Russell, American Legal History: http://www.houseofrussell.com/legalhistory/alh/docs/penitentiary.html.

6. Eastern State Penitentiary website, Timeline and History: General Overview: http://www.easternstate.org/learn/research-library/history.

7. Charles Dickens, *American Notes for General Circulation* (1842), quoted in Mary Hawthorne, "Dept. of Amplification: Charles Dickens on Solitary Confinement," *The New Yorker* online, May 29, 2009: http://www.newyorker.com/books/page-turner/dept-of-amplification-charles-dickens-on-solitary-confinement.

8. Even the U.S. Supreme Court noted the cruelty and inefficacy of solitary confinement in *In Re Medley* (1890), discussed in the "Perspectives" section of this volume by Stuart Grassian and Laura Rovner.

9. *Alcatraz History* website, Birdman of Alcatraz: http://www.alcatrazhistory.com/stroud.htm.

10. The Committee to End the Marion Lockdown, "From Alcatraz to Marion to Florence: Control Unit Prisons in the United States" (1992): http://people.umass.edu/~kastor/ceml_articles/cu_in_us.html. For more on Marion and the birth of supermax prisons, see Stephen C. Richards, *The Marion Experiment: Long-Term Solitary Confinement and the Supermax Movement* (Carbondale: Southern Illinois University Press, 2015) and Nancy Kurshan, *Out of Control: A Fifteen-Year Battle against Control Unit Prisons* (Berkeley, CA: Freedom Archives, 2013).

11. Prison Policy Institute, States of Incarceration, 2014: http://www.prisonpolicy.org/global/.

12. Deanna Pan, TIMELINE: Deinstitutionalization and Its Consequences, *Mother Jones* online, April 29, 2013: http://www.motherjones.com/politics/2013/04/timeline-mental-health-america.

13. For more of the development of and reasoning behind supermax prisons and control units, see Lorna Rhodes, *Total Confinement: Madness and Reason in the Maximum Security Prison* (Berkeley: University of California Press, 2004) and Sharon Shalev, *Supermax: Controlling Risk Through Solitary Confinement* (Cullompton, Devon, UK: Willan Publishing, 2009).

14. Department of Justice, Fact Sheet, Violent Crime Control and Law Enforcement Act of 1994, October 24, 1994: https://www.ncjrs.gov/txtfiles/billfs.txt.

15. Daniel P. Mears, *Evaluating the Effectiveness of Supermax Prisons*, Urban Institute Justice Policy Center Research Report, March 2006: http://webarchive.urban.org/UploadedPDF/411326_supermax_prisons.pdf.

16. Craig Haney, "'Infamous Punishment': The Psychological Consequences of Solitary Confinement," ACLU *National Prison Project Journal* 8:2 (Spring 1993), 3: http://www.probono.net/prisoners/stopsol-media/424927.Infamous_Punishment_The_Psychological_Consequences_of_Solitary_Confinement.

17. Cited in Commission on Safety and Abuse in America's Prisons, *Confronting Confinement* (New York: Vera Institute of Justice, 2006), 52–56: http://www.vera.org/sites/default/files/resources/downloads/Confronting_Confinement.pdf.

18. Scarlet Kim, Taylor Pendergrass, and Helen Zelon, *Boxed In: The True Cost of Extreme Isolation in New York's Prison*, New York Civil Liberties Union, 2012: http://www.nyclu.org/files/publications/nyclu_boxedin_FINAL.pdf.

19. See Jean Casella and James Ridgeway, "Woman Prisoner Sent to Solitary for Reporting Rape by Guard," Solitary Watch, May 3, 2010: http://solitarywatch.com/2010/05/03/woman-prisoner-sent-to-solitary-for-reporting-rape-by-guard/ and American Civil Liberties Union, "Worse than Second Class: Solitary Confinement of Women in the United States," April 2014: https://www.aclu.org/sites/default/files/assets/worse_than_second-class.pdf.

20. State of California, California Code of Regulations, Title 15: http://www
.cdcr.ca.gov/Regulations/Adult_Operations/docs/Title15-2015.pdf.

21. For more on California's SHUs, see Shane Bauer, "No Way Out," *Mother Jones* online, November/December 2012: http://www.motherjones.com/special-reports/2012/10/solitary-confinement-shane-bauer.

22. Keramet Reiter, "Parole, Snitch, or Die: California's Supermax Prisons & Prisoners, 1987–2007," ISSC Fellows Working Papers, Institute for the Study of Social Change, UC Berkeley, 2010: http://www.probono.net/prisoners/stopsol-reports/416661.Parole_Snitch_or_Die_Californias_Supermax_Prisons_Prisoners_19872007.

23. Testimony of Charles Carbone, California Assembly Public Safety Committee hearing on Security Housing Units, August 23, 2011: http://www
.whatthefolly.com/2011/08/30/transcript-charles-carbones-testimony-on-the
-harmful-impacts-of-solitary-confinement-practices-at-california%E2%80%99s
-secure-housing-units-shu-prison-facilities/.

24. See Margo Schlanger, "Prison Segregation: Symposium Introduction and Preliminary Data on Racial Disparities," *Michigan Journal of Race & Law* 241 (2013): http://papers.ssrn.com/sol3/papers.cfm?abstract_id=2237979. Also see Bonnie Kerness and Jamie Bissonette Lewey, "Race and the Politics of Isolation in U.S. Prisons," *Atlantic Journal of Communication* 22:1: http://dx.doi.org/10.1080/15456870.2014.860146.

25. See Laura L. Rovner and Jeanne Theoharis, "Preferring Order to Justice," *American University Law Review* 61 (2012): http://papers.ssrn.com/sol3/papers.cfm?abstract_id=2079776 and Human Rights Watch and Columbia Law School Human Rights Institute, *Illusion of Justice Human Rights Abuses in US Terrorism Prosecutions*, July 2014: http://web.law.columbia.edu/sites/default/files/microsites/human-rights-institute/files/final_report_-_illusion_of_justice.pdf.

26. Such is the case with the Angola 3's Herman Wallace and Albert Woodfox. See Wallace's piece in this volume, and James Ridgeway and Jean Casella, "Torturous Milestone: 40 Years in Solitary," *Mother Jones* online, April 17, 2012: http://www.motherjones.com/politics/2012/04/angola-prison-3-herman
-wallace-albert-woodfox-40-years-solitary-confinement.

27. E. Fuller Torrey et al., *The Treatment of Persons with Mental Illness in Prisons and Jails: A State Survey*, Treatment Advocacy Center and National Sheriffs' Association, April 8, 2014: http://tacreports.org/storage/documents/treatment
-behind-bars/treatment-behind-bars.pdf.

28. See, for example, James Ridgeway, "The Secret World of Deaf Prisoners," The Crime Report, September 29, 2009: http://www.thecrimereport.org/news/inside-criminal-justice/the-secret-world-of-deaf-prisoners, and "The Silent Treatment," *Mother Jones* online, March/April 2012: http://www.motherjones.com/politics/2011/12/deaf-prisoners-felix-garcia.

29. Human Rights Watch, *Ill-Equipped: U.S. Prisons and Offenders with Mental Illness,* October 23, 2003: http://www.hrw.org/reports/2003/10/21/ill
-equipped.

30. Ian Kysel, *Growing Up Locked Down: Youth in Solitary Confinement in Jails and Prisons Across the United States*, ACLU and Human Rights Watch, October 2012: https://www.aclu.org/files/assets/us1012webwcover.pdf.

31. Aviva Stahl, "Transgender Women in New York State Prisons Face Solitary Confinement and Sexual Assault," Solitary Watch, August 7, 2014: http://solitarywatch.com/2014/08/07/transgender-women-in-new-york-state-prisons-face-solitary-confinement-and-sexual-assault/.

32. National Immigrant Justice Center and Physicians for Human Rights, *Invisible in Isolation: The Use of Segregation and Solitary Confinement in Immigration Detention*, September 2012: http://www.immigrantjustice.org/sites/immigrantjustice.org/files/Invisible%20in%20Isolation-The%20Use%20of%20Segregation%20and%20Solitary%20Confinement%20in%20Immigration%20Detention.September%202012_3.pdf.

33. See Jean Casella and James Ridgeway, "Due Process Rights Routinely Suppressed in California Prisons," Solitary Watch, August 3, 2010: http://solitarywatch.com/2010/08/03/inmates-due-process-rights-routinely-suppressed-in-california-prisons/. Also see *Boxed In*, note 18.

34. See, for example, James Ridgeway and Jean Casella, "Oversight in British Prisons: Lessons for the U.S.?" The Crime Report, August 12, 2013: http://www.thecrimereport.org/news/inside-criminal-justice/2013-08-oversight-in-british-prisons-lessons-for-the-us.

35. Human Rights Watch, *No Equal Justice: The Prison Litigation Reform Act in the United States*, June 16, 2009: http://www.hrw.org/reports/2009/06/15/no-equal-justice.

36. American Civil Liberties Union, *The Dangerous Overuse of Solitary Confinement in the United States* (ACLU Briefing Paper), August 2014: https://www.aclu.org/sites/default/files/field_document/2014.10.30.stop_solitary_briefing_paper_updated_august_2014.pdf.

37. See American Civil Liberties Union Stop Solitary Project, Solitary Confinement: Resource Materials—Mental Health Effects of Extreme Isolation: https://www.aclu.org/files/assets/Solitary%20Confinement%20Resource%20Materials%2012%2017%2013.pdf#page=4. Also see Sharon Shalev, *A Sourcebook on Solitary Confinement*, Chapter 2 (London: Mannheim Centre for Criminology, London School of Economics, 2008): http://solitaryconfinement.org/uploads/sourcebook_02.pdf.

38. Maclyn Willigan, "What Solitary Confinement Does to the Human Brain," Solitary Watch, August 4, 2014: http://solitarywatch.com/2014/08/04/what-solitary-confinement-does-to-the-human-brain/. Also see Shruti Ravindran, "Twilight in the Box," Aeon, February 27, 2014: http://aeon.co/magazine/society/what-solitary-confinement-does-to-the-brain/.

39. Fatos Kaba et al., "Solitary Confinement and Risk of Self-Harm among Jail Inmates," *American Journal of Public Health* 104:3 (2014): http://ajph.aphapublications.org/doi/pdf/10.2105/AJPH.2013.301742.

40. Susan Greene, "The Gray Box," The Ochberg Society, January 24, 2012: http://www.ochbergsociety.org/magazine/2012/01/the-gray-box-an-original -investigation/, and Testimony of Anthony Graves before the Senate Judiciary Subcommittee on the Constitution, Civil Rights and Human Rights, Hearing on "Reassessing Solitary Confinement: The Human Rights, Fiscal, and Public Safety Consequences," June 19, 2012: http://www.judiciary.senate.gov/imo/ media/doc/CHRG-112shrg87630.pdf.

41. Allegra Helena, "Momentum Building against Juvenile Solitary Confinement," ACLU of Montana, October 12, 2012: http://aclumontana.org/ momentum-building-against-juvenile-solitary-confinement/.

42. Commission on Safety and Abuse in America's Prisons, *Confronting Confinement* (New York: Vera Institute of Justice, 2006), 55: http://www.vera.org/ sites/default/files/resources/downloads/Confronting_Confinement.pdf.

43. Susan Greene, "CO Prison Officials Acknowledge Chief's Murder Tied to Solitary Confinement Policies," *Colorado Independent*, July 8, 2013: http://www .coloradoindependent.com/128438/co-prison-officials-acknowledge-chiefs -murder-tied-to-solitary-confinement-policies.

44. Robert G. Morris, "Exploring the Effect of Exposure to Short-Term Solitary Confinement among Violent Prison Inmates," *Journal of Quantitative Criminology*, January 24, 2015: http://link.springer.com/article/10.1007/s10940-015 -9250-0#page-1.

45. See, for example, Testimony of Christopher Epps, Mississippi Commissioner of Corrections, before the Senate Judiciary Subcommittee on the Constitution, Civil Rights, and Human Rights, Hearing on "Reassessing Solitary Confinement: The Human Rights, Fiscal, and Public Safety Consequences," June 19, 2012: http://www.judiciary.senate.gov/imo/media/doc/12 -6-19EppsTestimony.pdf.

46. Commission on Safety and Abuse in America's Prisons, *Confronting Confinement* (New York: Vera Institute of Justice, 2006), 54: http://www.vera.org/ sites/default/files/resources/downloads/Confronting_Confinement.pdf.

47. Daniel P. Mears, *Evaluating the Effectiveness of Supermax Prisons*, Urban Institute Justice Policy Center Research Report, March 2006: http://webarchive .urban.org/UploadedPDF/411326_supermax_prisons.pdf.

48. Sal Rodriguez, *Fact Sheet: The High Cost of Solitary Confinement*, Solitary Watch, June 2011.

49. Jeffrey Ian Ross, "Is the End in Sight for Supermax?" *Forbes*, April 19, 2006: http://www.forbes.com/2006/04/15/prison-supermax-ross_cx_jr_06slate _0418super.html.

50. Atul Gawande, "Hellhole," *The New Yorker*, March 30, 2009: http://www .newyorker.com/magazine/2009/03/30/hellhole.

51. They include Susan Greene and Alan Prendergast in Colorado, Lance Tapley in Maine, George Pawlaczyk and Beth Hundsdorfer in Illinois, and Mary Beth Pfeiffer in New York. See James Ridgeway, "Fortresses of Solitude,"

Columbia Journalism Review, March/April 2013: http://www.cjr.org/cover
_story/fortresses_of_solitude.php.

52. "About Solitary Watch": http://solitarywatch.com/about/.

53. See "The California Hunger Strike Explained," *Mother Jones* online, August 27, 2013: http://www.motherjones.com/politics/2013/08/50-days-califor
nia-prisons-hunger-strike-explainer.

54. Victoria Law, "Two Years After Hunger Strike, California Settlement May Release 2,000 Prisoners From Solitary," *Truthout*, September 2, 2015: http://www.truth-out.org/news/item/32612-two-years-after-hunger-strike
-california-settlement-may-release-2000-prisoners-from-solitary.

55. Juan E. Méndez, *Interim Report of the Special Rapporteur of the Human Rights Council on Torture and Other Cruel, Inhuman or Degrading Treatment or Punishment*, August 5, 2011: http://solitaryconfinement.org/uploads/
SpecRapTortureAug2011.pdf. The report was presented to the UN General Assembly on October 18, 2011: http://www.un.org/apps/news/story
.asp?NewsID=40097#.UdsQoT5gaBg.

56. Document Serial No. J–112–80, U.S. Washington: Government Printing Office, 2012: http://www.judiciary.senate.gov/imo/media/doc/CHRG
-112shrg87630.pdf.

57. See Jean Casella and James Ridgeway, "Audit of Solitary Confinement in Federal Prisons: An Inside Job Reaches Foregone Conclusions," Solitary Watch, March 2, 2015: http://solitarywatch.com/2015/03/02/audit-of-solitary
-confinement-in-federal-prisons-an-inside-job-reaches-foregone-conclusions/.

58. Eli Hager and Gerald Rich, "Shifting Away from Solitary," The Marshall Project, December 23, 2014: https://www.themarshallproject.org/2014/12/23/
shifting-away-from-solitary.

59. See Samuel Weiss and Amy Fettig, "Supreme Court Justice Kennedy Denounces 'Human Toll' of Solitary Confinement and Invites Constitutional Challenge," *Solitary Watch*, June 23, 2015: http://solitarywatch.com/2015/06/23/
supreme-court-justice-kennedy-denounces-human-toll-of-solitary
-confinement-and-invites-constitutional-challenge/ and Jean Casella, "Pope Francis Denounces Solitary Confinement, Calls for Prison Conditions That 'Respect Human Dignity,'" *Solitary Watch*, October 26, 2014: http://solitarywatch
.com/2014/10/26/pope-francis-denounces-solitary-confinement-calls-for
-prison-conditions-that-respect-human-dignity/.

60. See Jean Casella, "Way Down in the Hole," Solitary Watch, Counterpunch, March 6, 2014: http://www.counterpunch.org/2014/03/06/way-down-in-the
-hole/.

Part I

VOICES FROM SOLITARY CONFINEMENT

ENDURING

A Sentence Worse than Death

WILLIAM BLAKE

William Blake is in his twenty-ninth year of solitary confinement, currently being served in the Special Housing Unit (SHU) at New York's Great Meadow Correctional Facility. Born and raised in upstate New York, he spent much of his youth in juvenile jails. In 1987, while in county court on a drug charge, Blake, then twenty-three, grabbed a gun from a sheriff's deputy and, in a thwarted attempt to escape, murdered one deputy and wounded another. He is now fifty-two years old, and is serving a sentence of seventy-seven years to life. Blake is one of the few people in New York held in "administrative" rather than "disciplinary" segregation—meaning he is considered a permanent risk to prison safety and is in isolation indefinitely, despite periodic pro forma reviews of his status.

The following essay earned Blake an honorable mention in the Yale Law Journal's *Prison Writing Contest. When published on the Solitary Watch website in 2013, the piece went viral worldwide—garnering more than half a million hits on its home site alone as well as being reprinted by numerous other publications and translated into several languages. Blake, who says that reading and writing are what sustain him, began receiving letters from all over the world. In December 2014, Blake was moved from one SHU to another; much of his correspondence was not permitted to follow him, nor were any of the fourteen hundred handwritten pages of the novel he was writing.*

"YOU DESERVE AN ETERNITY IN HELL," ONONDAGA COUNTY SUPREME Court judge Kevin Mulroy told me from his bench as I stood before him for sentencing on July 10, 1987. Apparently he had the idea that God was not the only one qualified to make such judgment calls.

Judge Mulroy wanted to "pump six bucks' worth of electricity into [my] body," he also said, although I suspect that it wouldn't have taken six cents' worth to get me good and dead. He must have wanted to reduce me and The Chair to a pile of ashes. My "friend" Governor Mario Cuomo wouldn't allow him to do that, though, the judge went on, bemoaning New York State's lack of a death statute due to the then-governor's repeated vetoes of death penalty bills that had been approved by the state legislature. Governor Cuomo's publicly expressed dudgeon over being called a friend of mine by Judge Mulroy was understandable, given the crimes that I had just been convicted of committing. I didn't care much for him either, truth be told. He built too many new prisons in my opinion, and cut academic and vocational programs in the prisons already standing.

I know that Judge Mulroy was not nearly alone in wanting to see me executed for the crime I committed when I shot two Onondaga County sheriff's deputies inside the Town of Dewitt courthouse during a failed escape attempt, killing one and critically wounding the other. There were many people in the Syracuse area who shared his sentiments, to be sure. I read the hateful letters to the editor printed in the local newspapers; I could even feel the anger of the people when I'd go to court, so palpable was it. Even by the standards of my own belief system, such as it was back then, I deserved to die for what I had done. I took the life of a man without just cause, committing an act so monumentally wrong that I could not have argued that it was unfair had I been required to pay with my own life.

What nobody knew or suspected back then, not even I, is that when the prison gate slammed shut behind me, on that very day I would begin suffering a punishment that I am convinced beyond all doubt is far worse than any death sentence could possibly have been. On July 10, 2012, I finished my twenty-fifth consecutive year in solitary confinement, where at the time of this writing I remain. Alhough it is true that I've never died and so don't know exactly what the experience would entail, for the life of me I cannot fathom how dying any death could be harder or more terrible than living through all that I have been forced to endure for the past quarter century.

Prisoners call it the box. Prison authorities have euphemistically dubbed it the Special Housing Unit, or SHU (pronounced "shoe") for short. In society it is known as solitary confinement. It is twenty-three-hour-a-day lockdown in a cell smaller than some closets I've seen, with one hour allotted to "recreation" consisting of placement by oneself in a concrete-enclosed yard or, in some prisons, a cage made of steel bars. There is nothing in a SHU yard but air: no TV, no balls to bounce, no games to play, no other inmates, nothing. There is also very little allowed in a SHU cell: three sets of plain white underwear, one pair of green pants, one green short-sleeved button-up shirt, one green sweatshirt, one pair of laceless footwear that I'll call sneakers for lack of a better word, ten books or magazines total, twenty pictures of the people you love, writing supplies, a bar of soap, toothbrush and toothpaste, one deodorant stick, but no shampoo.

That's about it. No clothes of your own, only prison-made. No food from commissary or packages, only three unappetizing meals a day handed to you through a narrow slot in your cell door. No phone calls, no TV, no luxury items at all. You get a set of cheap headphones to use, and you can pick between the two or three (depending on which prison you're in) jacks in the cell wall to plug into. You can listen to a TV station in one jack, and use your imagination while trying to figure out what is going on when the music indicates drama but the dialogue doesn't suffice to tell you anything. Or you can listen to some music, but you're out of luck if you're a rock 'n' roll fan and find only rap is playing.

Your options as to what to do to occupy your time in SHU are scant, but there will be boredom aplenty. You probably think that you understand boredom, know its feel, but really you don't. What you call boredom would seem a whirlwind of activity to me, choices so many that I'd likely be befuddled in trying to pick one over all the others. You could turn on a TV and watch a movie or some other show; I haven't seen a TV since the 1980s. You could go for a walk in the neighborhood; I can't walk more than a few feet in any direction before I run into a concrete wall or steel bars. You could pick up your phone and call a friend; I don't know if I'd be able to remember how to make a collect call or even if the process is still the same, so many years it's been since I've used a telephone. Play with your dog or cat and experience their love, or watch your fish in their aquarium; the only creatures I see daily are the mice and cockroaches that infest the unit, and they're not very lovable and nothing much to look at. There is a pretty good list of options available to you, if you think about it, many things that you could do even when you believe you are so bored. You take them for granted because they are there all the time, but if it were all taken away you'd find yourself missing even the things that right now seem so small and insignificant. Even the smallest stuff can become as large as life when you have had nearly nothing for far too long.

I haven't been outside in one of the SHU yards in this prison for about four years now. I haven't seen a tree or blade of grass in all that time, and wouldn't see these things were I to go to the yard. In Elmira Correctional Facility, where I am presently imprisoned, the SHU yards are about three or four times as big as my cell. There are twelve SHU yards total, each surrounded by concrete walls, one or two of the walls lined with windows. If you look in the windows you'll see the same SHU cellblock that you live on, and maybe you'll get to see the guy who has been locked next to you for months that you've talked to every day but had never before gotten a look at. If you look up you'll find bars and a screen covering the yard, and if you're lucky maybe you can see a bit of blue sky through the mesh, otherwise it'll be hard to believe that you're even outside. If it's a good day you can walk around the SHU yard in small circles staring ahead with your mind on nothingness, like the nothing you've got in that little lacuna with you. If it's a bad day, though, maybe your mind will be filled with remembrances of all you used to have that you haven't seen now for many years; and you'll be missing it, feeling the loss, feeling it bad.

Life in the box is about an austere sameness that makes it difficult to tell one day from a thousand others. Nothing much and nothing new ever happens to tell you if it's a Monday or a Friday, March or September, 1987 or 2012. The world turns, technology advances, and things in the streets change and keep changing all the time. Not so in a solitary confinement unit, however. I've never seen a cell phone except in pictures in magazines. I've never touched a computer in my life, never been on the Internet and wouldn't know how to get there if you sat me in front of a computer, turned it on for me, and gave me directions. SHU is a timeless place, and I can honestly say that there is not a single thing I'd see looking around right now that is different from what I saw in Shawangunk Correctional Facility's box when I first arrived there from Syracuse's county jail in 1987. Indeed, there is probably nothing different in SHU now than in SHU a hundred years ago, save the headphones. Then and now there were a few books, a few prison-made clothing articles, walls and bars and human beings locked in cages. And misery.

There is always the misery. If you manage to escape it yourself for a time, there will ever be plenty around in others for you to sense; and although you'll be unable to look into their eyes and see it, you might hear it in the nighttime when tough guys cry not-so-tough tears that are forced out of them by the unrelenting stress and strain that life in SHU is an exercise in.

I've read of the studies done regarding the effects of long-term isolation in solitary confinement on inmates, seen how researchers say it can ruin a man's mind, and I've watched with my own eyes the slow descent of sane men into madness—sometimes not so slow. What I've never seen the experts write about, though, is what year after year of abject isolation can do to that immaterial part in our middle where hopes survive or die and the spirit resides. So please allow me to speak to you of what I've seen and felt during some of the harder times of my twenty-five-year SHU odyssey.

I've experienced times so difficult and felt boredom and loneliness to such a degree that it seemed to be a physical thing inside so thick it felt like it was choking me, trying to squeeze the sanity from my mind, the spirit from my soul, and the life from my body. I've seen and felt hope becoming like a foggy ephemeral thing, hard to get ahold of, even harder to keep ahold of as the years and then decades disappeared while I stayed stuck in the emptiness of the SHU world. I've seen minds slipping down the slope of sanity, descending into insanity, and I've been terrified that I would end up like the guys around me who have cracked and become nuts. It's a sad thing to watch a human being go insane before your eyes because he can't handle the pressure that the box exerts on the mind, but it is sadder still to see the spirit shaken from a soul. And it is more disastrous. Sometimes the prison guards find them hanging and blue; sometimes their necks get broken when they jump from their beds, the sheet tied around the neck that's also wrapped around the grate covering the light in the ceiling snapping taut with a pop. I've seen the spirit leaving men in SHU, and I have witnessed the results.

The box is a place like no other place on planet Earth. It's a place where men full of rage can stand at their cell gates fulminating on their neighbor or neighbors, yelling and screaming and speaking some of the filthiest words that could ever come from a human mouth, do it for hours on end, and despite it all never suffer the loss of a single tooth, never get their heads knocked clean off their shoulders. You will never hear words more despicable or see mouth wars more insane than what occurs all the time in SHU, not anywhere else in the world, because there would be serious violence before any person could speak so much foulness for so long. In the box the heavy steel bars allow mouths to run with impunity when they could not otherwise do so, while the ambiance is one that is sorely conducive to an exceedingly hot sort of anger that seems to press the lips on to ridiculous extremes. Day and night I have been awakened by the sound of rage being loosed loudly on SHU gates, and I'd be a liar if I said that I haven't at times been one of the madmen doing the yelling.

I have lived for months where the first thing I became aware of upon waking in the morning is the malodorous funk of human feces, tinged with the acrid stench of days-old urine, where I ate my breakfast, lunch, and dinner with that same stink assaulting my senses, and where the last thought I had before falling into unconscious sleep was: "Damn, it smells like shit in here." I have felt like I was on an island surrounded by vicious sharks, flanked on both sides by mentally ill inmates who would splash their excrement all over their cells, all over the company outside their cells, and even all over themselves. I have seen days turn into weeks that seemed like they'd never end without being able to sleep more than short snatches before I was shocked out of my dreams, and thrown back into a living nightmare, by the screams of sick men who had lost all ability to control themselves, or by the banging of the cell bars and walls being done by these same madmen. I have been so tired when sleep inside was impossible that I went outside into a snowstorm to get some rest.

The wind blew hard and snowflakes swirled around and around in the small SHU yard at Shawangunk, and I had on but one cheap prison-produced coat and a single set of state clothes beneath. To escape the biting cold I dug into the seven- or eight-foot-high mountain of snow that was piled in the center of the yard, the accumulation from inmates shoveling a narrow path to walk along the perimeter. With bare hands gone numb, I dug out a small room in that pile of snow, making myself a sort of igloo. When it was done I crawled inside, rolled onto my back on the snow-covered concrete ground, and almost instantly fell asleep, my bare head pillowed in the snow. I didn't even have a hat to wear.

An hour or so later I was awakened by the guards come to take me back to the stink and insanity inside: "Blake, rec's over. . . . " I had gotten an hour's straight sleep, minus the few minutes it had taken me to dig my igloo. That was more than I had gotten in weeks without being shocked awake by the CA-RACK! of a sneaker being slapped into a Plexiglas shield covering the cell of an inmate who had thrown things nasty; or the THUD-THUD-THUD! of an inmate pounding his cell wall; or bars being banged and gates being kicked and rattled; or men screaming like they're dying and maybe wishing that they were; or to the tirade of an inmate letting loose his pent-up rage on a guard or fellow inmate, sounding every bit the lunatic that too long a time in the mind-breaking confines of the box had caused him to be.

I have been so exhausted physically, my mental strength tested to limits that can cause strong folks to snap, that I have begged God, tough guy I fancy myself, "Please, Lord, make them stop. Please let me get some peace." As the prayers went ungranted and the insanity around me persisted, I felt my own rage rising above the exhaustion and misery—no longer now in a begging mood: "Lord, kill those motherfuckers, why don't you!" I yelled at the Almighty, my own sanity so close to being gone that it seemed as if I were teetering along the edge of a precipice and could see down to where I'd be dropping, seeing myself shot, sanity a dead thing killed by the fall. I'd be afraid later on, terrified, when I reflected back on how close I had seemed to come to losing my mind, but at that moment all I could do was feel anger of a fiery kind: anger at the maniacs creating the noise and the stink and the madness; anger at my keepers, the real creators of this hell; anger at society for turning a blind eye to the torment and torture going on here that its tax dollars are financing; and, perhaps most of all, anger at myself for doing all that I did that never should have been done that put me into the clutches of this beastly prison system to begin with. I would be angry at the world; enraged, actually, so burning hot was what I would be feeling.

I had wet toilet paper stuffed hard into both ears, socks folded up and pressed into my ears, a pillow wrapped around the sides and back of my head covering my ears, and a blanket tied around all that to hold everything in place, lying in bed praying for sleep. But still the noise was incredible, a thunderous cacophony of insanity, sleep impossible. Inmates lost in the throes of lava-like rage firing philippics at one another for reasons even they didn't know, threatening to kill one another's mommas, daddies, even the children, too. Nothing is sacred in SHU. It is an environment that is so grossly abnormal, so antithetical to normal human interactions, that it twists the innards of men all around who for too long dwell there. Their minds, their morals, and their mannerisms get bent badly, ending far off center. Right becomes whatever and wrong no longer exists. Restraint becomes a burden and is unnecessary with concrete and steel separating everyone, so inmates let it go. Day after day, perhaps year after year, the anger grows, fueled by the pain caused by the conditions till rage is born and burning so hot that it too hurts.

Trying to put into words what is so unlike anything else I know or have ever experienced seems an impossible endeavor because there is nothing even remotely like it any place else to compare it to, and nothing that will do to you on the inside what so many years in SHU has done to me. All that I am able to articulate about the world of a Special Housing Unit and what it is and what it does may seem terrible to you indeed, but the reality of living in this place for a full quarter of a century is even more terrible still. You would have to live it, experience it in all its aspects with the fullness of its days and struggles added up, to really appreciate and understand just how truly terrible this plight of mine has been, and how truly ugly life in the box can be at times, even for just a single day.

I spent nine years in Shawangunk's box, six years in Sullivan's, six years in Great Meadow's, and I've been here in Elmira's SHU for four years now, and through all of this time I have never spent a single day in a Mental Health Unit cell because I attempted or threatened suicide, or for any other reason. I have thought about suicide in times past when the days had become exceedingly difficult to handle, but I'm still here. I've had some of my SHU neighbors succumb to the suicidal thoughts, though, choosing death over another day of life in the box. I have never bugged out myself, but I've known times that I came too close. I've had neighbors who came to SHU normal men, and I've seen them leave broken and not anything resembling normal anymore. I've seen guys give up on their dreams and lose all hope in the box, but my own hopes and dreams are still alive and well inside me. The insidious workings of the SHU program have yet to get me stuck on that meandering path to internal destruction that I have seen so many of my neighbors end up on, and perhaps this is a miracle. So thanks be to God for the miracle; I'd rather be dead than to lose control of my mind.

Had I known in 1987 that I would spend the next quarter century in solitary confinement, I would certainly have killed myself. If I took a month to die and spent every minute of it in severe pain, it seems to me that on balance that fate would still be far easier to endure than the past twenty-five years have been. If I try to imagine what kind of death, even a slow one, would be worse than twenty-five years in the box—and I have tried to imagine it—I can come up with nothing. Set me afire, pummel and bludgeon me, cut me to bits, stab me, shoot me, do what you will in the worst of ways, but none of it could come close to making me feel things as cumulatively horrifying as what I've experienced through my years in solitary. Dying couldn't take but a short time if you or the state were to kill me; in SHU I have died a thousand internal deaths. The sum of my quarter century's worth of suffering has been that bad.

To some judges sitting on high who've never done a day in the box, maybe twenty-five years of this isn't cruel and unusual. To folks who have an insatiable appetite for vengeance against prisoners who have committed terrible crimes, perhaps it doesn't even matter how cruel or unusual my plight is or isn't. For people who cannot let go of hate and know not how to forgive, no amount of remorse would matter, no level of contrition would be quite enough, only endless retribution would be right in their eyes. Like with Judge Mulroy, only an eternity in hell would suffice. But then, given even that, the unforgiving haters would not be satisfied that hell was hot enough; they'd want the heat turned up higher. Thankfully these folks are the few; in the minds of the many, at a point, enough is enough.

No matter what the world would think about things that they cannot imagine in even their worst nightmares, I know that twenty-five years in solitary confinement is utterly and certainly cruel, more so than death by an electric chair, gas chamber, lethal injection, bullet in the head, or even immolation could possibly be. The sum of the suffering caused by any of these quick deaths would be a small thing next to the sum of the suffering that this quarter century in SHU has brought to bear on me. Solitary confinement for the length of time that I have endured it, even apart from the inhuman conditions that I have too often been made to endure it in, is torture of a terrible kind. And anyone who doesn't think so surely knows not what they are thinking.

I have served a sentence worse than death.

Living in the SHU

C.F. VILLA

Cesar Villa, fifty-five, has been held in Pelican Bay State Prison's Security Housing Unit (SHU) since 2001. He grew up in San Jose, California, and was one of the thousands of young people given life sentences under California's three strikes law. Villa was sentenced to 348 years to life after his third conviction for robbery. He was "validated" as a gang associate in 2001 when another man in prison became an anonymous informant, telling gang investigators that the name "Pancho," which they found written in the wall calendar he had hanging in his cell, referred to Villa.

In California's prisons, "evidence" such as a letter, name, drawing, or possession of the wrong book is enough to "validate" someone as a gang member or associate, which results in indefinite placement in solitary confinement. Many "validated" prisoners have never committed a violent act in or out of prison, but they are deemed guilty by association. The only chance they have to return to the prison's mainline is to "debrief," which means providing information, often false, about other prisoners. Villa was re-validated by gang investigators in 2008, then again in 2013 when a corrections officer said he heard Villa hollering a phrase down the corridor in Nahuatl, an indigenous Mexican language banned at Pelican Bay.

THE FIRST WEEK, I TELL MYSELF: IT ISN'T THAT BAD; I CAN DO THIS. The second week, I stand in the dog run in my underwear shivering as I'm pelted with hail and rain. By the third week, I find myself squatting in a corner of the yard, filing my fingernails down over coarse concrete walls. My sense of human decency dissipates with each day. At the end of the first year, my feet and hands begin to split open from the cold. I bleed over my clothes, in my food, between my sheets. Band-Aids are not allowed, even confiscated when found.

Although I didn't realize it at the time, the unraveling must've begun. Now I ask myself: Can I do this? Not sure about anything anymore. My psyche had changed. The ability to hold a single good thought left me, as easily as if it was a simple shift of wind sifting over tired, battered bones.

Waking is the most traumatic. From the moment your bare feet graze the rugged stone floor, your face begins to sag, knuckles tighten—flashing pale in the pitch of early morning. The slightest slip in a quiet dawn can set a SHU personality into a tailspin: If the sink water is not warm enough, the toilet flushes too loud, the drop of a soap dish, a cup . . . In an instant you bare teeth, shake with rage. Your heart hammers against ribs, lodges in your throat. You are capable of killing anything at this moment.

This is the time it's best to hold rigid. This is not a portrait you wish anyone to see. Take a deep breath. Try to convince yourself there's an ounce of good left in you. And then a gull screeches—passing outside—another tailspin and you're checking your ears for blood.

And this is a good day.

Fourteen years have passed since I entered the SHU on gang valida-tion. This year I'll be fifty-five years old. When I first arrived I was attentive and, if you'll excuse the expression, bright-eyed. I thought I could beat "this thing," whatever "this thing" was. I confess—I was ignorant. Today, I can be found at my cell front, my fingers stuffed through the perforated metal door—I hang limp—my head angled in a daze. My mind is lost in a dense fog of nothingness. I'm withering away—I know it—and I no longer care.

Hopelessness is a virus I hide under my tongue like a magic pebble. If only that shiny stone could assist in deciphering warbled language in a cellblock full of grunts and floods of ignorance from convicts with-out tongues. Someone screams behind me, "Waste not, want not." But what's to waste when all you are is a virus that no one's allowed to touch. Concentration is an abstract invention for those with only half a mind—and half a mind is a terrible thing to waste.

If I were to imagine life outside of Pelican Bay, I'd have to imagine a hospital. And, between me and you, I don't like hospitals. I don't like the stench of sanitized sheets, industrial-strength ammonia. Gowns that open from the back. Polka dots and paper slippers. Looney tunes in looney beds, leather straps and leather masks. Shocks and shots and broken ribs.

Once, long ago, I adopted a miniature red Doberman. Naturally, I named him Red. Red had been abused so terribly that if I raised my voice he'd shake until he wet himself. I had to hold him to feed him; otherwise he'd starve. Maybe he thought he was so bad he didn't deserve food. So loathsome he didn't deserve to be held. It took a long time for him to warm to me. I think what did it was when I chose to sleep on the floor with him in my room. He must've seen me as his equal. I really liked the way he'd press his wet nose against my neck in the middle of the night. I think he was thanking me for treating him—dare I say—humanely. Like family. Like a friend. Today, I imagine life outside the SHU and I can't help but wonder, at seventy or eighty, who will want to hold and care for me?

The truth is we've been undone, unwound. The inside of our plastic skulls raked and routed. A composition of cracks and fissures where nothing will ever be the same again. The hardest thing about spending years in the SHU is that it's not "just" years. Call it what it is: a circle of perpetual sensory deprivation that spans an entire lifetime. Inmates have been confined to isolation based on gang validation since the early 1970s. Funny . . . when I think of validation, I still remember Fridays after work—cashing my paycheck—handing over a parking ticket to the bank teller and asking to be validated. How cool is this, I thought, validation for free!

The psychological damage does not fix itself. Does a rape victim stop being raped after the act? What about the boy who's been hit by a car, dragged for one hundred feet, dragged until the meat is scraped off his bones? Does he flinch at the sound of grating metal? It's the same damage a SHU inmate suffers when a chain is snapped around the ankles, cinched at the waist. When metal doors slam shut, tumblers in a lock spin. Loudspeakers blare through a silent cellblock. Although more suppressed, less visual, the damage is there.

The hardest thing? Nobody cares.

Worse? Nobody wants to.

The guards: our oppressors of humanity—a breed apart from others. Their leathery faces stink of feces. Their unwashed bodies oily, in crisp soiled uniforms. Imagine if you will: Before leaving your home—the key to getting beyond that door—you must expose yourself to a stranger. Strip naked and show him your genitals. Bend over and show him the inside of your anus. Does even the thought of this make you uncomfortable? Is it enough to startle your moral consciousness?

How would the observer react to this display before him?

What if he liked it?

What if he signed up to appear at your front door every morning to witness this very act? To force you to go through the motions slowly, cautiously—so he can inspect every fold of your skin with a leer?

Imagine this: Your family comes to visit you. Before this visit officers tear through your personal belongings: your underwear, cosmetics. They sit on your bed and read your letters. Confiscate books, pictures, magazines.

Your family notes tension on your face sitting across from them through the glass. You're thinking of your room being ransacked. The invasion. Your body language is rigid. Awkward. They ask, how are you? How do you keep a straight face—tell a lie—to your mother? Father? Your children?

On a whim, without provocation, reason, or justice, SHU inmates are accosted by these foul-smelling guards, plucked from their cells at random and thrown into freezing tanks empty of furnishings, fixtures, running water—handcuffed. Forced to defecate in a seatless chair in a bucket in restraints. If they refuse to turn over a stool sample large enough to please the indignant guard, inmates may remain handcuffed for days with no end. Inmates may even be subjected to forced penetration with surgical forceps—scraping the anal cavity—pinching tissue, skin, intestines. The more degraded the inmate, the more pleasured the guard or sergeant watching. Glee spilling from their faces, mixed with sweat. In every corner of the world, forcible penetration of the anal cavity with a foreign object is RAPE. In California's Pelican Bay SHU it's protection of public safety, smiles and all.

The hardest thing? Nobody cares.

Worse? Nobody wants to.

Indignity. That choking filament that can cut air down to quarters and turn eyes purple, puffy, and watery. Drown skin and soul in chemical agents, outrage, some post-traumatic flashing. Manic guards off their meds. That last good photograph stamped with a boot. Classification hearings postponed for potlucks. The daughter whose eyes fill when you ask innocently, who are you? Sons who are bullied and black-eyed at school because nobody, especially sons of law enforcement, likes the son of a felon. Summers that last for three weeks, winters for ten months. And somewhere in the middle you're caught praying for global warming. Sunburn blisters from two minute's warmth. Optical nerves damaged from light. Wrists that snap wringing clothes. Tendons that tear when reaching for a towel. Knees that don't have a leg to stand on. Teeth caught in toothbrushes. Toenails that fall off into socks—rattle like loaded dice. Ankles that buckle jogging in place.

A spontaneous nose bleed on that last clean sheet, laundered shirt. Filling the sink, the toilet, splashing across the floor.

Making your own funeral arrangements, notifying the next of kin— only to receive a return to sender: Unable to forward as addressed.

The only piece of mail you've received in years.

Seven-year-old daughters who think glitter is what father needs on his Father's Day card, but the mailroom disallows it because what they don't need is an over-excited prisoner.

Do I think it's possible to be a "normal" human being while in the SHU? Normal? Can we first focus on this "human being" thing? It seems I heard that phrase somewhere before. Oh yes, now I remember. Karl Marlantes described it best in his novel *Matterhorn*, when his protagonist is struck with a realization:

"He suddenly understood why the victims of concentration camps had walked quietly to the gas chambers. In the face of horror and insanity, it was the one human thing to do. Not the noble thing, not the heroic thing—the human thing. To live, succumbing to the insanity, was the ultimate loss of pride."

That's the protagonist I want to be.

And still, here I am. A decade later—the dog part of me grappled at the nape of the neck. Held under water, drowning. My tired limbs flailing. Poet Peter Blair, in his ode to the beautiful Donna Lee Polito, writes of five attempts at suicide: sleeping pills, tranquilizers, a bathroom razor, before racing blind out an eighth-floor window—her dark cropped hair wild in the wind—the bright splash below across railroad tracks. What I wouldn't give to know the freedom of that moment. What I wouldn't give to race blind for just half a block. I can understand the helplessness. How he must've held his breath so long, until he too understood—sometimes death outshines life. Then he lapped up every drop of water, every string of saliva, only to be jerked from the skin of water to again taste every sting of air.

Once you reach this inhumane way of living all you know is stooping. The curvature of the spine—remnants of ducking insults. I often stoop as I hear the jangle of the guards' metal keys, hatred flung from their foul mouths, as if I was the one responsible for everything bad that ever happened in their lives. You cannot call it sleepwalking when there's no place to walk. When all you do is paddle in a circle in your cell and moths and mosquitos and mice quietly watch the spectacle until you crawl back to bed with some restless something syndrome.

Each morning wakes the potential for disaster. Each morning starts with anger before the anxiety. Then there are those mornings when the spinal spasms buckle me and suddenly I'm on the floor, reaching for what? Irrational anger spills out in flashes. Sometimes it happens when you bite your cheek from chewing food too fast. When your jaw cramps and locks from chewing too slow. Unusual uncomfort for a mouth that doesn't see much action. Where talking to an inmate—talking at all—can extend SHU confinement another six years. If silence is golden, I'm chained to Fort Knox. Call me, Bernanke, to lower the rate. And someone please buy me a vowel.

In the SHU books are limited to ten. So I have to hide books under my pillow, my mattress, in envelopes, strapped to my waist. I wake up damp with sweat just to pore over another verse. One good chapter or stanza will set me straight. My best books I've read ten times over and still I'm hungry for another reading. A forty-nine-year-old eighth grader studying for his GED! I traded my favorite books for theories on algebra. I thought I hit gold when I found *Algebra for Dummies*. Then couldn't afford it. I studied signed numbers, two-step equations. Listened to lectures—on TV—on science, literature. Weeks before my last practice test, all my work was confiscated. "Who's the dummy now?" kept ringing in my head. And I'm spinning in circles. Oversensitivity to stimuli? Who's the dummy now?

In the SHU you're lucky to form a single thought at all. That's why I keep notes for everything. Notes on colors, names, words that look confusing, emotions, social protocol (should I ever meet another human being, I'd like to be ready), books, magazines, quotes, phrases . . . you name it, I probably have it on a note. When I'm nervous I do things backward. Why? Your guess is good as mine. Oh yeah, my reading level—documented at fifth grade. Maybe that's why I enjoy reading books ten times over. I never thought of that. And there you go—a single thought. I'm good for another six months.

The idea of someone touching me has me bouncing off the walls.

One evening a fight between two inmates broke out in front of my cell. At this point, guards do not come into the unit until the combatants are down. But this particular evening, the guard in the tower was having trouble (morally) pulling the trigger—close range—on her gun. So the inmates remained engaged in exchanging blows. That is, until another female guard rolled on the scene—livid. "What are you waiting for?" she shouted. "Shoot! They're just fuckin' animals. Shoot!" Four ear-splitting shots rang out before they went down. There was blood everywhere. On my cell door. The tier. The floor. The roof. And her voice: "Fuckin' animals" kept ringing in my head. My blood boiled. My fists swelled. I felt my face reddening.

An hour later I cooled. She's right, I thought. We're supposed to be animals. We're only here to die. The prison administration is paid to put us down. The undesirables. The malignant misfits who have no right to breathe.

Last year, SHU inmates joined in a hunger strike, advocating to be treated more humanely. One week into the strike, a burly red-haired guard came into the cellblock yelling, "You want to starve yourselves to death, go 'head. Ain't shit gonna change."

I didn't bother looking up from my book. I didn't laugh. I didn't get angry. However, one image did flash quickly: inmates in wheelchairs, on gurneys—crowded in a hallway—hollow cheeked, paper skin. Some slumped over. Some dying. Flies in swarms, in a black fog. My one good thought for the whole year . . . please let "mine" be a closed casket. Then I went back to reading my book.

Innocent in the Eyes of the Law

UZAIR PARACHA

Uzair Paracha is a Pakistani national who was a permanent resident of the United States when he was accused of providing material support to terrorists by conspiring to help an alleged Al Qaeda operative to enter the United States illegally. From the time he was arrested in 2003, when he was twenty-three years old, he maintained his innocence and refused to accept a plea bargain for as little as five years in prison. He was indicted on charges that could have brought him up to seventy-five years. While awaiting trial for two and a half years, Paracha was held at Metropolitan Correctional Center (MCC), a high-rise federal jail in lower Manhattan, a few blocks from New York's City Hall, surrounded by homes and offices. On the jail's tenth floor, suspects accused (but not yet convicted) in terrorism-related cases are held in extreme solitary confinement, often under Special Administrative Measures, or SAMs, a post-9/11 designation that places additional restrictions on communication both within the prison and with the world outside.

Because they were imposed after his interrogation, Paracha and his lawyers believed the SAMs—and indeed, Paracha's long stay in solitary confinement—were used coercively, to try to force a guilty plea. After he was tried and convicted on all counts in 2005, Paracha was sent to the federal government's only supermax prison, the United States Peniten-tiary, Administrative Maximum (ADX) in Florence, Colorado, which he says compared favorably to the tenth floor of MCC. He is now in the Communications Management Unit (CMU) at the maximum security Federal Correctional Institution in Terre Haute, Indiana.

UNTIL MY INDICTMENT I WAS KEPT IN SOLITARY CONFINEMENT IN THE Special Housing Unit, or SHU, at Metropolitan Correctional Center (MCC), at first pending classification, then under administrative detention. Overall it was the usual "secure running of the institution" stuff, something about my safety and that of other prisoners. Soon after my indictment I was placed on the Special Administrative Measures (SAMs) and moved to 10 South where I stayed until my trial. By the time I was placed on the SAMs in December 2003 I had been in their custody for nearly nine months. All the discovery evidence against me was obtained within the first couple of months, but the pressure to plead guilty to the eight years remained and so did the option to have them negotiated down to a single five-year charge. I kept refusing until the seventy-five-year indictment came in October 2003. The SAMs that came two months later prohibited me from many things, including talking to any other prisoner, and they were strongly enforced with frequent sanctions. My lawyers felt that the SAMs and harsh conditions that the SAMs unit (10 South) brought were part of the pressure because the offer was still on the table.

Ten South was a disturbingly quiet place. Things have probably changed a lot over the past twelve years, so I can't say how it is now, but back then it had only a few cells in the entire unit. There were cameras within our cells and sometimes the guards could be heard joking about our everyday behavior while they monitored us like lab rats. I remember them trying to joke around with us from their desks while we were using the toilet, for instance, because some cells were within hearing distance. The cells weren't all the same size, but two or three times as large as the average SHU cell. The bed, desk, and seat were concrete. The showers were inside the cells, which ran only hot or only cold water at a time (i.e., you couldn't mix the water temperature), so it took some time getting used to scalding hot or freezing cold water and I got burnt quite often. One camera had a clear video of the shower stall without a shower curtain or any other barrier for privacy. The other was either above the toilet or the bed. I myself knew of female guards who made comments on how some prisoners cleaned their private parts after using the toilet.

Our lights were completely controlled from outside and we had to ask the guards to turn our lights on or off. When we had particularly troublesome guards (please remember that the Iraq War was at its height and many of them were participating), they would turn our lights on in the middle of the night. The lights were large and very bright, and we wrapped our eyes with socks to sleep. The light issue was worse for those who were in cells that were beyond the guards' hearing distance, especially because most of them were lazy. There was a "night light," which was simply a big light fixture that never turned off. We argued that it made no sense to have this night light because they could turn all the lights on from outside whenever they wanted to anyway, but we got nowhere with this. The windows were huge but the glass was frosted so we had a lot of light but couldn't see a thing. It was a shade of white during the day, blue in the evening and early morning, black at night, and yellow when it snowed, as the snow reflected the streetlights. This was one way to estimate the time because they didn't allow any watches (except once for a few months and then they confiscated them and put clocks in front of our doors so we could know the time for prayers).

The heating was out of order during most of my time there because of some leak. My lawyer came to see me one day while he was wearing a business suit and he was very uncomfortable in the visiting area. He kept asking me how I was coping in this frigid temperature and I told him that it was possibly because my cell was worse. A few minutes into the visit I looked up from my papers and saw him standing on his chair looking for a heat source. He couldn't tolerate it so he cut the visit short and left in anger. He wrote a letter to the judge mentioning that my conditions of confinement looked like a deliberate attempt to pressure or punish me. He mentioned that I didn't have a sweater, hat, or jacket, while the guards were wearing all of these things because of the temperature in the unit. Within the unit the cells were the coldest places because the metallic sheets on the walls turned the cells into ice boxes, freezing us inside instead of insulating us from the outside weather, and food items would freeze if I kept them in some parts of my cell. The summers made the cells into ovens.

There was no mirror in the cell and we were not allowed to buy one through the commissary. We asked for razors when we needed to shave and we returned them when we were done. The guards also gave us a cardboard mirror, which wasn't really a mirror at all, so we just did without until they allowed us to get our small personal plastic mirrors out of our properties if we had them and we started borrowing mirrors from each other. If someone was leaving, he would give his mirror away. Still, we always tried to keep our usage of the mirror discreet because we didn't want to attract unwanted attention. I ended up with a small mirror that someone left me and I lent it to a neighbor who hadn't seen his own face for years. For me it was only several months. Over time such things were taking away our sense of identity.

A typical day in 10 South started with breakfast at anywhere between six and eight in the morning. Nothing really happened in the unit so I slept until lunchtime between ten and twelve. Then I did some exercises, showered, recited the Quran, did some reading, and it was usually evening by then. The daily prayers, daily chores like cleaning up the cell, having the meals, and attending to other daily needs like using the toilet took up a good portion of the day and that is all that happened on an average day.

When I was first moved to 10 South they withheld my property for about a month, including my clothing (thermals, sweatpants, and sweatshirts), all the books I had (I had dozens), and some food. The one thing I remember getting is the Quran. At that time it was the middle of winter in December and January, without heat. So I started memorizing the Quran to keep myself busy and distracted. Pretty soon it absorbed many hours of my day.

Initially I saw a lot of shakedowns (cell searches where they turned the whole cell upside down) because of a violent incident on a guard that took place in the unit a few years before I came. They were done every day or a few times every day, every time the meals were served. As the prisoner responsible for the incident left the institution they calmed down a bit. The recreation area was barely used (I'll explain why later). Other than legal visits we hardly ever left the cell until we were moved to a different cell (i.e., cell rotation).

We rarely saw anyone else. We saw the guards when they served the meals and they would also come over for small talk. We discovered that the guards wrote down a full account of each conversation in a register but that was our only opportunity for social interaction so we talked to them anyway. The senior administration people like the warden made rounds every few weeks. The SAMs prohibited us from talking to any other prisoner so we rarely and very cautiously talked to each other. I got a bunch of sanctions for just talking to other prisoners. You could spend days or weeks without uttering anything significant beyond "please cut my lights," "can I get a legal call/toilet paper/a razor," etc. Some of the guards would steer the conversation toward our cases and ask for details, but that was not common and our lawyers warned us not to talk about our cases, so it never became a serious problem while I was there. All of the cells were heavily monitored, which was well understood from the SAMs.

The SAMs also denied me access to radio and television news, they only allowed newspapers that were thirty days old, and the delayed newspapers were supposed to be censored. MCC claims it did not have the resources to censor radio or television so we had no access to radios or televisions at all. As for the newspaper, one of the prisoners had a subscription to the *New York Times* and they suddenly started censoring it. He was very vocal about the fact that the paper was two months late (not one month as per the SAMs), that even articles from the food section were missing, and when they censored an article they cut it out of the paper so the articles on the back side of the page were also missing portions and he couldn't read most of it. The rest of us got the hint and I stuck to ordering travel magazines with pictures of beaches. The unit didn't have a leisure library or law library. If we needed any policy or case law we had to specify to education and they brought it over in a few days. There was no list or database to choose from so we had to know what we were asking for. If I needed time to read the material I could ask for a copy and they made me a copy after charging me for it. Depending on the person who was helping out they sometimes didn't charge me if there were not a lot of pages to copy.

For leisure reading requests they brought a few books to choose from. I relied on my family to send me the books I wanted to read. Even though the rules weren't clear, the BOP sent every book and magazine to the FBI before I got them and this delayed them for months.

There were absolutely no educational opportunities for prisoners in the unit. I myself had just finished my master's but I wanted to get some typing lessons to improve my speed. They didn't trust me with any type of keyboard. Another prisoner wanted to brush up on his geometry but they didn't trust him with even a photocopy of a ruler. I never saw anyone getting any education while I was there.

As for my possessions, other than purchased clothing (two pairs of sweatpants, two sweatshirts, two thermal tops, two bottoms, some boxers) we had institutional stuff like orange t-shirts, an orange jumpsuit, orange socks, underwear, towels, and basic bedding. I should point out that we did not have jackets, sweaters, hats, pillows, woolen blankets (only two thin white blankets no better than bed sheets), combs, or toothbrushes over two and a half inches long. One day they took away our drinking cups and property storage bins because they did not trust us with any type of plastic. We couldn't have anything like a plate, knife, fork, bowl, spoon, or drinking cup even if it was plastic. Only a soft plastic spork (spoon and fork in one). There was little logic to this as our hot food meals came in microwaveable plastic trays so we just kept the food trays for food and used old milk cartons to drink from.

About one in ten guards treated us like normal human beings. About one in ten hated us with a passion and harassed us at every opportunity. One of the respectful ones explained the harassment as the others wanting a piece of the action in the war on terror. The other eight just treated us like extra dangerous criminals. They were all very scared of the upper-level staff, especially the unit manager. One of the guards told me that the unit manager had warned them that if they didn't report us for talking to each other then he would report them. So the guards would report me to avoid trouble for themselves. Then he would come over and sanction me and take away my calls and visits with my family, the two things that mattered most to me. Once he was out sick and we were relieved that someone else might sanction us instead of him but he called in and put some kind of hold on things (that was not allowed by policy) until he came back to work. A few of us complained about him specifically but we never got anywhere with that. Nothing more than a verbal reprimand. I never met a prisoner who didn't hate him.

Most prisoners did not have a problem with us Muslims but once in a while we would be around those who did not want to hear us praying and they would take the argument in the "you're a terrorist" direction. It always went in this direction. This was avoidable because prisons have designated areas to pray in privacy but SHU inmates have none of that. Overall I believe we were not in any more danger than the average prisoner because all prisons have large Muslim populations that give them a sense of safety among other prisoners.

Solitary confinement can affect a person in ways he may only realize with time. I had Lasik surgery a few years before my arrest and it went well. Yet my eyesight deteriorated threefold in the nine years I was in isolation. We couldn't see anything beyond a few feet in front of our doors and nothing at all from our windows in 10 South. I met several prisoners who had to get prescription eyeglasses for the first time in their lives while in the SHU. I mentioned this to the ophthalmologist in ADX and he told me that having your entire world just a few feet away weakens the eyesight.

After all these years, when I was once in an open yard under the sky for a few hours, I felt something similar to fear of heights, only I felt it in the sense that I might fall upward and I tried to lie down from time to time to calm my anxiety as I held the ground closer.

A similar issue was depth perception, which impacted my hand-eye coordination for months after isolation ended. Simple things like estimating the distance of a ball as it bounced in my direction took time to get comfortable with. More serious was what I would call depth perception in foot-eye coordination. More than once I tripped on the stairs after coming out of isolation. Once it was a young fellow who was two steps ahead of me who blocked my fall before I fell down the stairs. By now I am more confident on the stairs but for about two years I was constantly misperceiving the placement of the stairs and held tightly to the rails to be on the safe side.

I also developed breathing problems. If I lay down in bed it was hard to breathe and if I was half asleep or sleeping I would wake up with a jolt feeling like someone had given me an electric shock. The only thing that made it easier to breathe was if I ate less, so I stopped buying food from commissary and reduced my diet until I was eating a light meal or two (like vegetables, fruit, or cereal) every other day. I also exercised a little bit to help relieve some stress. My weight went down from about 140 pounds to below 112 pounds over seven weeks sometime around the summer of 2005. Even walking around within the cell became difficult. Eventually MCC showed me to a psychiatrist who diagnosed me as claustrophobic and prescribed the antianxiety pill Paxil for two years. The medicine allowed me to breathe comfortably in bed but I was sleeping fourteen hours a day and eating too much because of the medication. My weight went from 112 pounds to 172 pounds within months as they added multiple servings of a calorie-heavy nutritional supplement to my daily diet to help me recover my weight. I was always lean but the medication made me pudgy for years. By the time I finished the two-year prescription I was in ADX and medical services gave me the option to continue taking the pill. But based on my original discussion with the psychiatrist who first prescribed it I wanted to see if I could manage to breathe normally without it. When I stopped it I felt sharper and slept less, like coming out of a dream. There was a span of several weeks while I was in ADX when the problem came back and I was unwilling to eat my food. This time ADX force-fed me for several weeks. I didn't want to go back to taking the pills because I didn't want to depend on them, so after being force-fed for several weeks I did the bare minimum to prevent force-feeding.

If medical staff members determine that a prisoner should be force fed they first offer him a nutritional supplement to drink voluntarily. If he cannot or will not, they ask him to allow them to place restraints on him (refusal leads to use of force). If he accepts they take him and strap him to a chair. They ask him to hold some water in his mouth and then shove a lubricated tube up his nose (he can choose which nostril) until it reaches his stomach. While they are shoving it up his nose he should swallow the water slowly so that the tube goes down with less friction. Then they pour the nutritional supplement through the tube directly into his stomach. When they are done he holds his breath while they pull the tube out and if they know what they are doing it won't come out with a lot of blood on it. But this was at ADX and I was never force-fed at MCC.

Going back to MCC, another medical problem started while I was chewing food and suddenly felt like someone punched me on the side of my jaw like I broke something. The dentist told me it was temporo-mandibular joint disorder (TMJ), a stress-related clicking jaw prob-lem. There was no solution so I had to live with it, but over time it became a rare occurrence. These are the main physical problems I remember from MCC besides the stress-related muscle twitches I used to complain about regularly.

On March 22, 2005, my lawyers got a court order to appoint a fo-rensic psychologist to see the impact of my conditions of confinement and if I could still understand the nature of the charges against me and was able to properly assist in my defense. I was told it was to help im-prove my conditions somehow but the way my lawyers were speaking to the judge made me question their motives and I found out from my family years later that after nearly two years of constantly pressuring me to accept the plea offer the lawyers wanted to see if they could use that opportunity to take the decision out of my hands because of my state of mind and give it to my family who would plead guilty on my behalf. After the doctor's findings the judge decided to speak to me directly and determined that I was still of sound mind.

But the deafening silence of complete isolation all day every day and the constant awareness that someone is observing us through cameras 24/7/365 for years had an impact on each and every one of us and it was obvious. Generally it is about helplessness as we didn't have control over anything in our lives, our daily routine, the light, the water, etc. Isolation is also about privacy because we were all alone but there were constant reminders from the guards that we had absolutely no privacy.

In the SAMs unit, only a lieutenant had the authority to feed us or take us out so we had to ask for recreation when he came by during breakfast. It was common for him to say he was too busy at that time and that meant that no one was going for recreation that day. No single week went by in which every prisoner who wanted recreation actually got it; sometimes the recreation area was empty for a whole week or two. We were all supposed to go through a strip search and our cells shaken down. The recreation area was no bigger than the average cell in the unit but seemed larger because of the absence of a bed, toilet, desk, and shower stall. You couldn't see the outside and there was no access to open-air recreation for our unit. Because of these reasons it wasn't worth asking for recreation and over time everyone including myself stopped asking and it was seldom used. In the beginning I actually tried to come out as much as I could but then I stopped because I could wait for hours to go back to my cell (unable to use the toilet), then I would return to my cell with my stuff overturned and it took time to clean up and put my stuff back in order. I would discover that some of my stuff was missing. For all those reasons I just stopped.

The main focus of the SAMs was on our contact with the outside world. The SAMs required that all letters to or from me should be photocopied by the BOP and the copies were to be sent to the FBI for screening. They could redact parts of the letters if they wanted. MCC was supposed to keep the originals and if they got no objection from the FBI they were supposed to give me the incoming letters within fourteen business days. This is what the SAMs stated. In practice, the institution sent the originals to the FBI so all my mail (books, magazines, letters, etc.) took months to get to me. Depending on how busy the FBI was with its other responsibilities a letter could take four to six months to get a response.

In the thirty months I was at MCC I probably made no more than ten fifteen-minute calls. It took me months to get a number approved. After my SAMs I was told to reapply for the same numbers. Same number, same approving party, and no basis in the SAMs for this. Again it took months. The SAMs required my calls to be monitored by the FBI contemporaneously. I couldn't get a call unless an agent on my case came to MCC and listened to my call. I was allowed to get one fifteen-minute call a month, but if the agent was busy I lost my call for the month. The agents were usually too busy. Had I asked to speak in Urdu, the need for an interpreter would have made my calls even fewer, but I was fortunate that my entire family spoke English fluently, so I agreed to stick to English only.

The visits were also supposed to be monitored in the same way. The first problem was that MCC only allowed immediate family plus one friend who could be anyone I chose. My immediate family members were all in Pakistan, while I had my uncles, aunts, and cousins in the tristate area here. I asked to put my cousin on the visiting list as a friend but was denied. When I was placed on the SAMs it allowed no visits, letters, or calls with anyone but immediate family. But the institution did not fully enforce this rule and allowed letters from my cousins, uncles, aunts, and grandmother (who was living with us but didn't count as immediate family, according to them). They strongly enforced the rules on visits. In December 2004 the judge ordered the jail to allow me visits from my aunt and uncle.

When my aunt came to see me for the first time I mentioned that I got legal visits in the same exact place. She was already told to speak in English because the FBI was monitoring our visit and she saw the large cameras watching us, so she asked me how I was getting my legal visits in a place that was so heavily monitored. I had no answer. We were not allowed any physical contact here; a screen blocked us. My lawyers couldn't give or take anything from me during these visits, not even a paper, not even a business card. Everything had to be mailed in.

After my trial my SAMs were amended to allow me to talk to other prisoners and I was moved to a regular SHU. During this time a guard saw me talking to another prisoner and asked me about it. I explained that with my new SAMs I could talk to other prisoners and she walked away without a word. The next day I got sanctioned for talking to another prisoner and they took my visits and calls for nine months each. I reminded them that I was allowed to talk and I didn't do anything prohibited, but it was like talking to a wall. After MCC I was in solitary for around five and a half years and I never got a sanction in ADX.

MCC didn't have its own imam or Muslim chaplain. From time to time they hired one on contract and then he would leave in a few months and then another one came for a few months. Because they were on contract they had to be accompanied by the MCC chaplain who was present for all our conversations. They tried to come once a month but many times couldn't even do that. The visits were only for a few minutes and it was a rushed conversation through the cell door.

The attorneys could visit as much as they needed but the visits were non-contact. In fact, during my time in MCC and most of my time in ADX, I was not allowed physical contact (handshake, hug, etc.) with anybody.

When I was convicted of every single charge they actually made my SAMs more lenient. I faced the harshest part of my SAMs and incarceration while I was innocent in the eyes of the American law. The fact that they became lenient about a month after my conviction was counterintuitive and made the SAMs look more like a pressure tactic and less like any security measure, as was claimed.

On the Verge of Hell

JUDITH VAZQUEZ

Judith Vazquez was born in 1956 to parents who emigrated from Puerto Rico. She grew up in Harlem, and later moved to New Jersey. She became the first female licensed electrician in Jersey City, and also did plumbing, carpentry, locksmithing, and mechanics. In 1992, Vazquez was arrested and held at the county jail. She was tried in 1995 and sentenced to thirty years to life for first-degree murder, although she still maintains her innocence and is fighting her case. After trial, she was transported to the Edna Mahan Correctional Facility for Women (EMCF) in Clinton, New Jersey, where she currently remains.

At the county jail, Vazquez spent three years in solitary confinement before, during, and after her trial, without ever receiving an explanation or any due process. She also experienced several additional years in solitary during her time in the maximum security section of EMCF. In 2013, she was finally transferred to a minimum security section of the prison. Now fifty-nine years old, Judith Vazquez has two daughters and four grandchildren, two of whom she has never met.

MY FIRST THREE YEARS (1,095 DAYS) IN SOLITARY WERE PURE HORROR. I was put in solitary in the county jail the minute I was arrested, as I waited for trial.

After I arrived at state prison, I suffered years of rape by guards. I became pregnant and was forced to abort in my cell without any medical aid. Due to the depression and desperation I felt because I had nowhere to turn to for help, I then found myself back in solitary by my own choice.

The day after my arrest, after having bail set at court, upon my return to the county jail, the guards escorted me from population into another area. I was supposed to remain in population while I awaited trial, but they placed me in an area that held just three cells. These cells were meant for females only, and next door through a glass window you could see the men's side, which had more than ten cells. The three cells were empty; I was the only female there. I remember asking the officer why I was there; she said the judge had ordered I be placed there. I thought it was for a night or two, but it turned out to be a nightmare. I went in and never came out until three years later.

Why the judge placed me in this other area, as opposed to population, is beyond me. Many times, very late at night, some captain or lieutenant would open my door and look at me and say, "You are a pretty strong woman, Vazquez, a man would not survive all these years locked in like you have." I would respond, "You can go back and tell whoever put me here, the judge or the prosecutor, that you can put me in a closet for all I care but you will never break me!" They would laugh and slam the door shut. Deep down inside I was afraid, but I could not allow them to see my fear.

Being in this cell for three years felt like a survival task. Much of the food served to me was raw, such as the hot dogs. I would get a lotion bottle and shampoo bottle and put one on top of the other and put one end on the edge of the sink and the other end I would use to press the hot water button so it could stay running. I would then sit there and hold one hot dog under the running hot water for a long time until the hot dog would feel a little hot so that I could eat it, although knowing it was still not fully cooked.

Some late nights I would be awakened by the men yelling, asking the officers about getting help for a very ill male inmate, but no one would come. The next day the ill inmate was being carried out in a body bag. One night I heard screams from the men about a man hanging in his cell. Officers did not show up until thirty minutes later.

• • •

There are things that people use every day and take for granted. Things such as nature. Who would ever think that to be denied nature would be such a big deal? I had no open window. My window was about four inches wide and maybe three feet tall. My view consisted of just bricks and barbed wire. If I could see maybe a dime-sized piece of the sky, it was a lot. As time went by, I noticed a little plant growing from between the bricks. I would look at that plant every day. It was the only view of nature I had. Oh boy, did I love that plant. It was my buddy, my pal. I would watch the breeze blow it from side to side and I would close my eyes and pretend that wind was blowing across my face. I never thought I would crave nature so badly.

As time passed, I started to resent the plant. I wanted to be the one feeling that breeze. One day I couldn't take it anymore, so I grabbed a plastic garbage bag and sealed it around the window, covering it completely. I refused to look at the plant enjoying the breeze I craved. Months went by and the cell was dark all day long.

One day, I decided I had to tear down the plastic bag. I felt I had to find a way to get air! So I began to scrape the rubber seal that held the window to the frame. I used my fingernails to scrape and scrape for days, weeks, and months. It got to the point that my fingernails began to bleed. They hurt so bad that I would cry. But I needed some air. I believe it took about six months of scraping and bleeding before I finally made a tiny little hole. Wow . . . wait. . . . Sorry, I had to stop writing, my tears started to come down as I remember what I went through in that room. At times, I feel it is just past and forgotten, but I guess not.

The hole wasn't big enough so that I could feel a breeze come in, but it was big enough for me to hold my nose against it and inhale. Upon seeing this little opening, I acted savagely. I only had room to put one nostril at a time against the hole, and I would breathe in so hard. It gave me a sense of being human again. I had a secret in that room that the officers did not know about. It was my secret air supply, which was what kept me alive. I no longer felt jealous of the plant. If anything I sort of made the plant my friend again; it was all I had for company.

Thinking back about being in that cell brings tears to my eyes. Three years in a cell might not sound like so long to a civilian who has never been to jail. But I can tell you, those three years felt like a lifetime. It changes people. It turns you into someone you never thought you would be. Your life is just never the same. It's like when a soldier goes to war; there are things that will stay with that soldier forever, and he finds it hard to speak of and ends up having to live with PTSD. Well, being locked in a room for three years is just the same. It plays with your mind, with your emotions, with your life.

One day I felt I could not take it much longer. I felt the world closing in on me and without any control or knowing this was going to happen, I just busted out screaming, uncontrollably. I screamed without being able to stop. As I looked down at the floor, it seemed as though I was standing right at the edge of a cliff. The floor had somehow cracked open and for a moment or so I was not at the jail or in the cell. I was on top of the edge of some ledge where when I looked down I saw an endless pit of fire and darkness. I saw people screaming, crying, and burning.

In my eyes and thoughts I was looking at hell. I was right at the edge, and as I screamed I was trying to keep my balance. I was about to fall in and I managed to throw my balance where I fell back and landed sitting down on the floor and the pit had closed up and I was back in my cell. By then I was able to control this screaming and stopped and I was terrified and frightened from what I had just seen. I then rubbed my mouth with my hand, feeling I had drooled, and found blood on my hands. This screaming that unexpectedly burst out of me and that I was not able to control was so strong I actually bled from within.

The officers did not hear me because I could scream all I wanted and no one would hear or if they did, they ignored me. But what made this even more crazy was that at that moment when I had fallen back on my butt and sat there wiping this blood from my mouth, my door was opened by the guard and she had a priest with her! Somehow I guess the priest was at the jail that day, maybe seeing other inmates. I'm not sure, because I had never ever seen a priest there before. But the look on my face was so surprised, and he just looked at me as he saw me on the floor, and he asked me, "Are you OK?" Then he went on to tell me how he had heard about me being there and decided to come back and say hello and let me know if I needed him I could ask to see him.

I have no explanation for this. I was not sleeping and didn't dream this. I was up and pacing the floor with worries about how I was going to find help, or if I was there forever. But I never forgot what I saw. As a matter of fact, now that I have spoken on this for the first time, I may just sit down one day soon and draw this scene.

Although I overcame my claustrophobia in my jail cell, I developed another phobia—agoraphobia. When the day came for me to be transferred to the state prison, EMCF, the officers had to fight with me, and drag me out. I did not want to leave my cell. I had become used to this life of solitude. I feared being around people. I wanted to be in my cell all alone with my plant. I felt so dehumanized. Sorry . . . again I had to stop writing because my tears were coming down.

When I first arrived at the state prison in 1995 in general population, I felt like a space alien seeing our world for the first time. To see the green of grass and trees through the barbed wire and gates felt unusual. But what was really weird was to look up to the sky. It was huge, beyond huge! As I slowly spun around looking up, I can still hear myself saying, "WOW!" Other girls would look strangely at me. To see a television was even more odd. They had new shows I had never heard of, new commercials, new products in advertising. But these new visions did not last long because my eyes hurt so bad I broke down crying. To see all this light and color was too much for my eyes after spending three years in darkness.

Once you arrive to state prison, you are assigned a job. I worked steadily, but staying to myself. I worked and went right back to my cell. Then in 1998, I began to experience the sex abuse by the officers. I became pregnant and was forced to abort in my cell by the officer who abused me. I thought that day I was going to die. This abuse went on until 2001. By then I had sunk into a depression. In 2004, I became disabled and could not work anymore. With no job to go to, I had to remain in my cell all day and night. In maximum, there is very little movement. If you do not work or go to school then you must stay in your cell. I remained idle and again found myself in a form of solitary from 2004 to 2013.

In March 2013, I was classified from maximum to minimum and moved to what we call "grounds," and the transition was from night to day. When I was told I was moving to grounds, I had an anxiety attack. I was terrified! A couple of nurses were called to sit with me and calm me down. I told them, "Look. Imagine a shoe box. I am kept inside of it with the lid closed. Twenty years later, here you come and open the lid, pull me out, and tell me, 'Ok, Judy, go ahead, you are free of solitary.' AAAAAHHHHHH!!!"

These people have no idea of the damage they did to me by keeping me in this "shoe box" for so many years. They provided me with no therapy in getting one ready for such a big move—they think it's nothing. But I must say that the "grounds" is beautiful. Lots of trees, grass, and animals, and it's peaceful. I actually am allowed to go outside and walk. Something I had not done in more than twenty years! You should have seen me trying to walk; I looked like a nine-month-old baby taking her first steps. Still I walk funny. Mind you, for more than twenty years I basically just wore slippers and to wear shoes or sneakers feels odd to me. I feel I was actually dehumanized.

Even after months of these beautiful "grounds" I find I cannot cope or adjust. I find myself putting myself back into solitary. Sometimes, I fear I may not be able to get out of this solitary confinement "urge" I find myself having. As much as I want to go home, I fear walking out the front gates. I have sort of found myself sinking back into solitary. Not because "They" are putting me there. This time it is "Me" doing it to myself.

Supermax Diary

JOSEPH DOLE

Joseph Dole was born in Michigan and raised in Illinois, and has been incarcerated since the age of twenty-two. He continues to fight pro se against his conviction for what prosecutors called a gang-related double murder, for which he is serving a sentence of life without parole. Dole spent more than a decade in solitary confinement in the now-closed Tamms Correctional Center, a supermax prison in southern Illinois that became notorious for housing individuals with mental illness. Despite the prison being purpose-built for extreme isolation, much of Dole's piece describes the interactions—wanted and unwanted—among men on his "pod," who shout to one another from behind steel perforated doors or over cement walls in the exercise pens, or communicate via jailhouse sign language from afar through cell windows.

A self-educated jailhouse lawyer and journalist, Dole has published work in the anthologies Lockdown Prison Heart *and* Too Cruel, Not Unusual Enough, *as well as in the* Mississippi Review, *the* Journal of Prisoners on Prison, *and several other publications. His first book,* A Costly American Hatred, *was self-published in 2015. His latest book is* Control Units and Supermaxes: A National Security Threat. *Dole is the winner of four PEN Prison Writing awards. What follow are just some of the entries from the diary he kept in the spring and summer of 2011. He is now being held in Stateville Correctional Center, southwest of Chicago.*

THE FIRST TIME I EVER REALLY WROTE ANYTHING WAS SHORTLY AFTER I arrived at Tamms. I wrote an essay. I had never written an essay before, not even in school as far as I can remember. Yet, desperate for money, I tried my hand at it. There was an essay contest being put on by a death row inmate and a good Samaritan. The theme was "Who Am I?" I learned of the contest from another prisoner who yelled out the details from down the gallery. I had to send it in that night in order to make the deadline. I simply wrote down the first thing that came to mind. Surprisingly I won first place and fifty bucks, even more than the ten dollars promised to every entrant. More than anything, though, it inspired me to learn how to write better. In prison good writing skills are essential for just about everything—keeping in contact with your family (especially here in Tamms where they still won't allow us to make phone calls); presenting your appeals in concise, coherent arguments to the courts; advocating for change; filing grievances; etc.

In that first essay, I briefly touched on what it is like in prison. I wrote:

"Most people's conceptions of being locked up are completely wrong. It's not the physical things that you're without that make it so hard to be incarcerated for life. It's the fact that you're helpless to take care of your family when they're sick, to raise your children, to help in their times of struggle, and to give back to your community. Instead you're a burden, a charity case, someone to pity. It strips you of your self-esteem and your self-respect. That is what breaks a man, not the absence of good food, alcohol, sex, or any of the other inconsequential things we may often wish we had to temporarily give us pleasure."

I still find all of that true. Yet, after being confined and isolated for the past nine years in a supermax prison, I've also come to realize that the little things add up too. There are a million little stressors and injustices that prisoners must endure on a daily basis that can also break a man. These are what I will try to describe with this diary. Each one may seem minor, but the cumulative effect of them all is what drives so many here insane.

March 15, 2011 4:30 a.m.
When I went to see the nurse she informed me that the doctor will

not treat a hernia until it becomes strangulated and is a life-and-death situation. I was scheduled to see the doctor, "Dr. Death," nevertheless. We call him Dr. Death because of his complete lack of compassion for prisoners and his priority of saving his employer money over the lives or health of his patients.

When I saw Dr. Death, he told me, "You're alright. It's reducible." I asked him, "Shouldn't I get it repaired?" He responded, "Yeah, but we're not going to do it. You can get it repaired when you get out." I told him that I'm never getting out, as I have a life without parole sentence. He responded, "Oh, then you'll die with it." I then asked him, "What about the pain?" He said, "You're tough, you can handle it."

I'm working on only about three hours' sleep right now. Two guys on the wing "bugged up" last night, and were screaming and kicking on the door all night. If you've ever heard anyone slam steel against steel, you can imagine how loud and nerve-racking five continuous hours of that deafening noise sixty times per minute in close quarters would be. We say someone has "bugged up" when they lose it and start disturbing the wing. We call the guys who are more mentally disturbed "bugs." I'm not sure why. Maybe it is a reference to pests, or people bugging others or something? Who knows?

The prison vernacular is a hodgepodge of English, Spanish, and Ebonics, filled with innuendos, euphemisms, slang, etc. I've been in prison for more than a decade and half the time I still don't know what people are saying. What's worse is that my language skills are deteriorating to the point where sometimes my family can't understand what I'm saying or I no longer pronounce words correctly and don't even notice. Others have heard me talk on the wing without seeing me and have said they thought I was Latino because I have a Spanish accent. When did that happen? Do I really? I can't tell if I do.

March 19, 2011 5:40 a.m.
Usually it's quiet at this time of the morning. That's why I choose to write this diary around this same time each day. Today, though, Yip and Yap (two "bugs" on the wing) are screaming at each other. This on top of the background noise of door kicking and howls of the mentally ill on some other wing. I imagine it will be another busy day for the guards. All the noise is usually a harbinger of inmates flooding or trashing the galleries, if not inmates tearing toilets off the walls or throwing feces at each other and/or staff. Did you know that guys are being sentenced to an extra five years sometimes for throwing feces at

guards? That means if they serve those extra five years in Tamms the taxpayers are paying $450,000 to punish a guy for slinging urine or excrement at a guard.

It's never completely quiet on the wing unless a power outage occurs. There's a constant and loud white noise here at Tamms. It's the giant fan that struggles to circulate air in an otherwise hermetically sealed environment. You get used to it but only after some months. After a year or so there would be times that it would just really drive me crazy, though. Then after about two years it ceased to ever bother me. It adds to the difficulty in communicating with others on the wing.

Whenever they mace someone on the pod it spreads to every wing. So even if it's on the other side of the pod you're going to be coughing too. If you're on the same wing as someone who gets maced you too feel the full effects because you're in a sealed cement box of ten cells sharing the same air. The administrative directive concerning the use of chemical agents states that staff is supposed to move everyone not being maced off the wing before macing someone, but they never comply with that directive. (Why bother? Macing eight or ten prisoners is more fun than macing just one.)

March 21, 2011 5:00 p.m.

I tried to send a card to my stepmother but it was just given back to me because I have insufficient funds to pay for the postage.

Last Friday I received a letter from my mother telling me that while one of my stepmother's brothers was in the hospital getting open-heart surgery, her other brother died of a heart attack. I guess she had to call my sister to pick up my father. My father is mentally disabled and someone has to be with him at all times. He had a stroke/heart attack more than a decade ago and now can't remember anything past a couple of minutes ago. So he couldn't handle being in the hospital all that time and was driving my stepmother nuts. I'm completely useless in any type of situation like this. All I can do is send a card offering my condolences. Even then, only if or when I have the funds to do so. I can't call her, go help out with my father, help her with anything concerning the funeral, etc. I'm completely impotent to be of any assistance to anyone.

That is what breaks you. It's not just that American society views anyone who is in prison as evil, stupid, and worthless. It's that, with a life-without-parole sentence, you're daily reminded of just how impotent you are and always will be if you don't get out. You're forced to view every family tragedy as a spectator, but with all the emotions of being personally affected that are compounded because you also know you can't do anything for your family. You can't take care of them when they're sick, help them when they need a hand, or even attend a funeral. Being in a supermax with no phone calls also means you learn of the deaths of family and friends weeks after the fact in a letter. Letters you reread over and over hoping that you somehow misread it the first half dozen times.

March 27, 2011 9:10 a.m.
It's Sunday morning. Once again Yip and Yap are screaming at each other. I have my earphones in with the radio blaring, destroying my hearing. I'm trying to drown out the noise. Unfortunately, people have their cell lights on so it makes the radio really staticky.

My writer's block is gone. The music and yelling are making it difficult to compose my thoughts, but I'd like to expound on why I have such a hard time coping with being incarcerated with a life-without-parole sentence and confined in a supermax prison with the plethora of restrictions solitary confinement entails, for years and years on end.

What makes prison so hard is having ambitions, dreams, and goals, and wanting to do right and accomplish positive things. Prison is conducive to none of these. It's so much easier to not care about life, not learn, not grow intellectually, not mature. It's easier to just hate—hate life, hate people, hate yourself. Striving to do something with your life, especially under these conditions, makes every day that much harder. It's always easiest to destroy or ignore. Hardest to care and build up yourself, other people, society, etc. It's easier for people to give up—on themselves, their children, others. It's why society finds it so easy to automatically demonize and write off anyone convicted or even charged with a crime without even knowing for certain whether he or she is guilty, or the circumstances surrounding the incident. All they need to know is that he or she is a "suspect" or a prisoner, or arrested for X crime, etc. It's much harder to look into the situation before making a judgment, harder to have compassion, harder to deal with the societal ills or root causes of crime. It's so much easier to be smug and sanctimonious. Easier to be deliberately indifferent to what is happening in your community until it adversely affects you and then just scream for revenge, rather than to try to understand how things came about. I know, that's how I used to be in my youth. Selfish, indifferent, not a care in the world.

That's also the easiest way to do a prison bit. It's safest to only look out for yourself. It's easiest to not care about your family and their struggles. It's easiest to sit around and read urban novels and watch the idiot box all day, not doing the hard work to try to accomplish anything with your life. Not fighting for your rights or the rights of others, not sticking up for or lending a hand to anyone.

I can't live like that. I want to make a difference and accomplish as much as I possibly can with the remaining grains of sand that plummet all too quickly in my inner hour glass.

I want to be a good father to my two beautiful daughters. I can't do that from in here—no matter how much I try. A prerequisite to being a good father is being there for your child. I can't be there for them, so I fight with every ounce in me to change that. Oh how easy it would be to not write them every week when they don't write me for months. How much heartache and stress it would save me not to constantly worry about how their health, grades, and lives are, and how my being here is affecting them or how it will impact their lives in the long run. How easy it would be to give up on all my avenues of appeal and collateral attacks on my conviction and sentence and just quit on life, becoming a bunk potato for the next five decades.

It would be so easy to harden my heart and not worry about how my family is doing, not care about the thousands of problems facing our communities and country. It would be so easy to not study all these issues, not write proposals, articles, reports, etc. Not stress about how I am so powerless to make a difference from in here. It would be so easy to cease trying to understand others' points of view, to show compassion, or to forgive those who have done me wrong. It would be so easy to repay every wrong done to me with an equal or greater wrong.

March 28, 2011 6:14 a.m.

I'm really getting started late today. I just got out of bed about fifteen minutes ago and only got about five hours of sleep. Five interrupted hours of sleep, though, as Yip and Yap were sporadically going at it all night. These guys drive me nuts, but I get along with both of them and try to understand that not only are they clearly mentally ill, but also that a lot of what they do are clear symptoms of what is commonly referred to as "SHU Syndrome" (Secure Housing Unit Syndrome) and what we call Tamms Syndrome.

What cracks me up is that they are completely oblivious as to how much they disturb the rest of the wing. They were screaming at each other in the middle of the night and in the wee hours of the morning, and thirty seconds after they stop one of them calmly calls me, as if nothing has been going on, and asks me to spell a word for him—at five in the morning, when I know at least two other guys are trying to sleep.

Most days I feel like "information," you know, when you call 411? Or nowadays I guess it's more like "Ask Jeeves." Instead I'm like "Cell Seven, how may I help you?" All day every day guys are calling up here asking me to help them with stuff, or to ask me questions, or to look something up, etc. Some days I just have to tell everyone to stay off my door. Otherwise I'll never be able to finish what I need to finish.

One guy—Yip, one of the screamers—I have to intentionally be rude to for him to leave me alone. If I don't he will try and start a thousand conversations just so he can have something to do. He can't read past like a first-grade level. He has so little knowledge about nearly every subject imaginable that the majority of his questions are completely illogical, and even when they are coherent enough for you to understand them you need to explain a hundred other things first. The whole time, though, he's not really interested in the conversation. He just wants to hear someone talk. Whenever the conversation starts winding down, he'll ask another question that usually has no connection to what you were talking about, or just as often evidences that he didn't listen to anything you just said.

Why does he do it? Because he's in his cell with no TV and no radio, uneducated, and can't read or write to pass the time. So his choice is usually to try and get someone to talk to him or to scream at Yap, his nemesis. He is so desperate to talk to anyone that he drives the guards crazy hitting the emergency intercom button, stops the guards every time they come on the wing every half hour to make rounds (to make sure no one escaped or that no one else has killed himself), and every time he sees anyone come on the pod he screams at the top of his lungs, all to try to get them to come talk to him. Why they put him in cell #1 (the only cell that can see everything that happens out in the main area of the pod) is beyond me. They hate him screaming for people yet put him in the only cell that gives him a view to even know that someone has entered the pod. He knows every employee in the institution and nearly every mundane detail of their personal lives. The car they drive, which of their family members work for the IDOC, who they're dating, married to, etc.

March 30, 2011 6:03 a.m.
Yesterday I was talking to someone through the window on another pod. Because we are so isolated and compartmentalized from one another we communicate through the two strips of four-inch-wide, dirty window that sit in the wall about eight feet above the floor of our cells. In order to see out of them you have to stack either your property boxes, if you have any, or all of your bedding—folded up mattress, blankets, and pillow—and stand on it. The shorter you are the more difficult it is. Because the windows do not open, the only way to communicate is through sign language. The administration some years back prohibited sign language instruction books to try and hinder communication. That was a futile undertaking. The first guys down here weren't about to wait until everyone could order the same books, so they began developing their own sign language system. Or actually systems. Because there's so little movement and each wing can only see a couple other wings, a number of sign languages were developed autonomously. Therefore each inmate knows a few different systems, and can easily adapt to a new one in the beginning when speaking to someone new.

Anyway, the guy I was speaking to out of the window was telling me how they refuse to provide him surgery for his hemorrhoids and how embarrassing and degrading going to see Dr. Death was. First, they come and shake/strip him down then handcuff and shackle him in boxers and a t-shirt and take him out to a little medical station. It's located on the pod and is completely open to viewing by anyone entering the pod. All while he is held on either side by two guards who were not only cracking homosexual jokes at his expense, but who will also inevitably tell their coworkers and other inmates about his medical condition.

You would think that people can't just arbitrarily treat you like this, but in prison it's all too common. According to the Prison Litigation Reform Act (PLRA), prisoners can't sue if they can't prove a serious physical injury. While I could sue for the assault while handcuffed, I couldn't sue for the four days of humiliation. So, for instance, all the terrible photos everyone saw in the media about how prisoners in

Abu Ghraib were humiliated, they could do that to prisoners in the United States and we would have no recourse whatsoever because humiliation, debasement, and mental and emotional suffering are not actionable.

Why? Because everyone hates prisoners, so laws like the PLRA can sail through with little opposition. We (prisoners) can't even garner the same public sympathy from Americans that our enemies garner. I find it really ironic and hypocritical that society always expects prisoners not only to rehabilitate themselves and follow the rules and laws, both when they are in prison and after they are released, yet guards and administration officials constantly break the rules and laws with little to no accountability. What's that maxim? Something about how a society is judged by how it treats its least powerful citizens?

April 2, 2011 6:15 a.m.
I just realized that I'm nearly out of paper. Let's see. What's one other example of what it feels like to be incarcerated that I haven't touched on? I guess I'll briefly explain about women. For homosexual male prisoners I guess it's fortuitous that they have no desire for women. For heterosexual male prisoners, the absence of women increasingly gnaws at our essence more and more each day as the years pile up.

It's not the absence of sex that weighs so heavily, although that certainly weighs on us as well. Of course most heterosexual men have a primal urge to have sex and procreate that is as old as humanity itself. It is something that is encoded in our being. No, there is something even more devastating. After having experienced a woman's companionship and the anxiety of a new relationship with a woman and the joy it brings, you don't want to believe you will never experience them again. It's difficult to come to terms with the fact that I may never get to fall in love again. Never meet, love, and live a lifetime with a "better half" or "soul mate." Not having touched, smelled, or had the companionship of a woman for well more than a decade is so soul-decaying that I can't adequately describe the toll it takes on me.

I dream not about having sex, but rather the sweet mundane moments shared with the mother of my children that I hadn't realized at the time had been recorded in my brain. The most vivid recurring dream I have is of her getting out of the shower with a plush maroon towel wrapped around her petite frame from the swell of her breast to the thick of her thigh. Residual heat from the shower pulses out of her every pore. Her hair is wet, curly, and long. As she steps out of the bathroom, I kiss her warm, moist lips and then smell the hollow of her clavicle while I enfold her into me. Her smell can only be described as immaculate euphoria. She is unblemished by any tattoo, makeup, or hair product residue. That's the entire dream, just holding her. Yet, other than when I've held my daughters as babies, I know of no other moment that gave me such a feeling of peace, joy, and pure love, as I felt at that moment, and I get to relive that feeling every time I have that dream. It is the only time I have ever had such a feeling in prison, and every time I have that dream I always worry that I'll never again have a similar experience and am terrified that I'll cease having that dream.

I don't know how well I've been able to convey what it is like living out a life-without-parole sentence in prison. Reading over what I've written doesn't seem worthy of anyone's time. It actually seems like a pretty boring read. I suppose part of it is because I am the one who wrote it and lives this monotonous existence.

This diary is as close as I can come to conveying what it is like to live in a supermax prison with a natural-life sentence. I'm in a sea of madness during an eternal perfect storm of despair and heartache for the duration of my breaths, constantly conscious of the fact that nearly the entire country despises me without knowing anything about me other than I am a prisoner. I've survived thirteen years so far. Just forty or fifty more to go.

RESISTING

Writing Out of Solitude

*Born and raised in Detroit, Shaka Senghor was eighteen years old in
1991 when he shot a man in a fight that started over drugs. Sentenced
to up to forty years for second-degree murder, he served nearly twenty in
Michigan state prisons before being paroled. Senghor says he experienced
an "epiphany" in prison after receiving a letter from his eight-year-old son,
born while he was behind bars. "I realized that, although I was incarcerated, I had a responsibility to set an example for him." In this excerpt
from a longer essay about his prison experience, Senghor writes about the
knife-edge racial and interpersonal dynamics that play out behind bars,
and his struggle to maintain his spirit during his first stay in solitary.*

*Senghor began studying and writing while in prison, and after his
release he founded a mentoring program, the Live in Peace Digital and
Literary Arts Project, which encourages Detroit students to "take control
of their own destinies through literature," and which won grants from
the Knight and Open Society Foundations in 2012. He has since been
named a 2013 MIT Media Lab Director's Fellow and a 2014 W.K.
Kellogg Community Leadership Network Fellow. His memoir,* Writing
My Wrongs, *was published as an e-book in 2013, and his TED talk
has received more than a million views.*

THE SOUND OF THE SIREN PULSATES THROUGHOUT MY BRAIN. WHEN I reach the top of the steps I know there's going to be a problem—the officer standing in front of the bathroom door dislikes me. In his eyes, I don't fit the criteria of the complacent, subservient prisoner he's accustomed to dealing with. I'm not supposed to challenge his authority or quote policy; I'm supposed to walk past him with my head lowered, mumbling to myself, straight back to my unit for emergency count.

"Where do you think you're going?" he asks sarcastically. I tell him I need to use the bathroom.

"I don't think so," he says, letting another inmate enter in front of me. I know I have three choices: I can urinate on myself, urinate out my cell window, or walk past the officer and urinate in the toilet three feet away from me. If I take the logical choice, I will have to accept a ticket for "disobeying a direct order"—and this officer's wrath along with it. At minimum, he'll shake down my cell, throwing my belongings around. Still, being desensitized to the value of property, I'm not too concerned about that.

"That was an assault on staff," the officer says as I begin using the urinal. His words echo in my ears as I relieve myself. I'm vexed at the thought of a trumped-up assault charge. As I wash my hands, the officer and I exchange glances. "Give me your ID," he says, blocking my exit. I inform him that I don't have it on me. He smiles sardonically, and I realize he's enjoying this immensely. I attempt to slide past, and that's when I hear the word "nigger" and feel his hands on my chest—demanding I produce an ID that I don't have.

In my mind I hear the word "nigger" repeating again and again as I land each blow. A sense of calm overcomes me. The officer is on the floor and I'm choking him. I feel years of oppression sliding off me—four hundred years of oppression that African people have endured on this continent. I feel liberated, even as my hands are being twisted behind my back and I'm dragged off the unconscious officer.

As medics fight to save the officer's life, two other officers place burning cold handcuffs on my wrists and tell me I'm going to the hole. Before I leave the building, I glance behind me at the other prisoners—"captives" as I like to call them—standing around watching the show. What I see in their eyes makes my spirit buckle. I see contempt and anger, and it's directed at me, not the officers. In that moment something clicks. I realize that most of these men would kill each other at the drop of a hat, but they hate me for standing up for their humanity.

I twist and jerk as the two officers drag me to solitary confinement—what we call "the hole"—which I've always literally imagined as a deep hollow dug into the dirt ground. Instead, I'm thrown into a shower, the officer nearly breaking my arm as he pulls it out of the slot to remove the cuffs for a strip search. I had assaulted one of his co-workers, and he wants me to know he doesn't appreciate it.

As I'm led onto the cellblock known as the "Graves," I'm assaulted by the unbearable smell of human despair. Defecation, unwashed armpits, soggy toes, and spoiled booties mingle in the air with the pepper spray officers use to extract prisoners from their cells. "Graves" is called what it is because in here you're dead to everyone in the general prison population—the cells are so small it feels like being squeezed into a coffin. It's by far one of the worst places a human being can find himself.

As I'm escorted down the hall, I keep my head forward. The convict code says not to look into another prisoner's cell; we don't want to deny each other the last semblance of privacy. Not everyone stays true to this code, and it's often the cause of conflict, leading the "Peeping Tom" to be stabbed on the yard or flashed with genitalia. I have no desire to see another man shaking his private parts in anger, nor do I want to stab anyone or be stabbed, so I keep my head forward.

The tier is relatively quiet; most of the prisoners appear to be sleeping, although it can't be much past noon. I look around my dingy new cell in disgust. The cellblock windows are painted grey. The only natural light sneaks in in the rare event that one of the officers is nice enough to leave a window cracked. Otherwise, the only way to gauge time is when meals are passed out. The bed is six inches off the floor, the toilet stuffed behind a small footlocker. In order to sit down and take a dump, I have to remove my jumpsuit and fold my legs behind the locker.

Soon another prisoner who works as a porter arrives with a food tray. The portion is nearly half the size I'm used to on the mainline. I devour the small meal like a ravenous wolf and place my tray back on the bars. I've never liked milk so I leave the carton sitting on top of my locker. When the porter comes back he sees the milk and gives me a "Man, you crazy?" look. I shrug. "Hide it in your locker," he whispers, "unless you want to be on food loaf." I have no idea what "food loaf" is, but his tone sounds cautionary enough that I decide to take his advice.

I lie down and try to sleep until dinner, the hum of other voices drifting down the tier. I find myself thinking about how I'd arrived at this point. I'm too smart for this shit, I think angrily and stare at the paint-chipped ceiling. As I lie there, the thoughts I'd long been able to stuff down on the mainline by watching television or playing basketball now rush to the forefront of my mind. I think about how soft my girlfriend's lips used to feel against mine, how good it felt to guzzle down an ice-cold forty on a hot summer day, and the late-night laughter that used to echo through the 'hood as we sat on the porch at two in the morning playing the dozens. No matter how many times I close and open my eyes, this nightmarish existence is still here.

Hours later, I hear the chow cart squeaking down the tier. I retrieve my tray, suck down the bland slop they call dinner, and this time I drink the milk. The lights go out. Where my cell is, on the bottom tier, there isn't even enough light to stand at the bars and read, so I lie down and begin to pray for sleep.

"BOOM. BOOM. BOOM," a sound as startling as a shotgun echoes through the tier. Someone is kicking the lid of their footlocker over and over.

"Get y'all bitch ass up," another voice yells. "Ain't no sleep around here."

A chain of events unlike anything I've ever imagined is set into motion. The once-quiet hole transforms into an anarchic stronghold as inmates bang on their lockers and hurl racial epithets and disparaging homosexual remarks through the air like hand grenades. Trash and sheets are set on fire and flown across the tier. Other inmates stuff their toilets with sheets and flush until water cascades over the tier like Victoria Falls. I stare in disbelief as the floor quickly becomes a small wading pool. After a few initial attempts to restore order by turning off the water supply the officers give up and the mayhem continues till dawn.

Over the next couple days, I learn how to sleep through the mornings and afternoons because every night the war would start again. Throughout the day, officer after officer passes by to peer into my cell, like I'm an animal in a zoo; curious to see the "monster" that assaulted one of their own.

A lot of the prisoners at Graves do act like animals, or worse. They wage battle after battle against the officers and each other. Their weapon of choice is what's called "Weapons of Ass Destruction," feces-filled bottles hurled at anyone considered an enemy. Once squirted with a shit pistol, no matter how many showers you take, the thought and feeling of being drenched in another person's defecation is not easily forgotten. The smell hangs in the air like a miasmic cloud for days, and stands as a reminder for everyone else to be careful.

Officers do what they can to stop the wars. First, they drill shut the food slots on our cell doors. In response, several inmates go into Mac-Gyver mode and figure out a way to jimmy the locks open. One way is to slide a comb attached to a piece of string out of the top of the door while your neighbor guides your movements across the hall. Once the comb is lined up with the bolt, you pull it back and forth until the lock comes undone. After that, all that's left to do is slide a cable cord under the door, twist it around the knob, and continue twisting until the slot pops open. Then it's business as usual.

Every day I struggle to ensure I don't fall into these abysmal wars myself. First, I sit down to write to my son's mother, then my ex-girlfriend in Ohio. Before I know it, I'm writing to everyone I know. The hours pass quickly as I scratch out letter after letter with a dull two-inch pencil. When the third shift comes on at 10:00 p.m., I'm still immersed in writing. At midnight they cut the power off and I lie down to sleep, my fingers sore to the bone.

I realize writing is my escape. By writing I seek to understand what's happening around me. The chaos in the hole is an attempt for men to gain some semblance of control over their environment. When a fight breaks out between two prisoners it affects the whole wing. That way, others are drawn into it.

Whenever the officers do something that we feel is unjust, we respond by flooding the wing with water from our toilets until they come and cut it off. This is the only way we have of voicing our grievances and getting a response. The officers know if they don't pass out our mail in a timely fashion or if they serve us our meals cold, they'll have to wade through water until the porters come to clean it up. They know if they deny us showers, we'll beat on the doors relentlessly until they let us go. The way we see it, if we don't fight back, we might as well lie down and die.

One night a Latino prisoner set himself on fire, so desperate for escape from this pain and misery he would rather end his life through immolation. After days of harassment about his sexual orientation by guards, he woke everyone up in the middle of the night reciting a chilling rendition of the Lord's Prayer. The next day he set his cell on fire. The officers sprayed him with a fire extinguisher then took him to suicide watch where he set himself on fire again.

I have come to realize that I'll never leave this prison the same person I was when I came in. Although my reaction to this environment isn't expressed externally like some of the others, internal scars can be far worse. I start to keep a journal and between the thin pages of a note pad make sense of the person I've come to be. The officers have no interest in seeing me turn my life around; to most of them, I represent job security. The state has long ago given up on rehabilitation. If I'm ever going to become the man and father I was destined to be, I have to take a long and painful look at myself.

I begin to chart my anger, and my reaction to my anger. Through this process, I realize I'm not that different from those who use "Weapons of Ass Destruction." Inside of me burns that same rage, the rage that nearly cost an officer his life and could cost me the rest of my mine in prison. The same anger clung to my back when I was on the streets, leading me to take another person's life. The absence of a real relationship with my mother, my parents' divorce, how my mother would beat me for the littlest things . . . all of these things affected me as a child. The more I write, the more I feel a weight being lifted off my shoulders. I'm tired of living in a ball of anger and bitterness. I'm tired of hurting people.

Six months after the day they brought me to "Graves," the officers inform me that I'm going to be transferred. After a long bus ride, they bring me into the control center of a technologically advanced prison. Six or seven officers stand around glaring at me. One officer removes the black box that's wrapped around my handcuffs to prevent me from escaping. Another approaches me with a pair of handcuffs attached to what looks like a dog leash. It's the first time I had seen anything like it, and my immediate thought is that it is a violation of the Universal Declaration of Human Rights, which states that "No one shall be subjected to torture or to cruel, inhuman or degrading treatment or punishment."

The officers lead me down the tier on this "leash." One of them motions to the control bubble and the door to my new cell slides open. Once inside the spartan cell, for the first time in my life I feel completely alone. A flat green mattress is folded on top of a thick slab of concrete that protrudes from the side wall. Another shorter slab of concrete protrudes from the back wall over the concrete bed, which I discover is meant to be a writing surface or television. I roll the mattress out, place the sheets on it, fold the blanket, and then sit back.

Then a piece of paper attached to a string slides under my door. I don't know what it is so I just sit on my bunk staring at it. Then, a voice calls out my cell number and tells me to pull in the line. I climb down on my hands and knees, peek under my door, and see that the string leads under the door of another cell. As I begin to pull, I see a magazine slide out from under his door. I pull it in; attached is a short note from him introducing him as Lowrider and letting me know if I need something else to just holler.

The next day they move an inmate across from me named Reed. I jump down on the floor and watch under the door as the officers force him into his cell. I hear him yell to remove the mask from his face and see the officers walk away with something made of black mesh, like something out of a fetish magazine. Lunch comes and I hear the officers ask Reed if he wants his food loaf. He tells them to get the hell away from his door. I look down at the small rations on my tray, and despite how hungry I am I know I can't eat without offering to share them with Reed. I slide my "car" over to him on a string with a small note asking him if he wants to share my rations. Immediately he sends me a kite back with a note saying he does. I take half of my food, place it in a few envelopes, attach it to the line, and slide it back across to him. For the next two weeks, I share every meal with Reed.

One day I notice Reed getting a food tray like everyone else. One of the nice officers had left the window open on our cell door that morning. I hear Reed call me to my window so I step up. It's the first time I've seen him face to face.

"What's going on, Reed?" I ask.

"You know what?" he begins.

"Naw, what?" I ask.

"Man, you a bitch ass dick sucker. Now get your hoe ass on your bunk and lay down." Then he breaks out into a maniacal laughter.

I stand there with my mouth agape, not really believing what I heard. I feel my anger rise and burn red-hot. The first chance I get, I tell myself, I'm going to stab that piece of shit in the neck. I look at Reed with his face twisted and deformed by years of being subjugated. I imagine my own face, contorted with rage. No, I think, this is not where I'm meant to be. I'm too smart for this.

Loneliness Is a
Destroyer of Humanity

Jesse Wilson

Jesse Wilson was originally convicted of larceny and sent to prison in Mississippi for five years at the age of seventeen. Wilson recalls that he was "at war with the guards," and his behavior eventually landed him in the infamous Unit 32 at Parchman State Penitentiary. There, in 2007, he killed a man being held on death row. Sentenced to life in prison, he was sent to the United States Penitentiary, Administrative Maximum (ADX) in Florence, Colorado, where he wrote this essay in 2012. The federal government's only supermax, ADX holds about four hundred men in the most extreme isolation of any prison in the nation. It has been called "a clean version of hell" by one of its own former wardens. Wilson, now thirty-three, calls it "the end of the line."

Wilson writes of himself: "Past these tattoos and this penitentiary pain, I remain, a son, a brother, a friend, and a human being. It sometimes feels that is forgotten. But it's very true; I too have ideas, thoughts, passions, emotions, insights, and, yes, feelings. I laugh, love, cry, and, like every other person, I long for acceptance and friendship. I've learned over time and after my horrible experiences that prison is not a place to seek acceptance. Not very much good grows inside of cold concrete."

I REFUSE TO EMBRACE THE SOLITUDE. THIS IS NOT NORMAL. I'M NOT A monster and do not deserve to live in a concrete box. I am a man who has made mistakes, true. But I do not deserve to spend the rest of my life locked in a cage—what purpose does that serve? Why even waste the money to feed me? If I'm a monster who must live alone in a cage, why not just kill me?

Our country has thousands of its people confined to concrete cages. Years pass, lives pass. The suffering does not. Our families suffer most, watching us grow old and go crazy in a cage. This is my biggest pain, knowing my mother and sister suffer with me. I cannot see how this is helpful to society. Most men will spend years in a cage alone and be released back into society filled with hate and rage. It is an ugly truth. We as a country are blind to the reality of our prison system.

It has become normal. And we the inmates are voiceless. Our voices are not heard. If they are heard, the things we say are thought of as lies. I heard the head of the Bureau of Prisons testifying in Congress (on radio), saying they do not have insane inmates housed here. This is what should be thought of as a lie. I have not slept in weeks because of these nonexistent inmates beating on the walls and hollering all night. And the most non-insane smearing feces in their cells.

This place is horrific with the solitary, and the lack of communication outside these walls. I've been in prison without release for more than twelve years, and eight of them I've been in a cage walking around in circles. So I am pretty in tune with the concept of solitary. Prison. Cages and craziness.

Out my window I see into a concrete yard surrounded by red brick walls. There is a drain in the middle of it and out of it weeds are growing. I thought they were weeds until a few blossomed into these beautiful yellow and brown flowers.

Every now and then a pair of owls roosts on the security lights. This spring they had two babies. We watched them grow up and fly away. On any given day the sky here is breathtaking. The beauty out my window stays in my mind. I look around this cage at plain concrete walls and steel bars and a steel door, a steel toilet, and I endure its harshness because I am able to keep beauty in my mind.

The window helps greatly.

I'm in the hole so there is no TV. Books help me escape better than my words could ever explain. But most of all it's the love of my family, the memories of beauty, and the knowledge of humanity.

Loneliness is a destroyer of humanity.

A Tale of Evolving Resistance

TODD LEWIS ASHKER

*Todd Ashker, fifty-two, spent his teenage years "in and out of juvenile fa-
cilities" for various nonviolent infractions, and was imprisoned for burglary
at the age of eighteen. In 1990, he was convicted of second-degree murder
for killing another prisoner in what he describes as a "prearranged fight."
He was subsequently "validated" as a member of the Aryan Brotherhood,
an affiliation he continues to deny. Ashker has since been held in isolation
at Pelican Bay State Prison.*

*In 2013 the call for the largest coordinated hunger strike in American
history came from the Pelican Bay Short Corridor Collective, a political
alliance between the twenty "main representatives" of the prison racial
groups. Ashker is one of these representatives, along with Arturo Castellanos, Sitawa Nantambu Jamaa (aka Ronald Dewberry), and Antonio
Guillen. The four also published a joint letter calling for the cessation of
all hostilities among racial groups. The strike lasted sixty days and was
joined by thirty thousand people, a quarter of the state's prison population, garnering significant global attention. Ashker has successfully sued
the prison system at least fifteen times—earning people in prison the right
to hardcover books (with the covers torn off), limited mail correspondences
with individuals held in other facilities (his father is also incarcerated), and*

the right to keep the interest generated from prisoner accounts. Ashker was one of the lead plaintiffs in the class-action lawsuit filed by the Center for Constitutional Rights, Ashker v. Governor of California, which reached a ground-breaking settlement on September 1, 2015, that promises to significantly scale back the use of solitary confinement in California's prisons. According to the terms of the settlement, CDCR can no longer hold prisoners in isolation indeterminately or for more than ten years. In addition, "gang validation" is no longer a legitimate reason for placement in the SHU. As a result, an estimated 1,500 to 2,000 prisoners may qualify for release into the general population, including the 500 that have been isolated at Pelican Bay for over ten years. Ashker will be placed in a high-security unit where he'll able to interact face-to-face with other prisoners for the first time in twenty-five years.

Hell Week

I'VE NOW SPENT MORE THAN TWENTY-SEVEN YEARS IN SOLITARY CON-finement, aka Security Housing Units (SHU). My original six-year term started in 1984 and was eventually increased to twenty-one years to life. I've been personally subject to and/or witnessed almost every form of abuse imaginable. This is a summary inclusive of my evolving resistance and fight for human rights.

It was at Folsom State Prison that I learned that prison staff are the real enemy. Guards are far more prone to dirty, illegal moves than any convicted felons I've ever done time with. By "prison staff" I'm referring to custody, medical, and even the "free" staff, like plumbers and electricians. Top to bottom, they're all corrupt.

The staff at Folsom State Prison used to play different racial groups against each other by setting up yard incidents. They'd break up the fights by firing live rounds from their Mini 14 assault rifles into the crowd. In 1987 they encouraged the Africans to attack the whites and vice versa. During one incident, they shot my friend in the stomach, then planted weapons in the drain they later claimed were used in the melee. A guard was stabbed in the neck a few days later.

About a week later, a large group of staff took a group of us out of our cells, twenty whites and four Africans. We were then escorted one at a time with our hands still cuffed behind our backs, in nothing but our boxers and shower shoes, to a secluded area where they beat the crap out of us. They told us they were going to kill us and bury us behind the prison. I ended up covered with my own blood from head to foot, with a broken foot, cracked ribs, and my teeth through my lip.

As the guards escorted us to the medical clinic, one asked me what I was smiling about. "Well, for being killed and buried I feel pretty good," I replied. The sergeant told the guards to put me through another beat down for that crack. When what staff referred to as "hell week" was finally over, twenty-four prisoners were charged with assaulting staff. Not one guard suffered any consequence.

I was placed in one of the new Bedrock SHU cells as soon as the cement dried. We each were allowed to have a shoebox-sized amount of property, no shoes, no access to canteen and only half our food rations. We responded with a minor "dirty protest," each of us filling milk cartons with shit and piss, then slinging them all over the control booth windows every time we'd come out for showers. After about two weeks of having to clean up shit every day, staff began giving us our full food ration, plus extras.

The Roman gladiator pit–style fights sadistic guards set up continued at Bedrock. The Bedrock unit looked like a ward in a military hospital—men with "dead" arms and legs from nerve damage, others with colostomy bags, and one missing an eye. At least two men were shot and killed. The guards filed charges against us for these injuries, using the incidents to further the guard union's agenda—more supermax prison cells!

Within the first nine months in Bedrock, half the men there became "debriefers," informing on other prisoners to get out of there and into protective custody. Either you break, or you do all you can to survive.

Pelican Bay SHU

While at New Folsom SHU, on May 25, 1987, I entered a guy's cell for a prearranged fight. He'd challenged me to a fistfight to settle some fabricated beef. I had to accept; it was that or request protective custody, which I'd never do. His cellmate immediately placed a mattress over the door to block the control booth's view, hoping to keep the guards from shooting blindly into the cell.

The guy swung at me with an eight-inch knife. As we fought over it, two guards fired a total of three rifle shots through the mattress. The guy ended up stabbed, and took a bullet in his shoulder. He died an hour later at the outside hospital.

In California, if you're put in the SHU for killing someone, you get sent there for a maximum of three to five years. If you're a validated gang member, you can count on spending the rest of your life in the SHU. After I was validated, I was transferred from New Folsom SHU to Pelican Bay SHU on May 2, 1990. Upon arrival I was told by staff that the only way I'd ever leave was to parole, die, or debrief.

A few months later the control booth opened my cell door when a prisoner was on the tier who they'd allegedly overheard threatening me two days before. With the alarm blaring and eight or ten guards screaming "Shoot them" at the control booth, the two of us began exchanging blows. The guard shot me from about nine feet away. The bullet hit my right radius about one inch above the wrist, disintegrating more than two inches of the radius, and broke the ulna into ten separate pieces. My hand was barely attached to my wrist by a bit of muscle and skin.

At this time prison staff were desperate to fix a serious flaw in the cell-door security system. The state had just spent more than $217 million on Pelican Bay and staff needed to have documented support to accompany any request for additional emergency funds. Toward this end, they falsely claimed I'd opened my cell door myself.

After being shot, I spent five days in the outside hospital. The nurses were kind. For the first time in more than six years, I was treated like a human being. I had completely forgotten what that felt like.

Evolving Resistance

During my first few years of imprisonment, the only way I knew how to deal with the abusive conditions was violent resistance. For more than two decades, we'd all watched the guards successfully pit racial groups against each other to the point where being on "lockdown" was a common state of affairs. "Lockdown" means everyone is kept in his or her cell 24/7 without yard time or programing. It means higher security and more guard jobs and higher pay. It is in the interest of the guards' union to have violence in the prisons, resulting in more jobs, more dues-paying members, more political power in the state. This is all fodder for the fascist police state mentality that plagues our country today.

Part of the torture I've personally experienced during the past twenty-nine years of solitary confinement has been the repeated denial of adequate medication for the chronic pain in my permanently disabled arm. Adding insult to injury, staff periodically remind me that I "hold the key to get out of the SHU and receive better care for my arm . . . by debriefing."

In the late 1980s some of us in Bedrock started to recognize that the prisoner class was getting the short end of the stick. We decided to learn the law and use the legal system to rein in the California Department of Correction and Rehabilitation's (CDCR) illegal and abusive policies. From 1988 to the present I have been challenging prison conditions in the courts. I have been a named plaintiff or assisted in several cases resulting in positive rulings beneficial to prisoners.

The Short Corridor Collective

In 2006, they decided to isolate two hundred of the alleged "worst of the worst" prisoners at Pelican Bay into the "Short Corridor." Fortunately for us, the prison's definition of "the worst of the worst" includes many fine people. Many of us have been prison condition litigators and many are well read. All of us are long-term SHU prisoners who have been subject to the same type of torturous conditions for two or more decades. In the Short Corridor, we soon came to recognize and respect our racial and cultural differences. We shared reading material on history, culture, sociology, politics, etc. We came to recognize that we are all in the same boat when it comes to the prison staff's dehumanizing treatment and abuse—they are our jailers, our torturers, and our common adversaries.

My good friend Danny Troxell was also moved to the Short Corridor. Danny and I began reading political books, including Thomas Paine, Naomi Wolf, and Howard Zinn, then we would discuss them across the tier. Six other men often joined in and the conversation gradually shifted to our progressively punitive prison conditions.

In 2009, we were introduced to a sociology professor named Denis O'Hearn, who invited Danny and me to participate in a class at Binghamton University. O'Hearn sent us the books that were required reading by the class, and asked us some questions related to our opinions on the subject matter. One of the books was *Nothing But an Unfinished Song*, about Bobby Sands and the Irish prisoner hunger strikes of 1980–81. This book greatly increased my awareness of and respect for the power of peaceful resistance against oppression.

At first many of us in the Short Corridor opposed the idea of a hunger strike. Yet, when we realized how it'd been used effectively in other parts of the world, we decided it might actually gain us the widespread exposure we needed to force an end to long-term solitary. We talked with other prisoners in our pod area and everyone agreed with the idea. That's when the "Short Corridor Collective" was born and we articulated our five core demands. We spread the word via the grapevine about our plans to strike—making clear in our articles that no person or group was leading the protest and that this was to be a purely voluntary action.

In 2012 we wrote the *Agreement to End Racial Group Hostilities*, a call for a ceasing of violence between racial groups across the state. Then in 2013 the hunger strike, combined with work stoppage, began— more than thirty thousand prisoners answered our call.

The prison administration portrayed the Short Corridor Collective as "violent, murderous gang leaders, making a power play to *regain* control of the prison system by forcing prisoners to hunger strike." Despite this, I believe prison officials' efforts to turn global support against us backfired. After sixty days we agreed to suspend the strike in response to lawmakers Loni Hancock and Tom Ammiano's public acknowledgment of our issues and request for time to enable them to hold hearings and hopefully enact legislation.

We Hope the Tide Is Turning

We are not operating openly in a free system; we are in a protracted struggle against a powerful entity with a police state world view. It's difficult to keep a movement together when we are so isolated, con- strained, and surveilled at all times. CDCR counts on internal dis- putes and hopes for us to implode as a result of their increased pressure on us post–hunger strike. We all do the best we can.

We hope the tide is turning. Hundreds have been released to gen- eral population. That is a partial victory, but it's not nearly enough. We have held on for so long that change sometimes seems unlikely. We've become skeptical of hope, but that may be because there is a possibility we might win. The reason for our progress is our collective unity inside and outside the walls and the global attention our cause has attracted. Our support remains strong, and continues to grow, while we patiently wait and see if change comes via our collective ef- forts inside and outside these walls.

It's an honor to participate in our collective coalition. For the third time in twenty-nine years I have felt a sense of human connectedness.

This collective energy—inside and out—keeps us strong, positive, and alive. It gives us hope of one day having a glimpse of trees; feeling the warmth of the sun; receiving a hug, kiss, or handshake; sharing a game of basketball or checkers; tasting a hot meal that has flavor or feeling a bed that is warm.

We stand united as a prisoner class, not just for ourselves, but for those who are young and headed this way. I stand strong, united in solidarity with each of you.

Agreement to End Hostilities, August 12, 2012

To whom it may concern and all California prisoners:

Greetings from the entire PBSP-SHU Short Corridor Hunger Strike Representatives. We are hereby presenting this mutual agreement on behalf of all racial groups here in the PBSP-SHU Corridor. Wherein, we have arrived at a mutual agreement concerning the following points:

1. If we really want to bring about substantive meaningful changes to the CDCR system in a manner beneficial to all solid individuals, who have never been broken by CDCR's torture tactics intended to coerce one to become a state informant via debriefing, that now is the time for us to collectively seize this moment in time, and put an end to more than 20–30 years of hostilities between our racial groups.

2. Therefore, beginning on October 10, 2012, all hostilities between our racial groups . . . in SHU, Ad-Seg, General Population, and County Jails, will officially cease. This means that from this date on, all racial group hostilities need to be at an end . . . and if personal issues arise between individuals, people need to do all they can to exhaust all diplomatic means to settle such disputes; do not allow personal, individual issues to escalate into racial group issues!!

3. We also want to warn those in the General Population that IGI will continue to plant undercover Sensitive Needs Yard (SNY) debriefer "inmates" amongst the solid GP prisoners with orders from IGI to be informers, snitches, rats, and

obstructionists, in order to attempt to disrupt and undermine our collective groups' mutual understanding on issues intended for our mutual causes [i.e., forcing CDCR to open up all GP main lines, and return to a rehabilitative-type system of meaningful programs/privileges, including lifer conjugal visits, etc. via peaceful protest activity/noncooperation e.g., hunger strike, no labor, etc. etc.]. People need to be aware and vigilant to such tactics, and refuse to allow such IGI inmate snitches to create chaos and reignite hostilities amongst our racial groups. We can no longer play into IGI, ISU, OCS, and SSU's old manipulative divide and conquer tactics!!!

In conclusion, we must all hold strong to our mutual agreement from this point on and focus our time, attention, and energy on mutual causes beneficial to all of us [i.e., prisoners], and our best interests. We can no longer allow CDCR to use us against each other for their benefit!! Because the reality is that collectively, we are an empowered, mighty force that can positively change this entire corrupt system into a system that actually benefits prisoners, and thereby, the public as a whole . . . and we simply cannot allow CDCR/CCPOA – Prison Guard's Union, IGI, ISU, OCS, and SSU to continue to get away with their constant form of progressive oppression and warehousing of tens of thousands of prisoners, including the 14,000 plus prisoners held in solitary confinement torture chambers [i.e., SHU/Ad-Seg Units], for decades!!! We send our love and respects to all those of like mind and heart . . . onward in struggle and solidarity . . .

Presented by the PBSP-SHU Short Corridor Collective:

Todd Ashker, C58191, D1-119

Arturo Castellanos, C17275, D1-121

Sitawa Nantambu Jamaa (Dewberry), C35671, D1-117

Antonio Guillen, P81948, D2-106

And the Representatives' Body:

Danny Troxell, B76578, D1-120

George Franco, D46556, D4-217

Ronnie Yandell, V27927, D4-215

Paul Redd, B72683, D2-117

James Baridi Williamson, D-34288, D4-107
Alfred Sandoval, D61000, D4-214
Louis Powell, B59864, D1-104
Alex Yrigollen, H32421, D2-204
Gabriel Huerta, C80766, D3-222
Frank Clement, D07919, D3-116
Raymond Chavo Perez, K12922, D1-219
James Mario Perez, B48186, D3-124

[NOTE: All names and the statement must be verbatim when used and posted on any website or media or non-media publications.]

Dream House

HERMAN WALLACE

Born in New Orleans in 1941, Herman Wallace was sent to Louisiana's Angola Prison after being found guilty of bank robbery in 1967. While at the notorious plantation prison, Wallace, along with Albert Woodfox and Robert King, helped to create a chapter of the Black Panther Party, which began organizing against the system of sexual slavery run by Angola prisoners with the acquiescence of prison staff. In 1972, Wallace and Woodfox were charged with the murder of a young prison guard and placed in solitary confinement in Closed Cell Restricted (CCR) housing. They remained in solitary after they were convicted on highly dubious evidence, including an account from a lone eyewitness who was later shown to have been bribed. Together with King, who was convicted of a separate prison murder, Wallace and Woodfox became known as the Angola 3.

Robert King was released from prison in 2001, when his conviction was overturned, after twenty-nine years in solitary. Soon afterward, Herman Wallace, in his thirtieth year of solitary, began corresponding with a young artist, Jackie Sumell. For a graduate school project, she asked him to describe what kind of house he dreamed of living in. Over the course of several years, via more than three hundred pages of letters, the two designed "The House That Herman Built," which became an art exhibit including a scale model of Wallace's dream house and a full-sized model of his cell. The art project became the subject of a film, Herman's House, *directed by Angad Bhalla, which won an Emmy Award in 2013. The first section of the following piece are excerpts from telephone calls Bhalla recorded for the film and for a subsequent interactive project, "The Deeper They Bury Me." The second is Wallace's description of his dream house, from a letter sent to Jackie Sumell.*

In October 2013, after more than forty-one years in solitary, Herman Wallace was released from prison by order of a federal judge, after his conviction was overturned because of irregularities in grand jury selection. Three days later, he died of liver cancer at the age of seventy-one. Although his conviction, too, has been overturned, Albert Woodfox, now sixty-eight, remains in solitary confinement while the State of Louisiana prepares to retry him.

Life in CCR

MY CELL IS SO SMALL THAT I CAN ONLY MAKE FOUR STEPS FORWARD until I touch the door, and if I turn in an about face at any place in this cell I'm going to bump into something. It is really smaller than anybody's bathroom. It is smaller than an outhouse somewhere. But I am used to it, and that's one of the bad things about it.

I'm in it right now and each time that I sit up off the bed I have to watch how I stand up because I'll hit my hip on the table. It's just that close. As far as moving about, there is no movement. I have to wait until I go in the yard three days a week in order to stretch my legs out and oil up the joints in my knees. [I have] arthritis, and that has come from me being in this cell.

You have men who have been in here for more than twenty years. It's not just me and it's not just Albert. There are others. In each unit you can come out on the hall for an hour and you can move up and down the hallway and stop in front of any one prisoner's cell and talk with him and you can even touch him through the bars. It's not like that other building that we just left two months ago where there was a screen partition that prevents you from touching someone else.

From the unit that I am on the only thing that I can see outside of that window is a big hill with trees, so there is no life moving out there at all. But when I am on the yard I can talk with Albert through the window.

I guess you know fluorescent lights are bad on the eye after time, and I do think it has affected me and my eyes as well, so much artificial light. I keep my light on 24/7 because every cell has a switch to the light, and if we want the light on we have to holler up to the security guard to turn on the light within your cell. I don't like hollering at three or four in the morning, "Turn my light out!" I use a legal pad to make a cover over the light in order to block the light out when I don't want it on. If I'm resting and I wake up and I want to write I don't want to rely on security to turn my light on and off. I do it myself.

In all honesty, I know my memory has deteriorated a great deal, my intelligence. I can discuss, but when it comes to holding onto concepts, I have a problem trying to come up with the simplest of things and I have to go through the ABCs to remind myself.

I write hundreds of people that I communicate with here in the United States and abroad as well. And basically this helps me to maintain what little sanity I have left. It helps me maintain my humanity and dignity. So I can fight back on what these people are trying to do to Albert and myself from a mental perspective, not so much a physical one.

So that's how I spend my day in a cell: writing and reading and reaching out to people in the streets. And I reach out to them with heartfelt love, man, and it's hard. But just because I am in a cell it doesn't mean that I can't do things.

I'm surrounded by men who have committed suicide and men who constantly throw feces at one another. When you're caught up in this kind of mess it rubs up on you and it has that kind of effect that sends you off into some mental state. But I have been able to keep my dignity as a man and help a great deal of others around me, by helping them with their legal work and in some ways financially with their smoking habits and trying to keep them out of additional trouble among themselves.

In society, they take animals and they build what you call reserves, or they build open areas like in the zoo, and they build habitats for them so that they can live more comfortably, because they learned that animals being in a closed area is inhumane. But they treat human beings here in a worse way. They put people here in a six by nine cell; they are not going to put animals in a cage like that unless they are doing some experiment with the animals and trying to kill them. That is what they are doing to these men; they are killing them slowly and surely.

I have to follow rules and rules are changing every day. They tell me to do one thing and then say you have to do something else. These are the mental games that they play with inmates, and if you don't follow them, that justifies them to put you in a worse situation.

Stuff like that keeps me from letting my ego get out there, and challenging them, [which would] allow them to justify putting me in a worse situation than I'm in now.

I mean, you can make this cell smaller if you want, one quarter the size it is now, and I wouldn't suffer from that. Things like that don't get to me. Fear don't get to me. The only thing that does get to me is my lack of ability to educate myself because I don't have the type of people around me to take and discuss matters.

There is a lot about my life that is centered around a structure set up through the BPP during the early '60s. I'm not sure if I'm in my right mind or not, but it works for me in order to maintain what little sanity I do have.

My keepers believe I am the man of steel. Ripping and running in and out of your life as if this shit ain't real. Maybe my soul is that of concrete; maybe it is that of the wind; maybe it is that of fire; maybe it is the spirit of the people, the spirit of my ancestors. Whatever my keepers want my soul to be, the man of steel has always been free.

I have had dreams of me getting out of prison. I have had a dream where I got to the front gate and there are a whole lot of people out there. And, you won't believe it, but I was dancing my way out. I was doing the jitterbug, doing crazy shit, and people were laughing and clapping until I walked out that gate and I turned around and I looked and there were all the brothers waving and throwing up the fist sign. It's so real I can feel it even now, talking about it.

Script for an Audio Tour of Herman's House

In 1971, I became a member of the Black Panther Party for self-defense as a result of systematic discrimination, police brutality, murder, and the disproportion of African Americans in prison.

The struggle of survival for African Americans in the USA is not founded in any particular location. Our struggle is international.

For thirty-three years I've been kept in a very small cage because I refuse to renounce my political views.

At any rate, through the years of my imprisonment, Robert King and Albert Woodfox were also targeted and held in similar cages.

King won his freedom on February 8, 2001, and to this day continues to function as an ambassador for both Woodfox and myself.

Shortly before King was free, I met Jackie and we became very good friends. She has been fighting with every pulse in her veins to expose the cruelty Albert and I continued to endure. . . . Even though she knew I was being held in the supermax dungeon at Camp J, Jackie did not let that stand in her way and immediately contacted me explaining she wanted to build a house, but wanted to do so from the vision of the type of house I would like to live in, given the fact of my having lived in a cage for thirty years at the time of the offer. So Jackie and I set out to build this house. I outlined the house and gave her the idea of what each room should be and look like. So, allow Jackie and me to give you a complete audio tour of *The House That Herman Built.*

The drive connects with flagstone and brick walkway to matching indoor walls and chimney.

The house is built of wooden material and preserved by surrounding plants, primarily green plants because of the source of food and oxygen they provide for the house and the occupants living within.

The wraparound porch was not constructed for the purpose of beauty but rather to discourage stray animals from getting too close.

As we enter the first door to our right, this is our salon, with multiple black leather stools and a large matching sofa with updated magazines.

As we move toward the back of the house, we enter the library with matching sky blue chairs, sofa, and shelf of photos. Here we have a full wall of books and off to the far right corner of this library is our stationary computer and off to the left corner of this library is a display of various types of weaponry.

Leaving the library we will walk through the east wing hallway with magenta-color carpet. At the end of the east wing hall off to the right is our in-house guestroom. This room is equipped with a queen-sized bed, mahogany furniture with wall mirrors, and soft brown carpet.

Leaving the guestroom, as we move straight ahead, off to the right is our two-car garage, but here in this room is the pantry with two large storage areas. At the back door of our pantry is our marble floor patio. As you see, we have a huge oak tree—preferably oak to withstand strong hurricane winds. We have two connecting grills— one with parallel bars that give heat from charcoal and the other by electricity.

This chimney connected to the house here is really an escape tunnel, but we'll get back to this later. Moving back into the pantry, adjacent to the pantry is the hobby shop with various tools, machines, workshop tables, and a wooden floor. Off the southwest side of the hobby shop is a cherry-threaded spiral staircase that leads to the second floor.

Moving south of the west wall, we enter the kitchen with a small table for four. We have a sink with built-around cabinets, large microwaves that sit between the sink cabinet, and an extensive countertop. We have a double-door refrigerator against the east/south wall next to a pecan wood wall and base cabinets. We also have here on the west/south wall a pecan wood wall and base cabinet with pots, pans, and utensils hanging nearby. The kitchen is equipped with tile floor and everything is yellow.

Between the southwest and southeast base cabinets is a swing door that leads to our dining/conference room with a polished wooden floor. On the wall shared with the kitchen is our wall of revolutionary fame. And off to the right side this room is elevated by two six-inch steps to illustrate its importance over all other rooms. We have a sixteen-chair mahogany conference table with three large windows overlooking the front entrance, our beautiful garden. We have tan curtains to complement the painting of the house.

If you will notice, on the far side of the west wing flagstone wall is our living room that is entered by the door here on the west wing of the porch. It is equipped with blue carpeting and a violet seven-seat L-shaped sofa. Here in the far left corner is a three-piece entertainment set covering both the south and west wing walls with a medium-sized glass table in the center of the room.

This opening leads to our west wing hall, also with blue carpeting. Against the wall we have portraits of prisoners of war and those missing in action. At the northern end of the hall is our guestroom. It leads from the west wing hall servicing the bedroom wing and a portal connects with the kitchen and bathroom. The guestroom cabinetry is crafted of old cypress and a bank of three windows spans the room's rear wall overlooking the patio and lawn beyond. Next to the west wing guestroom is our white-and-blue-tiled bathroom equipped with glass shower slide doors, wall mirror and pecan wood base table, and silver rim shower rack.

As we move up the cherry-threaded spiral staircase, we encounter a pocket door that opens into the upstairs master bedroom with mirrored walls with yellow/orange leopard design carpeting, crystal mahogany, and African-style furniture. We have a small entertainment room adjacent to the master bathroom. It consists of a six-foot-by-nine-foot bathtub, which is the exact size of the cell I lived in for twenty-six years. It has a toilet with black-and-white tiger covering and silver towel racks. Inside this room, travertine stone is everywhere, in the vanity tops and flooring. A double walk-in closet is also featured.

The master bathroom is connected with the fully paneled bedroom with wainscot paneling and private access to the bath. The suite accommodations also include African statues, African masks, and black carpeting and blue light above the wall mirrors. Cyprus paneling and four glass doors lead to our luscious rooftop garden of tomatoes, string beans, peas, and other veggies.

Back in the master bedroom you notice the fireplace; I spoke of this earlier while downstairs in the pantry. This chimney is really an escape route from this room or behind the storage in the pantry. This escape tunnel leads beneath the patio to the swimming pool that displays a large reflection of a black panther. Beneath the bottom of the pool's concrete floor is the bunker for safety measures. If attacked, seriously attacked, the house can be set afire with more than enough time for you and your family to escape unharmed.

Off from the house is a guesthouse with two rooms and a bath. Both rooms are equipped with small beds, carpeting, portable laptop computers, telephones, and television sets. There is one large window for each room with outdoor lampposts for security purposes.

This is "The House That Herman Built" and I am so grateful that all of you could attend. Thank you.

A Nothing Would Do as Well

Thomas Bartlett Whitaker

Thomas Bartlett Whitaker, thirty-six, has been on Texas death row since 2007. He was found guilty of hiring a gunman to stage a home invasion and kill his family. His mother and nineteen-year-old brother died in the attack. His father, who survived, has forgiven him and visits him frequently. While on death row, Whitaker completed a bachelor's degree in English and sociology, graduating summa cum laude, and is studying toward a master's degree in humanities from California State University. He has also become a prolific jailhouse lawyer, whose cases include a class action suit against the conditions of extreme isolation and deprivation on Texas death row. Like many of the more than three thousand men and women on death rows across the country, those held on Texas death row are kept in solitary confinement while awaiting execution, some for decades (although, as this story illustrates, their paths do occasionally cross). The torment of awaiting death in such conditions is so extreme, and produces such extremes of behavior, that even the state's largest correctional officers' union now favors curtailing isolation on death row.

Whitaker is a prolific writer whose work appears on his website, Minutes Before Six, *maintained for him by people on the outside, which also features work by prison writers across the country. He has three times received first-place awards in PEN's Prison Writing Contest. A slightly longer version of the piece published here won the essay award in the 2014 contest.*

The first time I met Mad Dog, he nearly shot me with a hepatitis C–infected blowgun dart.

In just a few short years, the man had become legendary on Texas's death row. There weren't many officers working the deep end of 12 Building that he hadn't attempted to harpoon, burn, cut, or toss feces on. He was something of a cross between a British soccer hooligan and MacGyver: toss him a few pieces of random rubbish and in twenty minutes he'd be launching the penal equivalent of a Hellfire missile at whatever lawman happened to be unfortunate enough to be passing by.

Every few weeks those of us on Level 1 would hear the whisper stream kick into high gear over one of his hijinks, the officers themselves often the messenger pigeons. It didn't take a keen observer to notice how the men in grey walked softly around the rest of us after this happened, or the way they absentmindedly fingered their batons and gas sprayers in an attempt to maintain the illusory shield of authority that has been the true badge of prison guards since time immemorial.

For no other reason than because it suits the hang-em-high ethos of state (read: Republican) politicians, we the condemned live out the remainder of our days in solitary confinement. We live, eat, shower, and recreate alone, and barring some nearly miraculous misfiring of the well-greased machinery of death, the only human contact we will ever feel is that of the handcuffs being secured behind our backs. Inmates without major disciplinary violations are referred to as "Level 1 Offenders"; those with certain infractions are known colloquially as "Twos" or "Threes." The distinction is for the most part one without a difference, as, intentionally or not, the prison authorities have removed virtually all of the normal perks of good behavior in recent years. For reasons that aren't exactly clear even to the Classification Committee, if a Level 3 offender manages to make it ninety days without an additional breach of the rules, he is returned to a Level 1 pod. For people like Mad Dog, the only reason to behave for a time is to come up to Level 1 for a few breaths of fresh air and a trip or two to the commissary, before recommencing the war.

Needless to say, men like Mad Dog are not much loved by those of us with highly developed antibodies against drama. When the rumor mill began disgorging the news that he was going to be moving down the hall one Tuesday morning, I sent a few prayer-analogs out to whatever gods might be listening to keep him the hell off of D-Pod. True to form, the universe listened to me with patience and concern, and then deposited Mad Dog in the empty cell directly to my left. And people wonder why I don't bother with organized religion.

For several days, we saw neither hide nor hair of the man. After a while, he began going to the dayroom, and it was there that I got my first good look at him. His tats were about what you would expect from a skinhead, with all of the usual homages to Grade 3 thinking and broad-spectrum hatred. He pretty much ignored everyone, his disdain for calm inmates obvious. His eyes—when he actually deigned to look at you—were hard autobiographies, witnesses to horrors one preferred not to think about.

After a brief survey, I didn't pay much attention to him. Moral nihilist, psychopath, sociopath, DSM-IV code 301.7—whatever you choose to label such people, there is little point in joining them in conversation, in my experience. You might as well parlay with a wolf; in fact, that is pretty much how you have to deal with these types, by baring your teeth and letting them know that they might be the Alpha in the equation, but it is going to be costly for them to find out for certain.

Twice a week we are allowed two hours in a cage outdoors, where you can—if you are lucky—get a few rays of sunshine. The day he nearly shot me was just such a day for my section, and I was so focused on the promise of the crisp December morning that I failed to notice that he had asked a special favor of the officers to put him instead in one of the dayrooms immediately adjacent to the crash gate. I am usually not so careless, but I suppose, like everyone else, I had been lulled into a false sense of security by his apparent lack of kinetic energy. It wasn't until I was within twenty feet of him that I noticed that he was wearing his work boots instead of his tennis shoes, and by then it was far too late to do anything but freeze and think small thoughts.

He actually smiled as he brought the homemade blowgun up to his lips, waiting for the two escort officers on either side of me to notice their peril before unloading. His first dart zinged past me on my left, thwacking that guard in the neck. He instantly cursed and let go of my arm, rolling away in an attempt to use the stairs as a shield. The screw on my right was a newbie, and he merely stood there for a moment, gaping at this sudden and violent departure of his normal routine. He figured out the game plan as soon as a dart drove into his shoulder, and he ran screaming toward the corner of the section, stupidly boxing himself in.

I merely closed my eyes and turned my face away from the dayroom. I had been in these situations before, and I had learned that ducking and dodging were only going to increase my chances of taking a hit meant for someone else. Such projectiles are not terribly accurate, and because I didn't think he had any reason to take aim at me, there wasn't much for it but to give Mad Dog at least one immobile zone to remove from whatever targeting algorithm his warped brain was running.

After about thirty seconds and what sounded like several more direct hits, I peeked my eyes open and surveyed the damage. Mad Dog was standing there triumphant, looking like Moses coming down from the mountaintop with the new law. He was mocking the officers, letting them know that they could thank Captain B for their shiny new infections, since he had recently taken Mad Dog's radio. That was the worst of it, I think: that so much evil could have been unbottled over the appropriation of a twenty-dollar Chinese knock-off clock radio, which wasn't even contraband.

It didn't take long for a dense thunderhead of officers to converge, the institutional instinct for something-must-be-donery kicking into high gear. Lacking any other apparent options, the mob quickly began spraying Mad Dog with CS/CN gas pepper spray. It didn't faze him, but then, it seldom affects anyone but the guards. The ventilation system on the Row has been broken since the days when parachute pants were all the rage, so when anyone gets gassed, we all get gassed. This is unfortunate for the first ten or fifteen experiences, but eventually you build up immunity to the stuff. Instead of gagging like most of the officers, Mad Dog merely tossed the blowgun at one of the officers' heads and began to pace in the dayroom.

I was quickly pushed up against a wall and ordered to stay put. One didn't need to be Tiresias to see where this was going; the way he had so casually tossed his weapon away after everyone had arrived was enough to convince me that I ought to be moving along. I quietly whispered to the two officers standing behind me that maybe it would be best for the "safety and security of the institution" if they moved me outside. After a brief conference with a sergeant holding a hand-kerchief over his mouth, this was agreed upon. Before I passed the crash gate and lost sight of Mad Dog, I took one last glance backward. His face was radiant, like all of the pain of a lifetime had been washed away: the bodhisattva of prison terrorists.

From my position on the yard, I could see only the back rows of officers as they surveyed the situation. Gas masks were being handed out, so that the majority of them could at least find something else to do besides gasp and wretch all over themselves. Within a few minutes the extraction team showed up, covered in plastic body armor and shields, marching in cadence. None of them seemed to realize that a nice, fat crowd might have been exactly what Mad Dog desired.

They figured it out, though, after he dove under the table and produced the second blowgun, which had been taped under a seat. I saw a captain and a sergeant stumble backward, little red blossoms unfolding on their chests. As the mass exodus from the section commenced, Mad Dog began spraying the backs of the departing with bottles of liquefied feces. The extraction team got their share of this foul concoction as well, before they rushed the dayroom and clubbed him to the ground. With an incredible display of efficiency, the team quickly had him shackled and cuffed and were lugging him off the pod by his limbs within thirty seconds. He was fighting them all the while, a Hegelian abstraction run amok in the real world: the indefatigable and uncaring essence of his era personified.

After his departure, the screws paraded about, smug looks on their faces. These would fade, I knew, in short order, after the accounting of the matter had finally been tallied and had a chance to sink in. Not that anyone asked, but if I had bothered to add my two cents' worth to a trillion bazillion pounds of dead weight hurtling through space, I would have declared the match for Mad Dog, whatever the final outcome.

I didn't see the maniac again for several years, and, to be honest, he was not present in my day-to-day thoughts. I am seldom comfortable with the generally accepted explanations for why anyone does anything. In fact, I have been informed by several (usually annoyed) friends that I can be a touch neurotic about digging down for the hidden motivations behind the world of behavior. Occasionally, I would take my memories of that day down from the attic and dust them off. Having never traded a single word with Mad Dog, this was a purely academic exercise, an attempt to evade boredom for a few minutes. I wasn't content with concluding that he was simply mad as a meat axe, but lacking any real data, I had few other options but to dismiss him as virtually everyone else in his life had already done. Back in the attic he went, a man forgotten.

Three years later, I again found myself living on the same pod as Mad Dog. Having grown frustrated with his ability to burn tiny holes in the Plexiglas security shields affixed to the steel doors of F-Pod, the administration emptied out an entire section of other inmates on A-Pod and tossed him into a cell that had been sealed as tight as Pharaoh's sarcophagus. Thinking that they had finally solved the riddle of Mad Dog, they left him there to rot.

Considering the pious nature of Southerners in general and Texans in particular, one would think that maxims regarding the devil and idle hands might have made an appearance in someone's mind as this was being done, but apparently the bureaucratic imperative to follow orders at any cost has grown so sturdy in the Texas Department of Criminal Justice that it is now trumping even common sense. I have no way of knowing how many shanks or projectiles Mad Dog was able to conjure up while he had a section all to himself, but I do know that he somehow managed to get a handful of pens, five writing tablets, and some carbon paper. In the end, I think this proved far more disastrous for the system, although I do not believe Mad Dog ever saw things in this way.

Considering the shakedown team was hitting his cell every two hours, I have no idea how he was able to keep these items. I suppose that these officers must have assumed that he had gotten permission for them from someone up the chain of command—how else would he have gotten them, after all? Instead of resorting to fisticuffs every time they came to harass him, he somehow managed to bottle up his feelings and attempted to pour them out on paper in the form of grievances and letters to the Prison Board. I would later learn that he went through periods like this every few years, where he would fire off a rapid succession of grievances before retreating into the familiar territory of violence. This time around, he gave the method about three months of his time before he began to feel he was tilting at windmills. Just before he stopped, he petitioned the law library for copies of his entire grievance file. These he organized by type of complaint, and then bound everything up and sent them to a very different sort of audience.

This time, he sent them to me.

During the intervening years between our first and second contact, I had taken on the reputation as something of a "writ writer"—Texas prison slang for a jailhouse lawyer. This was an entirely unsought and undeserved honor because in reality I knew (and know) next to nothing about the law, and in general think that the entire concept of *stare decisis* is a bloody stupid and lazy way to go about the issue of solving problems or searching for objective truth.

I have no idea how Mad Dog learned of this, alone as he was in his modern oubliette. Neither do I have any idea how he managed to A) bend the corner of his solid steel door away from the concrete wall; B) fashion a fishing line, considering they were not giving him sheets or any clothing save for a paper gown; C) shoot said line across twenty feet of run, under the security door into C-Section; and D) send me nearly three hundred pages of handwritten notes plus copies of the more than 150 grievances he had written during his three years on death row. I hesitate to use the word *miraculous* to describe this feat, as that word has connotations that are somewhat abhorrent to a secularist like myself, but I really cannot think of any other term that is appropriate. The man was a wizard.

Reading through his litany of complaints was shocking on a number of levels. For starters, Mad Dog wrote in a nearly perfect Copperplate script, each letter graceful and efficient. In a world so rife with chaos, grime, and all the charm of a nuclear fallout shelter, looking upon anything with even the slightest hint of beauty is a rare occurrence. I can't really explain the feeling I got from simply looking over his letters; perhaps it is just one of those events that a clumsy wordsmith like myself is destined to forever fail at when attempting a description. All I can say is, if you lived in my world, you would understand. I had not expected this from a man who seemed to live by the motto of "in violence, veritas." Before I had even finished the first page, I had already begun to ponder the question of whether actions or words were judged by reputations, or the reverse.

Second, these were not the typical complaints one finds from prisoners. Generally, grievances are filled with almost nonsensical ramblings about the poor quality of the food or the radio reception. Most of Mad Dog's initial grievances dealt with a series of medical issues, namely that when he was arrested, the police broke both of his knees. While he was awaiting trial in the county jail, he slipped on some water left out by the mopping crew and injured his back. He was given medical braces for both knees and his back, and was allowed to wear these to trial. Upon his arrival at the Polunsky Unit, these had been taken from him, meaning that he had been unable even to walk to his cell. They refused to listen to him, and dragged him down to F-Pod on his first day, by his ankles no less. Under current regulations, not even an Ace bandage is allowed for death row inmates, and several of his initial grievances detailed the fact that the unit doctor was denying him even minor drugs like ibuprofen and acetaminophen; instead he was told that he could purchase said items on the commissary. Much as I did, Mad Dog arrived on the Row penniless, so such advice was less than worthless to him—and the unit was undoubtedly aware of this.

Mad Dog had gone out of his way to state each issue clearly in his grievances, politely even; he even tossed in some relevant case law from time to time. The guidelines for the grievance process specifically ask that inmates not do this—a convenient request, considering that the Fifth Circuit has tossed out about a million conditions lawsuits for having failed to exhaust the administrative grievance process specifically because the inmate did not "fully clarify" his exact complaint. He seemed to understand that an Eighth Amendment claim has both an objective and a subjective component, that medical negligence was not sufficient in and of itself, and that the standard he needed to shoot for was set in *Farmer v. Brennan*. I found copies of letters that he had sent to officials at the University of Texas Medical Branch, as well as to Texas Department of Criminal Justice big wigs in Huntsville. His collection of letters to the head warden of the Polunsky Unit was detailed, as was the fact that he had never received a single response from anyone.

One of these letters to the warden was particularly chilling. In it, Mad Dog once again explained that he was in serious pain and getting worse, and that he did not feel that anyone was listening to him. He ended the letter saying: "I have followed the rules you gave me when I got here. Yet you still will not respect that. What do I have to do to be heard around this camp? Do I need to share my pain with you?" Later, when he sent me his inch-thick disciplinary file, I found out that his first officer assault had occurred exactly fifteen days after this letter was sent.

Most remarkable to me, however, were the grievances regarding what he construed as violations of his First Amendment Rights to practice his religion. He had filed more than forty of these, and the claims were so bizarre that at first I suspected they were total fabrications. Until, that is, I read the accompanying documentation. Mad Dog, it turns out, was a legitimate Wiccan priest in the world, and I found a series of letters between him and the unit chaplain, in which the latter explained the process for ordering the approved accoutrements of his faith from free-world vendors. All of these letters were polite in nature. I also located several receipts from vendors licensed by the TDCJ to sell religious products; these receipts totaled nearly $700, and each item had been approved in writing by the chaplain, the warden, and the representative of the group of Wiccans paying for the order. When the items arrived at the unit, however, the mailroom confiscated them, deeming them a security risk.

This action was followed by a flurry of letters and grievances from Mad Dog, and I found several increasingly confused letters from the chaplain explaining that he had tried to obtain the items, but the mailroom chief was a staunch evangelical and thought the Wiccan faith Satanic. By the time the warden stepped in, the items had been destroyed. After this, nearly all of Mad Dog's correspondence to and from his connections in the outside world stopped altogether. When he tried to send mail to his attorney about this, these letters also managed to disappear.

I would be hard pressed to think of any issues more pointless to argue about than gods or the supernatural, but even I was ready to grab a pitchfork and march with the rest of the sans-culottes on the palace by the time I had finished reading this sorry account. There were so many obvious violations of the First Amendment's Establishment and Free Enterprise Clauses, the Religious Land Use and Institutionalized Persons Act (signed by President Clinton to protect the religious rights of those in prison), and its predecessor (the Religious Freedom Restoration Act), that I hardly knew where to begin doing my research.

It probably doesn't need to be mentioned by this point, but Mad Dog stabbed an officer the week after his final order of religious materials was destroyed. The grievance officers investigating these cases had clearly gone out of their way to deny him relief; one almost sensed a sort of sheepish regret or pity in their tone at times, as if even they felt bad about having to do their job. As in the dark ages of Christian scholasticism, these men and women were reasoning (if such it can be charitably called) with syllogisms that proved each other. Oftentimes, they would pick a single sentence out of an allegation, dispute it, and therefore conclude that the matter had been dealt with in its entirety. This was a common tactic statewide, I was to learn.

Few citizens of any political persuasion would be comfortable with a government agency policing itself, but that is precisely the situation in Texas prisons. The grievance process should use independent investigators, or at least have a few roaming inspectors tasked to keep an eye on everyone. Instead, these positions are filled from the general pool of whoever is currently in charge of maintaining the code of silence, with all of the results one would expect from such a state of affairs. In the only major survey of which I am currently aware, the State Auditors Office sent surveys to several thousand TDCJ inmates in 2004. More than 85 percent of them responded that the grievance process was completely and totally useless. Whatever this process was intended to be, by this point its only aim appears to be to pay the necessary lip service to the notion of due process required by federal law. I probably understand less than 2 percent of what Wittgenstein ever wrote, but as I delved into Mad Dog's grievances and reflected on the grievance system designed to address them, I couldn't help but agree with the philosopher that a nothing would do as well as a something about which nothing can be said.

It took me several months to dissect Mad Dog's issues. We who live in administrative segregation have no direct access to the law library. Instead, we must send request forms to the library for specific materials, even though this seemingly straightforward process is complicated by the fact that we are not allowed the actual materials, only copies of a very limited amount. It might take a week or two to read a single chapter in a large book, therefore. In addition, the clerks seem to take a great deal of pleasure in sending me cases I had never even heard of, let alone requested.

A picture eventually started forming, nonetheless, about the type of massive class action suit that would be required to cover all of Mad Dog's varied claims, and I was increasingly of the opinion that I was nowhere near capable enough to bring it to fruition. I reached out to some of the more knowledgeable men on the Row, hoping that their aggregated wisdom would be of some use. While I didn't end up getting much instruction, I did end up receiving a stunning amount of grievances. This started as a trickle, but quickly evolved into a torrent, amounting in the end to more than one thousand individual complaints. I am fluent in Spanish, and this number only continued to grow when I reached out to the guys who spoke no English; turns out, they had been filing legitimate discrimination suits for years, without having had any luck.

Getting all of this information was hellishly difficult. To pass a single sheet of paper from one inmate to another, one must deal not only with the steel doors and the roving officer teams, but also the multimillion-dollar camera system installed in 2010. To use the vernacular, it ain't no simple thing. Transferring a thousand grievances from hundreds of sources on five different pods was a nearly Herculean task, and I am still amazed that I only managed to catch one disciplinary case during the process.

It wasn't pretty, but *Whitaker v. Bell* was filed in the Eastern District of Texas on April 20, 2012. It was filed pro se, as I couldn't find a single attorney willing to take even the tiniest look at it. The principal defendants are the members of the Prison Board, the director of TDCJ's Institutional Division, the head of UTMB, and our idiot governor. It has about the same chances of prevailing as said governor does of becoming a socialist on the same day that he marries his secret longtime lover, Karl Rove.

Long before the suit was formally filed, Mad Dog had given up on the project, impatient with my lack of forward progress. I felt saddened by this, but by this point the suit had grown to be about something far larger than him or me. This thing gave me a new perspective, and helped me to understand things written by men like George Orwell and Victor Serge that I had long admired but seldom felt any real connection with. The suit gave me something to believe in and fight for, and I found within it a form of stoicism that kept me strong during all of the subsequent shakedowns and loss of mail. One does not go about Messin' With Texas in this fashion and expect for one's sailing to be smooth, after all. *Aetatis* 32, I finally discovered what it felt like to be a revolutionary. I am tempted at times to shout things like "c'est interdit d'interdire," but I don't, because my neighbors already think I am weird enough without adding kindling to the bonfire.

The first time I realized what I was feeling in this regard I began to understand Mad Dog's less-than-civil disobedience. I hadn't really had a chance during all of the preparation to give my full attention to the true human cost of a grievance system that exists in name only. There is no way to know what sort of offender he might have become had his voice been heard early on. Maybe he was always destined to be a troublemaker, but I do not believe so. Prison is not the Ritz-Carlton, and while I cannot say for certain, I believe that Mad Dog knew this. His expectations were not out of the norm, and certainly not outside of stated policy. His volte-face was in response to institutional indifference, and eventually he came to feel that the only appropriate response to a reign of terror was a rain of darts. It was the creature he had become that stalked my thoughts, a thing that need never have been.

Looking back on the day that he almost shot me, I see now the mutual comfort Mad Dog and the officers gave to each other. For his part, Mad Dog had come to see pain as an antidote to death and impotence, the path out of the wilderness. The hatred he received from the screws was better than nothing, and in any case there was often a touch of respect and maybe even admiration from some of them, heady stuff indeed. For their part, the officers were able to participate in the ages-old myth of the monster lurking just outside of the campfire's light, the almost-terror almost true, which made their tyranny acceptable. In the midst of monthly executions and cruelty beyond the conception of normal people, even prison guards need their justifications and mental salves. The Minotaur would have been lost without his labyrinth.

I've only been able to speak to Mad Dog on a few occasions, and only then for a brief few moments. Just before I filed in federal court, I found myself in a booth next to him in the visitation room. He had given up on using paperwork, and claimed he didn't really care about what happened in the courts. He was on Level 3 again, this time for having attempted to use paint thinner to incinerate another inmate. Exasperated, I locked eyes on him and asked him why he did these things. He paused for a moment, finally bringing his eyes up to mine.

"There seemed a certainty in degradation."

I recognized the quote as belonging to T.E. Lawrence, but I didn't call him on it. His eyes were keyholes into places that I would never—could never—go. Some stars you see in the sky died millions of years ago. Maybe people are like that too, although I'd like to believe that anyone can come back from the cold and be a better human being. I am certain that the prosecutors and the wardens and the public will shout until they are blue in the face that Mad Dog was a dead thing long before he arrived on the Row, but I know better. He had been a man when he arrived—a broken one, perhaps, badly in need of growth and redemption, but a man nonetheless. He had come to see himself as something less than human, a ghost wandering the halls, unheeded and miserable. What men believe to be real is real in its consequences, and in his role as a monster he finally found an audience willing to notice him.

I don't know who bears the brunt of the responsibility for what he became; I suppose there is enough blame to go around. I only know that he didn't need to become this . . . thing. For a time he tried to be human in an environment designed to kill one's humanity, to use the processes designed by the system to prevent violence. The process failed, and the result was apparent to all.

I had turned away from him in the legal booth, my mind drawing a blank on what to say to him that might bring him back from the nothing. People like him seldom pay me any attention in prison, so I suppose that I thought he had turned his attention to something else. When I looked back his way he was still staring at me, and we simply stood like that for a moment. When he eventually spoke, his voice was little more than a whisper.

"Why do you think I am like this?"

It didn't really sound like a question; there was no regret, or sorrow, or genuine tinge of curiosity. I didn't think he expected a complex answer in any case, as I'm pretty sure we both knew that a team of neuroscientists and psychologists could work on Mad Dog for a decade and still not have all of the answers. Instead, I removed a sheet of paper from my legal folder and wrote one quatrain from a poem by W.H. Auden:

> *I and the public know*
> *What all schoolchildren learn,*
> *Those to whom evil is done*
> *Do evil in return.*

He received this carefully and spent a moment looking it over. For the tiniest fraction of a second his face relaxed and his eyes softened and he seemed to shrink into himself as he breathed in. Then it was over, and he turned away from me, a dismissal if I ever saw one. He crumpled up my note angrily and tossed it away onto the floor. It was the last time we ever spoke.

SURVIVING

Weak as Motherfuckers

BRIAN NELSON

Brian Nelson, fifty, was born in Chicago and went to prison for murder in 1982 when he was sixteen years old. Nelson was later transferred to Tamms supermax prison after which he spent a total of twenty-three years in solitary confinement in various facilities. Although Nelson was never given a reason for the more than two decades he spent in isolation, he believes it was in retaliation for a lawsuit he won in 1989, Brian Nelson v. Ronald Haws, *which forced the Department of Corrections to build law libraries in every segregation unit in Illinois.*

At the time of this book's publication, Nelson has been out of prison for five years. He currently works with the Uptown People's Law Center in Chicago and is known as a tireless advocate and organizer against the use of solitary confinement. Nelson, who is a devout Catholic, says his favorite books are the Bible, the Harry Potter series, and "everything written by Thomas Merton." "Solitary still creates a lot of problems for me on a daily basis," Nelson writes. "I can't even ride the city train to work because I feel trapped." In fall 2014, he attended a protest in front of the Pontiac Prison but had to leave because he felt sick to his stomach. Nelson was incapacitated for days afterward by traumatic memories brought on by "the smell of the place." The following piece is based on an interview with Sarah Shourd in February 2014.

NOBODY GETS IT. EVERY DAY I CRY. I'M AFRAID OF PEOPLE, REALLY scared of people. Twenty-three years with no TV, no radio. Touched hands once with my mother in court. I'm not a human being, everybody wants to try drugs on me. I was in minimum security. I used to make guards' uniforms. I was the warden's fucking trustee. Then twenty-four hours later I'm at Tamms, two pairs of chains on my hands and feet. I can taste it. I can smell it. I can see it every single day. I like being away from people, I am so afraid of people. I used to love hangin' out, even my Mom—how do I tell my mother I'm afraid of her? The woman I love? How do I walk down the street with the prison mentality? No one knows what to do with me. What did they do to me? I went in at sixteen; I'll be fifty next month. I hate it out here. I'm afraid every fucking day.

I love going to work at 5:00 a.m. I'm the only one there and all I do is read letters from prisoners. I try to help them. My office is almost the exact same size of my cell. I need this space. I need a place to go where I can't see the fear in my mother's eyes, her terror at what's left of her son.

My brother criticizes me; it's the best thing. I need it. He keeps me on track. He made me stand in front of the mirror. "Look at yourself," he said, "look at where you were." He draws black lines on the mirror over my face like bars, then he wipes them away. "Look at where you are now." At first I didn't understand what he was doing. "Look where you were!" he shouts. "Now wipe it off, wipe it off!" He gets quiet. "Look where you are now. Look what you've accomplished in two years." Then he punches me in the head. "You've gotta wake up, man," he says. "I love you."

Somehow my brother gets how hard this is for me. How many people in the United States does this happen to? More than in the rest of the world combined. I didn't stab nobody; I didn't even catch a ticket. I went from being the warden's trustee—went in and out of the prison all the time—I had keys to their cars, scissors in my pocket. They never told me why I was transferred, but I know why; it's because I won a lawsuit. Last year, six months after my release, I had dinner with the director of the DOC [Department of Corrections] and still no one can tell me why. At the dinner, he says to me, "You've helped make a lot of change, you've helped a lot of people." "Yeah," I say, "but it's killing me."

No one wants to admit that we are weak as motherfuckers, that our brains beat us up. I tried to kill myself; the rope broke. I have so much survivor's guilt. I've never spent the night with a woman. I've never been involved with a woman, ever! I'm so screwed up, I don't think I can ever have a normal relationship. I'm your next door neighbor. I'm your next door neighbor! I didn't bomb anyone. I was a kid, a stupid kid that did a crime. I'm working my ass off, I'm fighting. Don't play that gangster shit with me, I tell the truth. What my brain did to my brain is not right. I flogged myself daily. I physically created pain in order to feel something. They used to find my back ripped open.

One guy I knew at Tamms comes over and we sit in the dark together. That's what we like to do. Just sit. There were years when I was the only person in the pod. If I lay down in my cell, I could see grass through the window at the end of the hall. When they found out I could see it, they put a plate over it. We are way worse than other countries. Nobody needs to be in solitary; just shoot me in the head and get it over with. Look what you've made me into. Look what I am! Look at me! You made me into this. I was a kid. A fuckin' kid.

You send me out here and put me on medication; if the doctor doesn't say I'm okay they'll put me back. I don't want medication. I want to be me. I pray every day to go to sleep, that means I want to die. Sometimes I walk through the worst neighborhoods and hope someone will kill me. Do it! I can't kill myself; I'm Catholic. I flash money. I want someone to blow my brains out. Ninety-nine percent of guys in solitary are coming home. I hate it out here and I hate it in there and what they did to me was wrong. I'm tired every day. I'm so tired.

Did you know they did this to McCain in Vietnam? He said it was worse than being hung upside down and being beaten till his legs were broken. McCain, McCain, don't let them do it to my brain. We're Americans, for chrissakes. We won't even let the UN torture guy in our prisons. We judge everyone else but not ourselves. My lowest weight was 110 pounds, down from 170. I paced eighteen hours a day. In zoos they have "habitat environments," but we don't do that for human beings. You know Plato's cave? That's solitary. He thinks the shadows are real. Hearing voices. Seeing things. You make up a make-believe world. The worst part is I think I'm still there. I'm so afraid I'm gonna wake up and be back there. I dare everyone to lock themselves in the bathroom for one weekend—I could be with a cellie and watch TV, but to be alone . . .

They bought me a Blizzard, right after I got out; a guy walked behind me and I lost it, started yelling at him. He stepped in my space; for so many years it was *my space*, me and my cell. I paced like a lion, cut open the blood blisters, and kept pacing. What's wrong with our system? It costs 20–30K to keep them in there and for the rest of their lives we pay for their medical treatment, social security. Walk into a room with me, wait five minutes, and I'll tell you how many lights there are, how many windows, speakers. I count everything. I do it just to be calm.

When I got home I dug holes of shit to buy my first car. I wanted to pay for it myself. A taxi driver totaled it. I sat by the road and cried. I cried and cried. What that taxi driver took away from me was not my car; it was my freedom. It was a Jeep Liberty. It was my liberty to go wherever I wanted. "You took my freedom," I screamed at him, "you took it from me!"

Scarred by Solitary

ENCENO MACY

Enceno Macy is the pen name of a formerly incarcerated man living in the Pacific Northwest, who asked that his real name not be used as he seeks to rebuild his life after his recent release from prison. Macy first experienced solitary confinement in a juvenile detention facility at the age of thirteen. At fifteen he was charged as an adult with felony murder, meaning he took part in a robbery during which the victim was killed by someone else, and spent nearly eight months in solitary in "involuntary protective custody" in a local jail while awaiting trial.

Once convicted, Macy, still age fifteen, was sent to adult prison, where he spent fifteen years in and out of solitary for various disciplinary infractions. He believes that corrections officers particularly targeted youth "to try and 'break' us." Macy wrote the following essay in 2012 during his last year in prison.

SOLITARY CONFINEMENT IS NO PLACE FOR A KID. I KNOW THIS FROM firsthand experience. As a young person in the criminal justice system, I was placed in solitary—locked down in a small cell for up to twenty-four hours a day—several different times before I was out of my teens. And although you can't see them, I bear permanent scars from this treatment.

I first experienced a kind of solitary confinement in juvenile detention, when I was thirteen years old. They referred to it as "room lock" because the facility didn't have separate cells for isolation. We would get sent there for bad language or being too loud, or for forgetting to ask permission to talk, get up from our seats, or change the card game we were playing—basically, for acting like kids. Where I was, the time in isolation would range from an afternoon to a few days. I know that in some juvenile facilities, children get locked down for weeks or months at a time.

When I was fifteen, I was accused of a serious felony, and while awaiting trial I was placed in "involuntary segregation" in county jail. I was put there solely because of my age and "for my own protection," but I was treated the same way as adults who were put in solitary for serious rule violations. We received two books a week, two sheets of paper, and a golf pencil. There was no access to any form of education or counseling for youth (or anyone else). In the wire cages we sometimes went to for exercise, the space was not much bigger than the cell and there was no room to run. I spent seven and a half months in those conditions.

Once convicted, I was sent to adult prison, where I experienced several stays in "disciplinary segregation," usually lasting a few months each—for fighting, leaving my job early, arriving back late from a meal, and copying out the lyrics to a song that they deemed "gang related," probably just because it was rap.

The guards were petty, and liked to single out youngsters who had a lot of time to do—to try and "break" us, I guess. Because of laws that gave mandatory minimums to teens charged as adults, there were many of us in our late teens going through this mental gauntlet. It was as easy as using profanity when speaking with a state employee to get a couple of weeks in "seg." In other words, actions that would qualify as everyday misbehavior for most American teenagers would get us placed in conditions that have been widely denounced as torture, especially when used on young people.

A typical day as a kid in seg involved a lot of sleep—probably sixteen hours on average. I'd wake up for breakfast, sleep until lunch, read for an hour or so, go back to sleep until dinner, pace back and forth, try to write poems or rap song lyrics, read, and wait/hope for mail—then go to sleep and do it all over again. In some of that time I might find someone I could talk to through the crack in my door. We had so little to do, we'd end up yelling insults at the guards just to vent our anger and restlessness.

I was ruled by sorrow, fear, and anger. Deep depression about missing people I used to know, and my mom. Fear about what might be coming next in my seemingly endless sentence. (I had no concept of what time really meant, so fifteen years felt the same as fifty.) Anger at those who I felt had wronged me. Back then I wasn't skilled in identifying my emotions, let alone dealing with them appropriately.

The only comfort was the daily letters my mom has written me since I came to jail. Otherwise there were no positives in my mind, no outlet to exercise the hurt and confusion. I was so lost. My mind was like a bowl of spilled popcorn, scattered into a hundred individually unique, fragile pieces. I never cut myself or attempted suicide, as I know a lot of kids in solitary do. But I did think about death a lot, and I had dreams of an apocalyptic world (and still do).

I know that solitary confinement caused me considerable psychological damage—or really, added to what was already brewing. It encouraged me to retreat deep into a demented reality where I was so alone, it made me feel as though I wasn't meant for this world. I still feel that way to this day—like I don't fit. On the clinical side, I was even more deeply depressed than I had been growing up. There was no counseling for this—just medication, but the only meds that made any difference were the ones that knock you out for days at a time.

Like most people who have served time in solitary as teenagers, I will someday be released from prison and resume life in the free world. We have no real idea of how such treatment affects a young mind. But because of solitary I will never be mentally right, I fear. More than ten years later, I think some of the effects have faded, but my panic attacks are so severe that they put me on antidepressants for PTSD. I still feel lonely and I have a hard time trusting, so I don't consider too many people my "friends." It's pretty lonely because of that, but I'm used to the feeling now.

I realize that inmates, even young ones, sometimes need to be separated from other inmates for safety reasons. But I don't think they should be put in segregation for things like talking back or being late for an appointment. And I don't believe solitary confinement is ever appropriate for teens the way it is practiced today. Kids need positive outlets whenever they are separated from others. They need some kind of program where they get counseling and periods to exercise their minds and emotions.

Recently, I was sent the summary from a new report by Human Rights Watch and the ACLU. It says that on any given day, there are hundreds of kids under eighteen in solitary confinement in America's jails and prisons. I know what they are suffering, and I wonder how many of them, like me, will bear the invisible scars of their isolation. It may be too late for us, but there is still time to save countless other children from this silent torture.

A Fragile Shell of
Who I Used to Be

BARBRA PEREZ

Barbra Perez is a thirty-six-year-old Cuban-born trans woman who works for a lighting and electrical company. She has lived in the United States since she was three years old. On the morning of February 3, 2014, Immigration and Customs Enforcement (ICE) arrested her in her driveway as she was leaving for work. They informed her she was being taken into custody over an arrest that happened fourteen years prior, in the year 2000. After being held for two days at the Davidson County Jail in Nashville, Tennessee, Perez was transferred to LaSalle Immigrant Detention Center, a privately owned, for-profit facility operated by GEO Group, in Jena, Louisiana, where she was held for more than two weeks. Like many transgender women in custody, she was housed with men and then placed in solitary confinement, or administrative segregation, "for her own protection."

Many ICE detention centers are run by for-profit companies like GEO Group and Corrections Corporation of America (CCA). When awarded federal contracts to run immigration detention centers, companies are asked to commit to keeping all the cells (often referred to as "beds") in their facilities occupied at all times, including in the solitary confinement units. Many human rights organizations have criticized this policy as creating an economic incentive to detain more immigrants and to mete out the harsh punishment of solitary confinement. The following piece is drawn from interviews with Sarah Shourd conducted in early 2015.

WE ARRIVED IN JENA, LOUISIANA, IN THE MIDDLE OF A FREEZING NIGHT. We'd been driving for twelve or thirteen hours, and it felt like we'd reached the end of the earth. The other prisoners were sitting together in the back, but they had me singled out, chained hand and foot in a cage made of thick Plexiglas near the front of the bus. When the officer came in to check our names off his list, he asked how many males and how many females were on the bus. The driver pointed to me and replied, "Twenty-seven and a half males," which was followed by raucous laughter at my expense.

The detention center was called LaSalle. I'd been brought there after three terrible days at a local jail in Tennessee where my "captor" informed me that bail would be unequivocally denied and that I would remain in custody for a minimum of three months. He said if I agreed to take the order of deportation, the judge would release me immediately. When I was taken upstairs to strip, I wasn't allowed to keep my sports bra or panties. This was the first time I'd worn men's undergarments since I left my parents' house in 2002. Mortified, I asked the nurse about my hormone shots. She assured me I would get them once the board approved. Then an officer came to escort me to what he lovingly called the "Sissy Pod." It was protective custody, but as far as I could tell none of the men there even identified as gay. I was the only woman.

In my normal life no one questions my gender or sex. I never thought of myself as a boy in the first place, but now I've been living outwardly as a woman since my early twenties, more than fifteen years. Nothing prepared me for the experience of being exposed and imprisoned alongside other men. They all looked at me like I was the closest thing to a "real" woman they'd ever seen behind bars.

A few days later, when I arrived at LaSalle, I was taken straight to Ad Seg [Administrative Segregation]. It was loud in there, people screaming and banging on the walls of their cells. The staff's treatment of me ranged from indifference to open hostility and disgust. Once I asked for a spoon, and the guard slammed my cell door in my face and walked off. Most of the detainees were Mexican, immigrants like me, but I didn't know what they were in Ad Seg for. There was a guy across from me making obscene gestures—asking me to show him my breasts. Their version of keeping me safe was putting me side by side with what that facility determined to be the worst of the worst. That night I lay down and tried to sleep on the cold metal cot with only a thin sheet to protect me.

After just a few days in there I became a fragile shell of who I used to be. I was given no recreation time. A shower only every other day. The phone was attached to a hand truck, which would be wheeled to you at the guards' leisure. In that mental state, I started doubting who I was. There was no one to talk to, no way to process what was happening to me. The anxiety and helplessness started to break me down, which is exactly what it's designed to do.

In my regular life, I tend to isolate myself anyway because I've always been different. Looking like and living as a woman for so long, then being incarcerated as a man, just kind of stripped me to the core and made all my insecurities flood to the surface. Whether it's in immigration detention or federal prison, transgender women are viewed as freaks. Men see you as an easy target, assuming you won't fight back, so sexual harassment is constant and assault is rampant. Prison staff say there's no other way to "safely" confine transgender women, but they're either simply unable to understand our experience, or they don't want to.

I had no idea what would happen to me or what lay ahead. When I was suddenly released twenty-four days later I'd lost seventeen pounds. I was handed my hormones along with my property, so they must have had them the entire time and just not wanted to give them to me. At the time I had no idea what was happening on the outside, but I soon found out my friends, family, and the Transgender Law Center has been raising hell for me. They basically made it a royal pain in the ass for ICE to continue holding me. The fact that I'm Cuban makes me practically undeportable, I was costing them a lot of money for my expensive medication, and they knew I didn't belong there in the first place.

I later learned that I was abducted in order to fill a "bed mandate." LaSalle has to have a certain number of heads in a bed at all times in order to continue getting its funding, and nationwide ICE facilities need to have 34,000 detainees a day to fill their quota. GEO is a private corporation getting a government subsidy for running the detention center and I was another warm body to fill that bed. So, I was used. They put me through all that not because they gave a rat's ass about what I did or didn't do; I was a means to an end.

In my mind I know that they can't ever do what they did to me again, but a year later I still feel I've lost some of the security I once had. I try not to, but I find myself looking out the window of my apartment every time I hear a car slowing down. I have a letter from my attorney saying that ICE determined that "it was no longer in their interest to hold me." Even though I know the charges are dropped, I still feel uneasy.

I don't want my detention to be a defining moment for me. I don't want to feel like they won, basically. Last year I spoke at a Not One More rally in DC, standing on stage and outing myself as a trans woman in front of thousands of people. It was truly beautiful. I felt part of a cause that we all believe in, that immigrants are Americans, that we all deserve to be treated with dignity—the opposite of what I felt inside that place.

The Freshman

GALEN BAUGHMAN

Galen Baughman, now thirty-two years old, was arrested at the age of nineteen and charged with engaging in sexual activity with a fourteen-year-old boy. After he had completed his prison sentence, the Commonwealth of Virginia sought to have him civilly committed for an indefinite period of time, claiming he was still a danger to society, and he spent several more years in custody. He won his freedom in court in 2012 but remains on the sex offense registry.

Since his release, Baughman has become an advocate against the excesses of sex offender laws in the United States. He has lectured in a variety of venues, trained grassroots advocates across the country, and lobbied legislators. In 2015, he was named a Soros Justice Fellow by the Open Society Foundation for a project focused on ending the practice of civilly committing youth as sexually violent predators. He is also working for a coalition of LGBT rights organizations, developing a federal strategy advocating against policies that foster the permanent marginalization of people convicted of sexual offenses. His writing has appeared in the Washington Post, Playboy, *and a number of other print and online publications.*

I WATCHED THE FIREWORKS FROM A SMALL SLIT WINDOW IN MY CELL IN Arlington, Virginia. Across the Potomac River, six hundred thousand people were celebrating Independence Day on the National Mall. The bright, dynamic explosions above Washington felt tiny and other-worldly through the barred Plexiglas. I was alone, and about as far from free as I could get.

For almost nine years I had been locked away from the world, half of that time in solitary confinement. I was twenty-seven, but this odyssey began for me as a teenager. It's the world I had known for almost the entirety of my adult life. I did my best not to think of the happy memories I had had as a child with my family on the Mall for the 4th of July. Nothing came of that but bitterness and the deepest sense of loss. While looking back was painful, looking forward was almost impossible—for me, there was no end in sight to my isolation. In a neat file beneath the bunk in my cell sat an update sheet from the state. On it, where my release date was supposed to be, it simply read: "No date." Nestled in the same file, a petition from the attorney general of Virginia, seeking to civilly commit me as a sexually violent predator.

When I was nineteen, I fell in love with a boy who was sweet and smart and quirky. He would read me his poetry and talk to me late into the night about everything and anything, and it always seemed interesting. We told each other our secrets, and he made me laugh. We were best friends. One night we stayed up late, talking quietly together after our friends had fallen asleep in the room around us. It was my last night back home on break before returning to college for the spring semester. He kissed me for the first time, and asked me if I would have oral sex with him. He was a freshman in high school.

We never thought that night would lead to a prison cell, or that the next decade of my life would be spent mired in a criminal justice system designed to crush my humanity.

My charge sheet read Carnal Knowledge of a Minor and Crimes Against Nature, and I was told that I needed to be kept in protective custody for my own safety. They gave me no choice in the matter and, as a preppy gay white kid in a terrifying jail, I was inclined to believe them. Everyone has heard stories of what can happen to "sex offenders" in prison. I would spend twenty months in solitary at that jail before I was transferred into the prison system, where I was placed immediately in general population.

Over the course of my nine years of imprisonment, I was held at six different prisons in Virginia, as well as three jails in as many states. I was moved around quite a bit: I spent time at those six prisons during just four and a half years; the rest of my time I was held at a jail in solitary. The only time I was confined to isolation during my nine years of imprisonment was when I was fighting a legal case—when the dehumanizing, destabilizing psychological effects of that environment could provide the greatest advantage to the state.

I had a lot of time to reflect on my situation in solitary, to be penitent. It's hard to be sorry for loving someone; it's nearly impossible to feel sorry for being loved. Sitting alone in a stark cell, as days turned into weeks and months turned into years, the power and hatred of the state was palpable to me. They had taken everything they could take: my freedom, the future I had built for myself. They can even rob you of your dreams. The fantasy of giving up and ending my suffering was seductive. I had ideas of how to do it, but no concrete plans: I realized how dangerous those might be, given my position.

There came a point, as the monotony of my existence in solitary drew on and on, where I found myself wondering if this ghostlike existence was real. Each day was so much like the last that I caught myself wondering if maybe I had died in my cell and simply didn't know it; I could think of no worse hell than an eternity condemned to haunting that jail.

The darkness that comes with solitary confinement is pervasive: it seeps into your soul, clouds your brain, and stains the pages of letters you send from your cell. It is the least natural place you can ever find yourself. It is institutional, bleak; often made of concrete, steel, and cinder block. My walls were painted grey. The only stab of color in the space was a wooden desk set into the wall and a tiny sliver of blue out the window, on sunny days. For more than four years of my imprisonment—the entire time I was held at the local jail in Arlington—I wasn't allowed to go outdoors. Every moment of my life was spent in this building.

My isolation wasn't accompanied by the normal advantages of solitude: there was virtually no quiet, and very little peace. A television blared in the dayroom most days and sometimes late into the night. Vents running through the building carried the sounds of anger, boredom, and desperation from cell to cell. It was common for other prisoners to talk through the vents, standing on their sinks to yell between cells, like small children tying cans to strings to play telephone. The effect was similar to an old-fashioned party line broadcasting on a speakerphone that you couldn't hang up, next to your bed, in a room you couldn't ever leave.

The guards jokingly referred to my unit as "the penthouse." We were on the top floor of the tower that housed the jail. My unit was small, only eight cells. This compounded the isolation. Sometimes each cell had a soul in it—but there were long stretches when only a couple of people were in the unit. There was an entire month, near the end of my time behind bars, when I was the only person in the unit. For that month, on a day-to-day basis, the only other humans I got to see were the guards—who didn't seem to count for some reason.

A prisoner's job is to escape. I don't mean the *Mission Impossible*–style prison breaks that we all probably dream of as prisoners. Such things almost never happen anymore, and when they do they nearly always end in tragedy. As a prisoner, I can remember feeling that anything would be justified to secure my freedom. This is a natural result of placing humans in cages. The human spirit abhors captivity.

In solitary, freedom meant escaping into my mind. Each and every morning I awoke and lay my plans of escape: I found things to study to challenge my mind, I listened to NPR religiously on a small radio I was able to buy off of the commissary, I corresponded regularly with many pen pals through lengthy missives chronicling my adventures and memories and plans for the future, I made careful plans for how I would use my precious little out-of-cell time every day, and I read just about anything I could get my hands on. I was very fortunate to have the intellectual and educational resources to be able to escape those confines into my head. Reading gave me characters to befriend, allowed me to explore worlds beyond my small cell, and provided a distraction from my situation.

For the first several years of my imprisonment I took the *New York Times*. Reading the paper cover to cover every day helped me stay grounded to the real world. Closely following the developments in the news (including three full presidential election cycles) tethered me to reality. The only section I didn't read was the sports section, which the guards regularly stole for their own amusement; occasionally it would reappear a week later, stuffed into the current edition, as if no one would notice.

When I was in general population at a turn-of-the-century penitentiary in rural Virginia, a few years into my imprisonment, I saw a man at the property window sending newspapers home to his wife. The papers were more than six months old. After I finished reading each newspaper, I would pass it on to the first person in line behind me and Big John would pass it on in turn to another prisoner. This way, the *New York Times* would wind its way through the prison, lovingly passed from reader to reader. I would sometimes pass by a bunk and notice someone reading a headline I recognized from weeks or months before. So hungry were the other men for intellectual stimulation and connection to the outside world. Mine was perhaps the most valuable subscription to the *Times* in the world.

The driving force behind my success in solitary was the intentional cultivation of a sense of purpose in my existence. The same skills that had helped me succeed as a young person in the free world—having goals and a drive to work toward those goals—sustained me in those harshest of circumstances. It is up to us to bring meaning to our suffering. Without that sense of purpose, such immense darkness can destroy a person's soul. I have seen some turn to religion to provide that sense of purpose. I turned instead to a study of my own mind and experience, and I refused to allow this experience to make me forget who I was. If I came to solitary because I was loved, I would carry that love through to the other side.

It's hard to explain what it means to be labeled a *sex offender* in America today—to be relegated to the most despised segment of society, outcast, and forced to live as a pariah. The solitude I endured behind bars would echo after my release in the isolation caused by the sex offender registry. But before I could confront that, I had to secure my release.

On my twenty-sixth birthday, three weeks before I was scheduled to be released from prison after completing my sentence of six and a half years, I was told I wouldn't be going home. Instead, the Commonwealth of Virginia was seeking to impose a second prison sentence—this time in civil court—alleging I was too dangerous to be released because of some alleged psychological problem. They call this civil commitment, but it's really a form of imprisonment for imaginary future crimes—things the state claims you *might* do in the future.

The Supreme Court considered the constitutionality of these laws in 1997 and held in a split decision that these laws were permissible because civil commitment was for the purpose of treatment and not punishment. I don't believe them. I was held in solitary confinement for two and a half years past my mandatory release date without a trial under the Civil Commitment of Sexually Violent Predators Act. It doesn't get more punitive than that. And because these laws are *civil* in nature (not criminal), the power of the state is not checked by the normal protections of criminal law. When my lawyers argued to the state supreme court that my constitutional right to a speedy trial had been flagrantly violated by a string of continuances caused by the state—leading to twenty-eight months in jail past my release date— the attorney general's office responded that I had no right to a speedy trial under these laws and the state could hold me indefinitely without a trial.

After years of waiting I was given my trial, and something happened that had never happened before in the history of the law in Virginia: The jury unanimously agreed that I was not a "sexually violent predator" and should be released.

"What's this like for you, now . . . after everything . . . ?" I looked at my new friend, curly haired and handsome, full of so much goodwill and joy. We were sitting above Times Square in a trendy, expensive lounge—a treat before the big show, after spending our chilly Sunday morning in line for rush tickets on Broadway. The restaurant was opulent and modern, jutting above the most iconic intersection in the world, with views on three sides of the frenetic energy below. He was nearly the same age that I had been that first night in a barren cell, alone; yet it is impossible to imagine him there in my place. Sometimes it's hard now to imagine that I was there . . . and for so, so long.

"When I was there, in that place, I always felt like this is where I belonged; and now that I am here, in places like this with friends like you, I *know* that this is where I belong."

The Metro car pulled to a stop at the Court House station, underground beneath the tower where I spent four years of my life. I looked up as a face I recognized sat down in the seat beside me. He wasn't wearing his uniform, but the steel-toed black work boots were a dead giveaway. It always amused me that sheriff's deputies usually change into civilian clothes before leaving the jail, trying to shed the evidence that links them to their work. He looked right at me and I smiled, but he couldn't see the prisoner whose cell he used to pass once an hour for twelve-hour shifts. Those who are part of the system have the hardest time seeing how these systems rob all of us of our common humanity—prisoner and guard alike.

As I sat shoulder to shoulder with my former jailor, an otherwise anonymous millennial on the subway in a suit, I thought about the three years since I won my trial and freedom, and all that I had accomplished in that time as an advocate against the extreme, counterproductive, and dehumanizing policies that had almost succeeded in crushing me.

I often think of the nineteen-year-old lover in the tower in Virginia and wonder if he would be proud of me, or surprised at how he turned out. I still feel the echoes of the horrors I've endured, but they are woven into the fabric of who I have become, and I am immeasurably stronger because of it. That kid lives in me still somewhere, and I like to think he would be content knowing that his pain bought a chance for some other teenage boy to be spared the hell he was made to endure.

Because I Could Laugh

DOLORES CANALES

Dolores Canales, fifty-five, lives in Orange County, California. She was arrested for burglary at the age of eighteen and spent a total of twenty years in prison, including several stints in solitary confinement. Her son, John Martinez, has spent fourteen years in solitary confinement and is now confined at Pelican Bay. In 2011, the first of three major hunger strikes erupted in California's prisons, and Martinez immediately joined. After a second hunger strike in 2012, Canales co-founded California Families to Abolish Solitary Confinement (CFASC), which played a central role during the state's third and largest hunger strike in 2013, arguably the largest in U.S. history.

Canales and CFASC organized demonstrations, sat on the mediation team with prison officials to negotiate the terms of ending the strike, and constantly found ways for families on the outside to stay involved. In 2014, Dolores Canales was named a Soros Justice Advocacy Fellow to support her work as founder of the Family Unity Network of Imprisoned People. The following piece is based on an interview with Sarah Shourd in October 2014.

My Son Still Looked the Same

MY SON, JOHNNY, WAS THIRTY-SIX YEARS OLD WHEN I FINALLY WAS granted a visit. I hadn't seen him for twenty years, but he mostly looked the same. It was crazy to me, all that time and so much had happened—but my son somehow looked the same.

I was eighteen when I got arrested the first time, same age as Johnny. It was for residential burglary—that was 1979. Now, I think about how I would feel if I knew someone had been in my home when I wasn't there. Just knowing that possibility I would feel unsafe. And yet when you're doing it, you're not thinking about that. You're just thinking about how you can feel better.

My granddad was one of the first Latino homeowners in Anaheim, California. We go all the way back to the orange groves. He was a foreman, with his own truck and crew at the packinghouse. I can still remember that truck in the backyard. They had a house over on Philadelphia—he grew up there with thirteen brothers and sisters. All of them have good jobs now, college and the rest of it. Only one brother went to prison. On my mom's side I have an aunt who partied all the time—she had five kids and four of them ended up addicts. Both my brothers have been locked up—one of them is dead now. If I try to add up how long I spent in prison, I come up with about twenty years. Heroin. That's what it was. Heroin, for all of us.

He Used to Tell Me I'd Never Be Nothing

Both times I spent six months in the hole. The drug investigator was this fat man with a mustache. He would chase me around the prison yard trying to catch me using drugs. Then he'd use this little card to measure my pupils and send me away for drug testing if they were off. He tried to make me look like I was part of this big drug cartel, but I never wanted to sell anything. I just wanted to stay loaded. He used to tell me I'd never be nothing—anything but a lowlife dope fiend. He hated me, probably because I was on drugs every day, but maybe, maybe it was because I could laugh.

My first long stint in solitary was in San Bernardino. When it was hot I'd put a wet sheet on the floor and lie down on it naked, trying to catch the air coming in from a crack under the door. They had a window in the women's pod, but when they left it open all the flies would come in, so they let us cover it with cardboard from our lunch boxes. Then in the winter it was unbearably cold, from one extreme to the other. No AC, no heat, no extra clothes, no nothing. Sometimes you could get the nurse to request an extra blanket for you, but you really had to complain. That was about it.

In our SHU (Special Housing Unit, a term they use for solitary confinement), we could have private conversations with the person next to us—we'd call them our vent partners. We could even see each other a little bit through the holes in the vent. When you looked out the door, if you stood one way, you could see each other's eyes. I used to like to do this thing with the other girls. "I'll be Aretha Franklin," I'd say. We'd laugh and I'd sing, "What you want, baby, I got it." Then all together we'd be like, "Sock it to me. Sock it to me. Sock it to me." The staff would trip out on us because we'd really be doing it. That way we'd have fun, make each other laugh, and pass the time.

I was with women before it was popular. One relationship I had with a woman inside lasted fifteen years. When I got arrested at eighteen I was still with my husband, but I left him for my new girlfriend. After that, I was only with men if it had a purpose, if I was using them for something. There was this older lady at Anaheim City Jail, Maria, she was in her thirties. We were in the same cell and she was talking about how her "old lady" was gonna show up in court and how her "old lady" was going to be there for her. I was so sheltered, I thought she was talking about her mom! And then she said, "That Cher's a fine bitch." I'd never really looked at women like that, but when she said it I thought, yeah, she is pretty.

I was petite and I had this really long hair. They let us wear our own things at that jail, so I would wear a bandana wrapped around me as a blouse, that's how tiny I was. And Maria used to tell me, "You're going to have a girlfriend." And I would say, "No way, I'm not attracted to that." But she was right, the girls started to come to the fence to talk to me—I thought one girl was cute because she looked so much like a guy. So I had a girlfriend before I even got out on the yard.

Does That Make Them a Gang? I Don't Think So

I never used drugs when I was pregnant with Johnny, not once. When I was young, my mom was always out partying and my dad was in prison, so my aunt Nena raised me. When I turned fourteen, though, my mom remarried and decided to take me back. The big mistake she made was not letting me see my Nena—she said I always came back from those visits with an attitude. After that I just hated her forever.

Then, just a few years later, it was my Nena raising Johnny while I was doing drugs and locked up. Johnny's childhood was hard because they lived in extreme poverty; they had to survive off what my Nena made working in the laundry at a motel. I look at pictures of when he was little, and I can see his shoes or his shirts were old looking. Even when I was out on parole, Nena was real protective of Johnny. If I wanted to take him shopping or out to eat, she had to come along. She was afraid I'd take him from her like my mom did with me, but I knew I could never do that to her.

When Johnny was seventeen, I started driving him to work, then my dad said no—Johnny needs to get to work on his own. For two days Johnny didn't show up at his job at all; he was just hanging out with his friends. One of the guys got in an argument with another guy who said something about his mom. They went to demand an apology, a fight broke out, two of the guys were stabbed. One died the next morning. This was in 1994, when all of the gang laws were being passed. The cops said that because they lived in Placentia and went to Fullerton High School they were in a gang. I'm not trying to downplay the stabbing—a life was lost, you can't take that back. My son lived in Placentia all his life, went to school, worked . . . he was even enrolled in a forestry program that he went to after school. Johnny was there, but he didn't stab anyone. So, was he hanging out with the guys from Placentia? Yes, absolutely. Does that make them a gang? I don't think so.

There's No Tomorrows for Us

In 2001, I was forty-two years old. I was potentially facing twenty-five years to life because of the three strikes law. Johnny had been in solitary at Pelican Bay for almost six years at that point. When I was in the hole it was a nine-month-maximum sentence. I knew I'd get out. For my son it's indefinite—because he's validated as a "gang associate" and that's how it works in California.

Every six years they revalidate him. The only evidence they used the first time was his name. They found it written in a note that somebody else had in their cell. People hear this and they don't want to believe it—that in California someone can be put in solitary confinement indefinitely for something so small—not even close to violent.

That they're put there just for associating—which all of us who have loved ones in there know is unconstitutional. The lawyers know it. Johnny didn't even write the note, but his name was in it, and that's enough for them.

I used to think the same thing about terrorists—who cares if they're being tortured? They must have done something awful. Now that's what people say about gang members, about people like my son— "they're gang members, who cares if they're getting tortured?" It's easy to condone what we do to them if we're convinced they deserve it because of who they are. The public is told these policies keep them safe. It's so easy to buy into that when you don't know all the truth.

One day I was lying on my bunk listening to a group of friends talking. I was miserable and no matter how many drugs I did, I was still miserable. I realized everyone inside had some kind of a plan. They were like, "Tomorrow I'm going to get on methadone. Tomorrow I'll turn myself in and detox." We all had a plan for tomorrow, but tomorrow was never gonna come. There's no tomorrows for us. I realized nothing was going to change.

As Soon as I Got a New Denial I Would Start Again

April 6, 2001, is my sobriety date. I never used once after that. From that point on, all I wanted was to get out of prison and be a good mom. I was on a mission. In 2009 it finally happened—the judge let me out on parole—then my mission was to visit Johnny. They denied me four times. The first time they said I didn't submit my whole arrest record. So I went to the police station to get a printout. Then they said I had a recent arrest. I didn't; it was somebody else who used my name. So I got that cleared up. Then I mailed in the request certified. I had letters of recommendation and everything . . . and it all just disappeared: "Lost," they said. After that I decided to drive to Corcoran and hand in the application myself. As soon as I got a new denial I would start again. They said I had three felonies in ten years, but they were just going by the wrong date.

Then one day Johnny got a letter under his cell door. He was expecting a denial, so he didn't even open it right away. He set it on his desk and started preparing a legal challenge in his head. He opened it later that night—July 20, 2011—and it was my approval.

I made plans to come up the weekend of August 8. My friend from church paid for my flight, but that morning I got a voicemail saying it was canceled. So we started looking for other flights. I found one out of Burbank, but then it looked like I'd miss my connection in San Francisco. Somebody texted me, "Have a great visit with your son." I texted back, "I don't know if I'm gonna make it." She put my situation on Facebook and all of a sudden I had people I didn't even know reaching out to help: "We're not going to leave without you." So that way I found a ride, all 364 miles from San Francisco up to Pelican Bay State Prison.

I was really worried that I'd start crying as soon as I saw him. I got through security and walked into the visiting booth, but as soon as I sat down I just started laughing. Then Johnny started laughing too and it was so crazy because it was such real, unbelievable laughter. I hadn't seen my son for twenty years and here we were laughing.

And he really did look the same. Being in solitary, they get almost no sunlight. They're not making a lot of facial expressions either, so they don't get wrinkles. So he looked similar to how he did when he was eighteen at thirty-six—twenty years later. It was like, "wow." I honestly couldn't believe it.

That's the Beauty of the Law, Mom

Now I take the trip to visit him on average every four to six weeks. Every time I see Johnny he tells me how proud he is of me—he doesn't go on and on about what a terrible mom I was, or how things could have been different. All he ever says is he's glad to have me back. Once or twice he's written me a letter where he talks about how bad the conditions are—how Pelican Bay is designed to make men go crazy or drive them to suicide. Even when he does talk about difficulties, he kind of laughs it off. I wish Johnny told me more, but he doesn't want to worry me. He always puts on a happy face.

Being that he's a jailhouse lawyer, Johnny's really focused on his case. He spends a lot of time helping other prisoners with their legal work. He gets a legal journal and sometimes we like to talk about what he's reading during our visits. Once, he was talking to me like that and he says, "That's the beauty of the law, Mom." And I just sat there staring at him. He can't even get out of this gang validation, but that's my son; he still loves the law.

Johnny's conditions are far worse than anything I ever experienced.

His cell is windowless; all he can see is the cement wall across from his cell—he can't even see other prisoners. When I went to yard, it was with other women and I was outside; my son exercises alone. The only physical contact he has is with the guards; the only time he looks at someone face to face is through glass. And this has been going on for more than a decade; it's indefinite.

When the prisoners first went on hunger strike in 2010, I hated the idea. I was already worried enough; I didn't want to think about them starving. When I told Johnny that, he looked at me and said, "Mom, what else are we supposed to do?" I realized he was right; they had no other way to change things. Throughout history sacrifice has always been the only way for the people at the bottom of society to make change. But the longer it went on, the more difficult it was—would all this suffering amount to anything? Would they let them die? I had to admit to myself that that could happen.

I Just Walked up to the Podium

My friend and I found out about an event on this prisoner solidarity website, so we drove out to South Central L.A. When we got there a lot of organizations were standing around handing out paperwork, so much paperwork. By this time the hunger strike had grown to the point where almost ten thousand prisoners were participating, and the media was starting to pay attention. We came to this meeting for one purpose, to talk about what we could do to support them. That wasn't happening, so we got up to leave.

Then someone asked if I wanted to speak. I said no, I came to hear from other people. Then I realized I had the Core Demands in my pocket—written up by the Pelican Bay Representatives—my son had mailed them to me. So I just walked up to the podium. "The SHU does not discriminate," I began, "it entombs all races. The Five Core Demands of the Pelican Bay Hunger Strikers are:

1. Eliminate group punishments and administrative abuse.

2. Abolish the debriefing policy and modify active/inactive gang status criteria.

3. Comply with the recommendations of the U.S. Commission on Safety and Abuse in America's Prisons and end long-term solitary confinement.

4. Provide adequate and nutritious food.

5. Create and expand constructive programming.

Then everyone applauded and I just sat back down. That was another one of those big moments in my life: like quitting drugs, seeing Johnny again . . . there was no going back after that day.

Then the Short Corridor Collective put out the *Agreement to End Hostilities*, signed by different racial groups. I thought—wow—this is revolutionary. Having been inside myself, I understood how significant it was. So we organized rallies, I learned to do media interviews, and then the whole thing took on a life of its own. The more I researched, the more I realized this wasn't new. There have been advocates, lawsuits, and even hunger strikes going on against prison conditions in California for decades. We were part of a movement, and we were inching closer, which just made us want to fight harder.

The hunger strike lasted three months. They agreed to stop when they were promised a legislative hearing and a new step-down program that would offer a way out of the SHU. Some people have gotten out, but there's been no meaningful change in conditions for my son. They've been allowed to order additional items from the canteen and given a few extra comforts like shorts, bowls, a pull-up bar, and a handball. Also, the visits have been expanded to three hours instead of what used to be an hour and a half. These things make a difference, but they're still in solitary.

We families realized we needed to form a group and keep organizing. So we started a group called California Families to Abolish Solitary Confinement (CFASC). Now we drive up together, sometimes a busload of us, to visit our husbands, boyfriends, sons—in some cases, it's grandfathers. Some people haven't been able to afford the trip for years—sometimes they're too sick, sometimes they're just scared to make the trip alone—one mom hadn't seen her son for a decade before she found CFASC. So we do it together. For these men, a visit from their families can totally turn their lives around.

A Story Behind Every Answer

Of course I worry. I worry that this is our moment, right now, when we still have the public's attention, which will inevitably fade. I worry they'll never let him out of the SHU and if they do how long will it take? Sometimes I wake up in the middle of the night and I feel like I'm in there with him. I feel his loneliness; he's been in there almost fourteen years now, how can anyone bear that? My son deserves to be a free man, but that's not even what he's asking for—he just wants out of solitary where he has a chance to do better, improve himself.

His first two years as a baby he was always with me, up until I started getting arrested. I just can't help but think that if he'd had a good mom—a really good mom—growing up, things would have been so different. He probably wouldn't be spending his life in prison. So there's that. I don't let it consume me. I try to take what we have now and go forward with it.

It's either laugh or be pissed off all the time. Don't get me wrong. I spent a lot of years just being angry—but that's what kept me using drugs. That wasn't letting me grow and succeed and move on. There just aren't simple answers. There's a story behind every answer. It's a life.

Invisible

FIVE MUALIMM-AK

Five Mualimm-ak was born in Ethiopia in 1975 and moved to the United States with his family at the age of twelve. Both of his parents were radical political activists, and his mother died awaiting trial in federal prison when Mualimm-ak was nineteen. Mualimm-ak entered the New York State prison system in his early twenties with a sentence of thirty-three years to life for a series of drug offenses. He served a total of twelve years, five of them in solitary confinement, before the majority of his convictions were overturned and he was released on time served for possession of a weapon.

After leaving prison in 2012, and while living in a homeless shelter for nearly two years, Five Mualimm-ak has become a leading advocate in New York against mass incarceration in general and solitary confinement in particular. He has worked with the Campaign to End the New Jim Crow, and is a founding member of the New York City Jails Action Coalition and the New York State Campaign for Alternatives to Isolated Confinement. In 2015, he launched his own advocacy group made up of formerly incarcerated people, the Incarcerated Nation Corporation. The following piece is based on a series of interviews with Jean Casella in 2013 and 2014.

As kids, a lot of us imagine having superpowers. I was an avid comic book reader, and I often imagined being invisible. I never thought I would actually experience it, but I did. It wasn't in a parallel universe—although it often felt that way. While serving time in New York's prisons, I spent 2,054 days in solitary confinement. I was out of sight and invisible to other human beings—and eventually, even to myself.

After only a short time in solitary, I felt all of my senses start to diminish. There was nothing to see but grey walls. In New York's so-called Special Housing Units, or SHUs, most cells have solid steel doors, and some don't have windows. You can't even tape up pictures or photographs; they have to be kept in an envelope. To fight the blankness, I counted bricks and measured the walls. I stared obsessively at the bolts on the door to my cell.

There was nothing to hear except empty, echoing voices from other parts of the prison. I was so lonely that I hallucinated words coming out of the wind. They sounded like whispers. Sometimes I smelled the paint on the wall, but more often, I just smelled myself, revolted by my own scent. There was no touch. My food was pushed through a slot. Doors were activated by buzzers, even the one that led to a literal cage directly outside of my cell for one hour per day of "recreation."

Even time had no meaning in the SHU. The lights were kept on for twenty-four hours. I often found myself wondering if an event I was recollecting had happened that morning or days before. I talked to myself. After a while, I began to get scared that the guards would come in and kill me and leave me hanging in the cell. Who would know if something happened to me? The space I inhabited was invisible to the outside world, just like I was.

People in the SHU become so desperate for contact with another human being that they find ingenious ways to make contact. One of them is called "fishing." You would start by pulling narrow strips off your bed sheet and tying them together into a fishing line. Then you'd need a counterweight to tie onto the end of your line. Little packets of shampoo made a good counterweight, if you could manage to smuggle them out of the shower.

To start fishing, you would shoot your line out from the crack under your cell door. Then someone next door, or across the tier, shot out his own line with his counterweight across your line, and tried to snag it and pull the end into his cell. Once you had a fishing line set up you could attach things to it for the person on the other end to reel in. That's how we would communicate, using "kites," which are notes attached to the line. Or we'd share things that someone else needed.

Books and magazines—any reading materials, really—were prized items to share. To fish with a book, though, you'd need to tear it into pieces small enough to fit under the door. We would pass books down the tier, section by section, until everyone who could read had read it. It wasn't much, but it made us feel a little less bored, a little less helpless, and a little less alone.

I try to explain to people how the sensory deprivation and the absence of human contact affects a person. I try to make them see how much we need human validation. The very essence of life is human contact, and the affirmation of existence that comes with it. Losing that contact, you lose your sense of identity. You become nothing. That's what I mean when I say I became invisible even to myself.

Anyone lacking familiarity with our state prison system would probably guess I must have been a pretty scary, out-of-control prisoner. But I never committed one act of violence during my entire sentence. Instead, a series of "tickets," or disciplinary write-ups for prison rule violations, were punished with a total of more than five years in "the box."

In New York, guards give out tickets like penny candy. During my years in prison, I received an endless stream of tickets, each one more absurd than the last. When I tried to use artwork to stay sane, I was ticketed for having too many pencils. Excess pencils are considered sharpened objects, or weapons. Another time, I had too many postage stamps, which in prison are used like currency and are contraband.

One day, I ate an entire apple—including the core—because I was starving for lack of nutrition. I received a ticket for eating the core because apple seeds contain arsenic. The next time I received an apple, fearful of another ticket, I simply left it on the tray. I received a ticket for "refusing to eat."

During the five years I spent in the box, I received insulin shots for my diabetes by extending my arm through the food slot in the cell's door. ("Therapy" for prisoners with mental illness is often conducted this way, as well.) One day, the person who gave me the shot yanked roughly on my arm through the small opening, and I instinctively pulled back. This earned me another ticket for "refusing medical attention," adding time to my solitary sentence.

My case is far from unusual. A 2012 study by the New York Civil

Liberties Union found that five out of six of the thirteen thousand SHU sentences handed out every year are for nonviolent misbehavior, rather than violent acts. This brutal approach to discipline means that New York isolates its prisoners at rates well above the national average.

On any given day, some 3,800 people are in isolated confinement in the state, many for months or years. Those accused of more serious prison offenses, and those deemed an ongoing risk to "safety and security," have been held in solitary for twenty years or more. In handing out these sentences-within-sentences, prison officials act as prosecutors, witnesses, judge, and jury. There is no defense counsel.

Using this form of punishment is particularly absurd for minor rule infractions. But in truth, no one should be subjected to the kind of extreme isolation practiced in New York's prisons today. I have no doubt that what is going on in prisons all over our state and our country is torture. Many national and international human rights groups—including UN Special Rapporteur on Torture Juan Méndez—agree. Yet it continues, unseen and for the most part ignored by the public.

Everyone knows that prison is supposed to take away your freedom. But solitary doesn't just confine your body; it kills your soul. And it makes it hard to ever live among other people again.

Because of the way I left prison, based on the outcome of a court case, I had no advance notice of my release date. I was in Upstate, a supermax prison way up by the Canadian border. I was in solitary confinement when a guard came to my cell one morning and said, "No breakfast today. You're getting out." I was handcuffed and searched, and then brought to the gate, where I was uncuffed, asked to sign a paper, and given a bag of my property and $40.

Then I was outside, by myself. It was 7:00 a.m. I just stood there for a long time until a van came to take me to the bus station. It was like a dream. They gave me a ticket and I climbed onto the bus, and I was so overwhelmed that I slept for nine hours. When I woke up I was in the Port Authority Bus Terminal, which has to be one of the most crowded, crazy places in the world.

I remember folding up right there in the bus station. I didn't know it at the time, but I was having my first panic attack. I was sweating, and I could feel my heart beating in my chest and my eyes darting back and forth. I just slid down to the floor in a corner. And in that moment, all I wanted was to be back in a safe, confined place, knowing exactly what was around me, far away from all those people.

I remember a homeless guy coming up to me and asking if I was okay, and then he said, "Oh, you just came home." I don't know whether he'd been incarcerated himself, or had just seen things like this before in the bus station. But he knew what was happening.

The police came, and I told them I just got out. They escorted me out of the bus station. It's sad, but it made me feel comfortable again—being escorted by people in uniforms, and being told what to do.

Then suddenly, I stopped walking. At first I didn't understand why I'd stopped. But then I saw that there was a huge yellow line running in front of the doors to the bus station. I had spent the past twelve years of my life in supermax or max, where there are yellow lines on the floor everywhere, and you are never allowed to cross a yellow line without permission. No matter where you're going, you have to stop at the yellow line. And if you go one step beyond, it's a club over your head.

That day, I was in such bad shape that the police sent me straight to the hospital, to Bellevue. And I didn't get out of there for several days. I was supposed to immediately report to parole once I reached the city. So within a day of leaving solitary, I had violated parole—and I ended up being sent back to prison.

The next time I got out, I was leaving from general population, not solitary, and I had a mental health diagnosis—I am bipolar—so I was able to get some help, although it wasn't easy. The system is stacked against formerly incarcerated people in so many ways, making it nearly impossible to get housing, jobs, or public assistance. If you've been damaged by solitary confinement and can barely function in the free world, then it's even harder. That is why the first goal of my new organization, the Incarcerated Nation Corporation, is to develop re-entry resources specifically for people getting out of solitary—to help them navigate the system, and get the special support and mental health treatment they need. There are programs for victims of other kinds of torture, so why not solitary confinement?

For me, recovering from solitary has meant fighting against solitary and other aspects of mass incarceration. When I first got out, I lived in a shelter on West 25th Street. When I went to organizing meetings around stop-and-frisk, and later solitary confinement, I always wore a suit, and if people asked me where I was living, I'd just say, "In

Chelsea," and then they would assume I was fine. After a while a few of my friends in the movement started to question me, saying, "Where you really living?" And I let some people get a little closer to me.

Still, you never completely recover from solitary confinement. You just learn to live with the scars it leaves behind. The scars may be invisible, too, but they're no less painful or permanent than physical scars. Even now that I'm out of prison, I suffer major psychological consequences from those years in isolation.

I know that I have irreparable memory damage. I can hardly sleep. I have a short temper. I don't like people to touch me. I can't listen to music or watch television or sports. I'm only beginning to recover my ability to talk on the phone. I have a hard time feeling connected to people. Even though I am a free man now, I often feel as though I remain invisible, going through the motions of life.

One of my greatest comforts has come from meeting other people who had been in solitary or had worked with people coming out of solitary, who took the time to say, *There's nothing inherently wrong with you. It's the system that creates people like you. I've seen a thousand people act the same way you're acting.* That was necessary for me because it let me know that the problem was bigger than me, that it wasn't just my problem.

In New York City, we have managed to make some progress, banning children from being placed in solitary confinement and setting some limits on how long others can be there. But we still have a long way to go. In New York State, we have written the most progressive piece of anti-solitary legislation in the country, the Humane Alternatives to Long-Term (HALT) Solitary Confinement Act, which is gradually gaining support. My goal is for New York to become a model for the rest of the country. It's what keeps me going.

I believe it's very important for people who are formerly incarcerated, who have experienced solitary firsthand, to have leadership roles in the movement to end solitary. That's one way that we can ensure that we—and the torture we endured—are never invisible again.

Part II

PERSPECTIVES ON SOLITARY
CONFINEMENT

Psychiatric Effects of Solitary Confinement

STUART GRASSIAN

Dr. Stuart Grassian is a board-certified psychiatrist and a former member of the faculty at Harvard Medical School. For more than three decades, Grassian has been studying the psychological and neurological effects of solitary confinement. He has interviewed hundreds of incarcerated individuals and was the first to conclude that people held in prolonged prison isolation exhibit a specific "constellation of symptoms" that suggests a discrete illness caused by solitary confinement. Grassian's findings have been cited in several federal court decisions, and he has lectured and given testimony on the subject at venues across the country.

SOLITARY CONFINEMENT—THAT IS, THE CONFINEMENT OF A PRISONER alone in a cell for all, or nearly all, of the day with minimal environmental stimulation and minimal opportunity for social interaction—can cause severe psychiatric harm. It has indeed long been known that severe restriction of environmental and social stimulation has a profoundly deleterious effect on mental functioning; this issue has been a major concern for many groups of patients including, for example, patients in intensive care units, spinal patients immobilized by the need for prolonged traction, and patients with impairments of[1] their sensory apparatus (such as eye-patched or hearing-impaired patients). This issue has also been a very significant concern in military situations, in polar and submarine expeditions, and in preparations for space travel.

The United States was actually the world leader in introducing prolonged incarceration and solitary confinement as a means of dealing with criminal behavior. The "penitentiary system" began in the United States, first in Philadelphia, in the early nineteenth century, a product of a spirit of great social optimism about the possibility of rehabilitation of individuals with socially deviant behavior.[2] The Americans were quite proud of their "penitentiary system," and they invited and encouraged important visitors from abroad to observe them.[3] This system, originally labeled the "Philadelphia System," involved an almost exclusive reliance on solitary confinement as a means of incarceration and also became the predominant mode of incarceration, both for post-conviction and also for pretrial detainees, in the several European prison systems that emulated the American model.[4]

The results were, in fact, catastrophic. The incidence of mental disturbances among prisoners so detained, and the severity of such disturbances, was so great that the system fell into disfavor and was ultimately abandoned. During this process, a major body of clinical literature developed that documented the psychiatric disturbances created by such stringent conditions of confinement. The paradigmatic psychiatric disturbance was an agitated confusional state that, in more severe cases, had the characteristics of a florid delirium, characterized by severe confusional, paranoid, and hallucinatory features, and intense agitation and random, impulsive, often self-directed violence. Such disturbances were often observed in individuals who had no prior history of any mental illness. In addition, solitary confinement often resulted in severe exacerbation of a previously existing mental condition. Even among inmates who did not develop overt psychiatric illness as a result of solitary confinement, such confinement almost inevitably imposed significant psychological pain during the period of isolated confinement and often significantly impaired the inmate's capacity to adapt successfully to the broader prison environment.

It is both tragic and highly disturbing that the lessons of the nineteenth-century experience with solitary confinement are today so completely ignored by those responsible for addressing the housing and mental health needs in the prison setting. For, indeed, the psychiatric harm solitary confinement causes had become exceedingly apparent well more than one hundred years ago. Indeed, by 1890, with *In re Medley*,[5] the United States Supreme Court explicitly recognized the massive psychiatric harm caused by solitary confinement:

> This matter of solitary confinement is not . . . a mere unimportant regulation as to the safe-keeping of the prisoner. . . . [E]xperience [with the penitentiary system of solitary confinement] demonstrated that there were serious objections to it. A considerable number of the prisoners fell, after even a short confinement, into a semi-fatuous condition, from which it was next to impossible to arouse them, and others became violently insane; others still, committed suicide; while those who stood the ordeal better were not generally reformed, and in most cases did not recover sufficient mental activity to be of any subsequent service to the community.[6]

The consequences of the Supreme Court's holding were quite dramatic for James J. Medley. Mr. Medley had been convicted of murdering his wife. Under the Colorado statute in force at the time of the murder, he would have been executed after about one additional month of incarceration in the county jail. But in the interim between Mr. Medley's crime and his trial, the Colorado legislature had passed a new statute that called for the convicted murderer to be, instead, incarcerated in solitary confinement in the state prison during the month prior to his execution.[7] Unhappily, when the legislature passed the new law, it simultaneously rescinded the older law without allowing for a bridging clause that would have allowed Mr. Medley's sentencing under the older statute.[8]

Mr. Medley appealed his sentencing under the new statute, arguing that punishment under this new law was so substantially more burdensome than punishment under the old law as to render its application to him ex post facto.[9] The Supreme Court agreed with him, even though it simultaneously recognized that if Mr. Medley was not sentenced under the new law, he could not be sentenced at all.[10] Despite this, the Court held that this additional punishment of one month of solitary confinement was simply too egregious to ignore; the Court declared Mr. Medley a free man and ordered his release from prison.[11]

Dramatic concerns about the profound psychiatric effects of solitary confinement have continued into the twentieth century, both in the medical literature and in the news. The alarm raised about the "brain washing" of political prisoners of the Soviet Union and of Communist China—and especially of American prisoners of war during the Korean War—gave rise to a major body of medical and scientific literature concerning the effects of sensory deprivation and social isolation, including a substantial body of experimental research.[12] This literature as well as my own observations has demonstrated that, deprived of a sufficient level of environmental and social stimulation, individuals will soon become incapable of maintaining an adequate state of alertness and attention to the environment. Indeed, even a few days of solitary confinement will predictably shift the electroencephalogram (EEG) pattern toward an abnormal pattern characteristic of stupor and delirium.

This fact is not surprising. Most individuals have at one time or another experienced, at least briefly, the effects of intense monotony and inadequate environmental stimulation. After even a relatively brief period of time in such a situation, an individual is likely to descend into a mental torpor or "fog," in which alertness, attention, and concentration all become impaired. In such a state, after a time, the individual becomes increasingly incapable of processing external stimuli, and often becomes "hyperresponsive" to such stimulation. For example, a sudden noise or the flashing of a light jars the individual from his stupor and becomes intensely unpleasant. Over time, the very absence of stimulation causes whatever stimulation is available to become noxious and irritating. Individuals in such a stupor tend to avoid any stimulation, and withdraw progressively into themselves and their own mental fog.

An adequate state of responsiveness to the environment requires both the ability to achieve and maintain an attentional set and the ability to shift attention. The impairment of alertness and concentration in solitary confinement leads to two related abnormalities: the inability to focus, and the inability to shift attention. The inability to focus (to achieve and maintain attention) is experienced as a kind of dissociative stop—a mental fog in which the individual cannot focus attention and cannot, for example, grasp or recall when he attempts to read or to think. The inability to shift attention results in a kind of "tunnel vision" in which the individual's attention becomes stuck, almost always on something intensely unpleasant, and in which he cannot stop thinking about that matter; instead, he becomes obsessively fixated upon it. These obsessional preoccupations are especially troubling.

Individuals in solitary confinement easily become preoccupied with some thought, some perceived slight or irritation, some sound or smell coming from a neighboring cell, or perhaps most commonly, by some bodily sensation. Tortured by it, such individuals are unable to stop dwelling on it. In solitary confinement, ordinary stimuli become intensely unpleasant and small irritations become maddening. Individuals in such confinement brood on normally unimportant stimuli, and minor irritations become the focus of increasing agitation and paranoia. I have examined countless individuals in solitary confinement who have become obsessively preoccupied with some minor, almost imperceptible bodily sensation, a sensation that grows over time into a worry, and finally into an all-consuming, life-threatening illness.

Individuals experiencing such environmental restriction find it difficult to maintain a normal pattern of daytime alertness and nighttime sleep. They often find themselves incapable of resisting their bed during the day—incapable of resisting the paralyzing effect of their stupor—and yet incapable of any restful sleep at night. The lack of meaningful activity is further compounded by the effect of continual exposure to artificial light and diminished opportunity to experience natural daylight. And the individual's difficulty in maintaining a normal day-night sleep cycle is often far worsened by constant intrusions on nighttime dark and quiet, such as steel doors slamming shut, flashlights shining in his face, and so forth. There are substantial differences in the effects of solitary confinement on different individuals. Those most severely affected are often individuals with evidence of subtle neurological or attention deficit disorder, or with some other vulnerability. These individuals suffer from states of florid psychotic delirium, marked by severe hallucinatory confusion, disorientation, and even incoherence, and by intense agitation and paranoia. These psychotic disturbances often have a dissociative character, and individuals so affected often do not recall events that occurred during the course of the confusional psychosis. Generally, individuals with more stable personalities and greater ability to modulate their emotional expression and behavior and individuals with stronger cognitive functioning are less severely affected. However, all of these individuals will still experience a degree of stupor, difficulties with thinking and concentration, obsessional thinking, agitation, irritability, and difficulty tolerating external stimuli (especially noxious stimuli).

Moreover, although many of the acute symptoms these inmates suffer are likely to subside upon termination of solitary confinement, many inmates—including some who did not become overtly psychiatrically ill during their confinement in solitary—will likely suffer permanent harm as a result of such confinement. This harm is most commonly manifested by a continued intolerance of social interaction, a handicap that often prevents inmates from successfully readjusting to the broader social environment of general population in prison and, perhaps more significantly, often severely impairs inmates' capacity to reintegrate into the broader community upon release from imprisonment.

Many inmates housed in such stringent conditions are extremely fearful of acknowledging the psychological harm or stress they are experiencing as a result of such confinement. This reluctance is a response to the perception that solitary confinement is an overt attempt by authorities to "break them down" psychologically and, in my experience, tends to be more severe when the inmate experiences the stringencies of his confinement as being the product of an arbitrary exercise of power, rather than the fair result of an inherently reasonable process. Furthermore, in solitary confinement settings, mental health screening interviews are often conducted at the cell front, rather than in a private setting, and inmates are generally quite reluctant to disclose psychological distress in the context of such an interview because such conversation would inevitably be heard by other inmates in adjacent cells, exposing them to possible stigma and humiliation in front of their fellows.

1. 889 F. Supp 1146 (N.D. Cal. 1995), rev'd and remanded, 150 F.3d 1030 (9th Cir. 1989).

2. An excellent history of the Philadelphia System is found in Norman Johnson et al., *Eastern Penitentiary: Crucible of Good Intentions* (1994).

3. See David J. Rothman, *The Discovery of the Asylum* 81 (1971). See also Gustave de Beaumont and Alexis de Tocqueville, *On the Penitent System in the United States and Its Application in France* and Charles Dickens, *American Notes and Pictures from Italy* (Leonee Ormond Ed., Everymans Library, 1997 [1842]).

4. Rothman, 96–101.

5. 134 U.S. 160 (1890).

6. Ibid., 167–68.

7. Ibid., 162–63.

8. Ibid., 166.

9. Ibid., 162.

10. Ibid., 166.

11. Ibid., 174.

12. Albert D. Biderman and Herbert Zimmer Eds., *The Manipulation of Human Behaviour* 2–3, 35 (1961).

How to Create Madness in Prison

TERRY KUPERS

Dr. Terry Kupers is a psychiatrist with a background in psychoanalytic psychotherapy, forensics, and social and community psychiatry. A former member of the faculty at the Wright Institute in San Francisco, he is also a Distinguished Life Fellow of the American Psychiatric Association. Among the foremost national experts on the mental health effects of solitary confinement, Kupers has worked with incarcerated people in several states and has testified on the subject in many class action suits. He is the author of four books, including Prison Madness. *Here, he places the use of solitary confinement in the context of the rise of mass incarceration.*

IT'S WORTH PAUSING FOR A MOMENT TO CONSIDER HOW WE CREATED AS much madness as exists today in our prisons. Perhaps, after exploring how we arrived at this dreadful state of affairs, we can strive to reverse the process and foster sanity, at the same time developing humane and effective prisons.

In the era of mental asylums, when individuals suffering from serious mental illness were confined in large public psychiatric hospitals, institutional dynamics came under the spotlight. Erving Goffman, Thomas Scheff, and other "sociologists of deviance" hypothesized that institutional dynamics had a big part in driving patients to regress into impotent and bizarre aggressive behaviors while clinicians were side-tracked into self-fulfilling biases in diagnostics.[1] An example of their theory: A young man is brought to the asylum by family members who consider him "crazy"; he protests loudly that he is not crazy and in fact it is the parents who want him locked up who are actually the crazy ones. The psychiatrist interprets his increasingly loud protests as signs of the very mental illness being ascribed to him, and he is involuntarily admitted to the asylum. As he realizes he is being deprived of his freedom, his protests become louder and more desperate. The staff take his emotional protests as further evidence confirming the diagnosis of psychosis; he is placed on a locked ward, and deprived of most familiar means of expressing himself; he does something irrational such as throwing a chair through a window in order to express his outrage over being deprived of his freedom; the staff are even more convinced of his "madness" and lock him in an isolation room with no clothes and no pens or writing materials. Being even more incensed and more desperate to express himself, he smears feces on the wall of the isolation room and begins to write messages with his finger in the smears on the wall. Of course, Goffman and Scheff were very concerned about the self-fulfilling-prophecy aspect of the staff's diagnostic process, and they warned poignantly that incremental denial of freedom to individuals within "total institutions," whether they actually suffer from a bona fide mental illness or not, leads them inexorably to increasingly irrational and desperate attempts to maintain their dignity and express themselves.

Today, because of recent interconnected historical developments —including de-institutionalization, reduced resources for public mental health services, and relatively less sympathy in criminal courts for defendants with psychiatric disabilities—serious mental illness is more likely to be acted out in prisons than in asylums.[2] In fact, in the United States, there are more people suffering from serious mental illness in jails and prisons than there are in psychiatric hospitals. And the bizarre scenarios enacted in correctional settings today can make the "back wards" of 1940s asylums look tame in comparison.

Consider as an example the scenario where the disturbed/disruptive prisoner winds up in some form of punitive segregation, typically in a supermaximum security unit where he remains isolated and idle in his cell nearly twenty-four hours per day. In the context of near-total isolation and idleness, psychiatric symptoms emerge, even in previously healthy prisoners. For example, a prisoner may feel overwhelmed by a strange sense of anxiety. The walls may seem to be moving in on him. (It is stunning how many prisoners in isolated confinement independently report this experience.) He may begin to suffer from panic attacks wherein he cannot breathe and he thinks his heart is beating so fast he is going to die. Almost all prisoners in supermaximum security units tell me that they have trouble focusing on any task, their memory is poor, they have trouble sleeping, they get very anxious, and they fear they will not be able to control their rage. The prisoner may find himself disobeying an order or inexplicably screaming at an officer, when really all he wants is for the officer to stop and interact with him a little longer than it takes for a food tray to be slid through the slot in his cell door. Many prisoners in isolated confinement report it is extremely difficult for them to contain their mounting rage, and they fear losing their temper with an officer and being given a ticket that will result in a longer term in punitive segregation.

Eventually, and often rather quickly, a prisoner's psychiatric condition deteriorates to the point where he inexplicably refuses to return his food tray, cuts himself, or pastes paper over the small window in his solid metal cell door, causing security staff to trigger an emergency "takedown" or "cell extraction." In many cases where I have interviewed the prisoner after the extraction, he confides that voices he was hearing at the time commanded him to retain his tray, paper his window, or harm himself.

The more vehemently correctional staff insist the disturbed prisoner return a food tray, come out of his cell, or remove the paper from the cell door so they can see inside, the more passionately the disturbed prisoner shouts: "You're going to have to come in here and get it (or me)!" The officers go off and assemble an emergency team—several large officers in total body protective gear who, with a plastic shield, are responsible for doing cell extractions of rowdy or recalcitrant prisoners. The emergency team appears at the prisoner's cell door and the coordinator asks gruffly if the prisoner wants to return the food tray, or do they have to come in and get it? While a more rational prisoner would realize he had no chance of withstanding this kind of overwhelming force, the disturbed prisoner puts up his fists in mock boxing battle position and yells, "Come on in, if you're tough enough!" The officers barge in all at once, each responsible for pushing the prisoner against the wall with the shield or grabbing one of his extremities. The prisoner is bruised and hurt, but when a nurse examines the shackled prisoner and asks about injuries, he responds that they hardly scratched him.

This kind of "cell extraction," which occurs in some supermaximum security prisons as often as ten times per week and reminds one of the scenario sociologists of deviance described in 1950s asylums, is not the only outbreak of madness within correctional institutions. Officers in facilities of all levels of security tend to yell at prisoners and tend to threaten prisoners with harsh reprisals if they do not obey orders quickly or thoroughly enough. Prisoners in whom anger has mounted because of the extremity of their situation typically respond in an angry tone, perhaps meeting swearing with swearing. Or they mutilate themselves repeatedly, or they smear feces or throw excrement at staff. With each angry, bizarre act on the part of prisoners, correctional staff become more harsh and punitive, less interested in listening to the prisoners' expressed grievances, less concerned about prisoners' pain and suffering, and more quick to respond to the slightest provocation with overwhelming force.

The recipe for creating madness in our prisons is easy enough to explicate; one merely needs to identify the steps taken to reach the current state of affairs. Here is the recipe:

Begin by overcrowding the prisons with unprecedented numbers of drug users and petty offenders, and make sentences longer across the board.

Dismantle many of the rehabilitation and education programs so prisoners are relatively idle.

Add to the mix a large number of prisoners suffering from serious mental illness.

Obstruct and restrict visiting, thus cutting prisoners off even more from the outside world.

Respond to the enlarging violence and psychosis by segregating a growing proportion of prisoners in isolative settings such as supermaximum security units.

Ignore the many traumas in the pre-incarceration histories of prisoners as well as traumas such as prison rape that take place inside the prisons.

Discount many cases of mental disorder as "malingering."

Label out-of-control prisoners "psychopaths."

Deny the "malingerers" and "psychopaths" mental health treatment and leave them warehoused in cells within supermaximum security units.

Watch the recidivism rate rise and proclaim the rise a reflection of a new breed of incorrigible criminals and "superpredators."

I will briefly discuss these successive steps to madness, starting with the massive prison crowding that began in the 1970s and continued to swell prison populations exponentially until, just after the new millennium, the prison and jail population in the United States climbed to more than two million—and it keeps on growing. There was convincing research at the time that prison crowding caused increased rates of violence, psychiatric breakdown, and suicide in correctional facilities.[3] One had only to tour a prison to understand how the crowding bred violence and madness. Consider the gymnasium that had to be converted to a dormitory with bunks for two hundred prisoners. A prisoner cannot move more than a few feet away from a neighbor, and lines form at the pay telephones and the urinals. With tough men crowded into a small space and forced to wait in lines, altercations are practically inevitable. The next prisoner in line begins to harass the prisoner on the phone, saying he's been on too long, the man on the phone turns and takes a swing at the other, and there's a fight. Of course, open expressions of rage and frequent eruptions of violence tend to push individuals prone to psychiatric breakdown over the edge. Often they become preferred victims of the violence. The more violence, the more madness, and the crowding exacerbates both.

The steady rise of prison crowding since the 1980s has been driven by calls for "tougher sentences," especially in the context of a widely proclaimed "War on Drugs." More defendants are put behind bars for longer terms, and a growing number of new laws require incarceration for drug use, drug dealing, and a whole list of crimes associated with illegal drugs.[4]

As it turns out, the theory that led to incarcerating more drug users was entirely foolhardy. Prison is not good for people with a substance abuse problem. Studies show that those who enter prison with a drug problem will leave prison with the same drug problem. And, with budget cuts, the actual amount of substance abuse treatment in prison has been declining over the past two decades. Prisoners who are not provided intensive substance abuse treatment will not transcend their drug habit while incarcerated, but as many as 60 percent to 80 percent of those who complete an intensive drug treatment program in the community will be "clean and sober" after three years.[5] What sense does it make to "violate" a drug user's parole and send him or her back to prison because of "dirty" urine on an unscheduled test?

A reasonable alternative to incarceration, a drug treatment program in the community, would require a fraction of the expense to the state, and the diversion of people who commit low-level, drug-related crimes would vastly improve the crowding problem in the prisons. Yet, from the 1980s until the present, the sentences have grown longer, drug treatment programs have been cut, the rate of parole violation has climbed precipitously, and the recidivism rate has been rising.

The next misstep was the dismantling of rehabilitation and education programs inside the prisons. A turning point occurred with the publication of Robert Martinson's 1974 essay, "What Works? Questions and Answers about Prison Reform."[6] Martinson ran some numbers and announced that rehabilitation programs have no positive effect on recidivism rates. This was the research that conservative pundits and politicians had been waiting for, and they made Martinson famous as they legislated a drastic turn from rehabilitation to harsher punishments. The article Martinson published in 1979, qualifying and recanting his rash overgeneralization, never received the media attention that had been showered on his earlier castigation of rehabilitation.[7]

In the 1979 article, Martinson confessed his 1974 methodology had contained serious flaws. He had tried correlating the presence of any kind of rehabilitation program in a prison with the overall recidivism rate, and found no significant correlation. In 1979, he argued that a better method would have been to correlate the availability of specific programs with the recidivism rates of prisoners whose needs were matched by those programs, and that this more nuanced research would clearly show that rehabilitation programs are effective to the extent they are directed at appropriately motivated and capable subpopulations of prisoners. But it was too late. The argument for longer sentences and harsher punishments had already come to dominate the public discussion about crime, and consequently Martinson's recantation received very little notice. With calls to "stop coddling" prisoners, prison education programs were slashed, weights were removed from the yards, the quality of prison food declined, prisoners were deprived of materials for arts and crafts, and so forth. Later in 1979, a dismayed Martinson took his own life.[8]

With crowding and the dismantling of rehabilitation and education programs, American penology took a wrong turn, a tragic misstep that has yet to be corrected and is causing irreparable harm. Frank Wood, the former Minnesota commissioner of corrections, commented:

"When you take away television, when you take away weights, when you take away all forms of recreation, inmates react as normal people would. They become irritable. They become hostile. Hostility breeds violence, and violence breeds fear. And fear is the enemy of rehabilitation." There was a moment in the mid-1980s, when prison violence was totally out of control, when it would have been possible for corrections departments to admit they had made a mistake and to reverse the crowding while reinstating rehabilitation and education programs. But instead of taking the advice Wood and many other experienced penologists offered, legislators and correctional administrators decided to "lock up" the prisoners they deemed troublemakers ("the worst of the worst"), and proceeded with increasingly shrill demands for absolute control inside prison walls. The supermaximum security unit was born. Before exploring that development, I will turn to another disastrous misstep in late twentieth-century penology: the incarceration of a growing number of people suffering from serious mental illness.

The Federal Bureau of Prisons estimates that at least 283,000 prisoners have significant emotional problems and need treatment.[9] Reasons for the expanding prevalence of mental illness in correctional settings include the shortcomings of public mental health systems, the tendency for post-Hinckley (the man who attempted to assassinate President Reagan) criminal courts to give less weight to psychiatric testimony, harsher policies toward drug offenders, including those with dual diagnoses (mental illness plus substance abuse), and the growing tendency for local governments to incarcerate homeless people for a variety of minor crimes.

The fact that a growing proportion of prisoners suffer from serious mental illness has not led to proportional enrichment of prisons' mental health treatment capacities. There is a tendency to focus precious mental health resources on those who suffer from an obvious "major mental illness," including schizophrenia, bipolar disorder, and severe depression. While prisoners suffering from these conditions deserve comprehensive mental health services (which they are unlikely to receive, given current budget constraints—their treatment is often limited to cell confinement with psychiatric medications), other disorders, including anxiety, phobia, obsessive-compulsive disorder, and post-traumatic stress disorder (PTSD), can cause as much suffering and disability. PTSD is especially important because we know that prisoners, on average, have suffered from a lifetime of severe traumas, including the domestic violence they witnessed or fell victim to as children, the violence and deaths they saw on the streets, and the violence they experienced as adults prior to incarceration.[10] Then, as convicts, they experience new traumas, including beatings, sexual assaults, and time in solitary confinement. Because of inadequacies in correctional mental health programs, oft-traumatized prisoners receive woefully inadequate treatment for PTSD and depression. All of this compounds the problem of crowding, of course, and exacerbates the madness.

Then, added to the mix, departments of corrections attempt to limit and restrict visiting. This can take the form of shortened visiting hours, requiring family members to wait in long lines to see their loved ones. It can take the form of increasingly intrusive searches, which cause humiliated family members and friends to visit less often. It can take the form of severe restrictions on mail and packages from home. Or it can take the form of punishing prisoners who violate prison rules with loss of visitation—a practice that clearly violates international human rights standards. These obstacles to visitation, combined with the fact that prisons are usually built far from the big cities where most prisoners' families reside, have the overall effect of decreasing the number and quality of prison visits. Because research clearly demonstrates that prisoners who can sustain quality contact with loved ones over the length of a prison term are much more likely than others to succeed at "going straight" after they are released,[11] these obstacles to quality contact with friends and family tend to increase the general level of madness within the prisons.

Then, in crowded facilities where rehabilitation programs are sparse and prisoners are relatively idle, the worst traumas and abuses are reserved for prisoners suffering from mental illness. It is not difficult to figure out the reasons for this unfortunate dynamic. Consider the prison rapist's options in selecting a potential victim. He wants to choose his victim well; the wrong choice might lead to lethal retaliation. If he rapes a gang member, or even a prisoner with friends, he would be forever vulnerable to deadly retribution. But if he selects a prisoner with significant mental illness, a loner who would not likely have friends who might enact revenge, he is more likely to get away with the rape and avoid retaliation. Thus prisoners with serious mental illness, especially if they are not provided a relatively safe and therapeutic treatment program, are prone to victimization by other prisoners.[12] In women's prisons, rape and sexual assaults are more often perpetrated by male staff, but women who have experienced earlier traumas and those suffering from mental illness are likewise singled out for victimization.[13] And of course the repeated traumas they are forced to endure in prison make prisoners' mental disorders and their prognoses far more dire.

By the 1980s, when the rate of violence was clearly rising precipitously in the prisons and too many disruptive prisoners were suffering from serious mental illness, the response on the part of the corrections system to the resulting violence and chaos was to vilify the "worst of the worst" among prisoners, the ones presumably responsible for much of the violence, and lock them up in near-total isolation.[14] The supermaximum security prison, where prisoners are almost entirely isolated and idle in their cells just about all of the time, was designed to diminish prison violence. There is ample evidence that long-term cell confinement with almost no social interactions and no meaningful activities has very destructive psychological effects, including but not limited to worsening mental disorders and extraordinarily high rates of suicide.[15] And newer research suggests that the turn toward supermaximum/isolated confinement for a growing proportion of prisoners is not reducing the violence inside prisons.[16]

Individuals in long-term segregated prison housing tend to develop psychiatric symptoms, if not full-blown decompensation, and they universally report the buildup of uncontrollable rage. Of course, even as departments of correction rely ever more on supermaximum security and other forms of punitive twenty-three-hours-per-day cell confinement, only about 6 to 10 percent of entire prison populations are in segregation at any given time. But a much greater percentage of prisoners spend time in segregation during their prison term, and the presence of harsh segregation units within a prison or prison system has a chilling effect on the entire population.

A disproportionate number of prisoners with serious mental illness wind up in punitive segregation. For some, it is a matter of their mental illness leading to irrational acts and rule violations; for others, it is a matter of losing control of their emotions and getting into altercations; and for others, it is a matter of breaking down only after being consigned to segregation for a lengthy period of time. I am often asked whether prisoners with serious mental illness are selectively sent to punitive segregation, or do the harsh conditions of isolation and idleness cause psychiatric decompensation in a vulnerable subpopulation of prisoners. Of course, both mechanisms are in play. The result is that whenever I tour a supermaximum security facility in preparation for testimony in class action litigation about harsh conditions of confinement or the adequacy of mental health services, I discover a very large proportion of prisoners confined therein to be exhibiting the signs and symptoms of serious mental illness.

Of course, the presence of prisoners with serious mental illness in supermaximum and other segregation units heightens the noise level and the overall chaos. Prisoners who are not suffering from mental illness tell me it is extremely difficult to sleep in a unit where several prisoners are up all night shouting and crying. And when a prisoner with mental illness flings excrement at an officer and the cell extraction team comes on the unit and sprays mace on that disturbed/disruptive individual, the prisoners in neighboring cells experience the effects of the mace that wafts into their cells even though they have done nothing to provoke an assault by the guards. In other words, the disproportionate placement of prisoners with serious mental illness in supermaximum security units tends to exacerbate the general level of pandemonium.

Then, the same conditions that worsen psychiatric disorders make treatment problematic. Psychotropic medications are not very effective when the patient is confined to a cell. The clinician has little if any opportunity to develop a therapeutic relationship or even educate the patient about the illness and the need for medications, and there are no group therapies nor psychiatric rehabilitation programs. Yet this is precisely the situation in many jails and prisons. In supermaximum security units, the psychiatrist might even be forced to interview prisoners at their cell doors with absolutely no confidentiality.

The failure of prisoners suffering from serious mental illness to respond positively to the minimal mental health treatments available in segregation settings (typically psychiatric medications with cell confinement) is often blamed on their "badness," or their psychopathy. Alternatively, their exacerbated mental illness and shockingly frequent attempts at self-harm are dismissed as inauthentic or "malingered."

Meanwhile the frustrated staff, who cannot figure out how to improve the situation, suffer massive burnout and become all the more insensitive to the plight of their wards.[17] They find themselves losing control of their tempers and resorting to ever more harsh and punitive measures in a desperate attempt to control an impossible situation. Then, in response to the harshness and seemingly arbitrary and disrespectful actions by security staff, prisoners become more disturbed, more enraged, and capable of even more bizarre actions such as flinging excrement at staff or repeatedly mutilating themselves. The bottom line is that we seem to have reproduced some of the worst aspects of an earlier époque's snake pit mental asylums in the isolation units of our modern prisons.

Is this kind of madness an inevitable aspect of prison life? If that were the case, there would really be little reason to think about what kinds of changes in the way prisons are run might diminish the madness. Or does a significant proportion of the madness arise from mismanagement of the prisons? If so, the situation could be improved—that is, better management would lead to less madness. To the extent correctional and mental health professionals throw up their hands and proclaim that the troublesome prisoners are incorrigible, there is no improving the situation. The most that can be accomplished is isolation of the troublemakers—but that really does not solve the problem because eventually most of them will be released from prison and, without any treatment or rehabilitation, they will pose a huge menace. The next step in this cynical, failed strategy is to change the laws to permit indeterminate civil (psychiatric) hospital commitment following completion of a determinate prison term. That strategy is being pursued in many states today, but the result is that the forensic psychiatric hospitals are becoming crowded and the madness bred of prison mismanagement is beginning to infest the mental health facilities.

A better plan would be to admit that mistakes have been made and that corrective action is needed. We need to reverse each step in the recipe I have delineated for creating madness in the prisons. And the process can be reversed. At the risk of appearing overly simplistic, I can offer a very schematic outline of that reversal here:

Crowding can be reversed by effective utilization of diversion programs and redesigning sentencing guidelines. Mental health courts and drug courts are requiring treatment in the community as an alternative to incarceration. Many other forms of diversion are possible. The trend toward harsher sentences can be ameliorated in rational ways to provide the kind of community treatment and rehabilitation needed by many of the individuals who currently populate our prisons. Of course, to accomplish this huge goal, social policies and priorities need to be reexamined. Homelessness contributes to high incarceration rates, as does unemployment. The social safety net that has been incrementally dismantled for decades needs to be strengthened and glaring social inequities need to be addressed.

Rehabilitation and education programs in the prisons must be reinstated and greatly expanded. It's simply not fair, and not accurate, to cut the programs that might help prisoners "go straight" and then blame the prisoners for their failure to do so without benefit of the needed programs.

Individuals suffering from serious mental illness in the community must be provided not only quality treatment in the public sector, they also need supported housing, help finding work, and so forth. If this plan were effected, far fewer of them would find their way into the jails and prisons. But there will still be prisoners suffering from serious mental illness, and they need quality mental health treatment within penal institutions.

Departments of correction must support visitation in every way that makes sense. Instead of cutting down on the hours for visits and making visitors submit to humiliating searches, departments of correction should set up free transportation for families and encourage conjugal/family visits and even home leave for prisoners who do not pose a significant security risk.

Instead of segregating problematic prisoners in supermaximum security units, a richer collaboration between security and treatment staff is needed wherein the more problematic the prisoner the more creative the staff becomes in effecting a management and treatment strategy tailored to help that prisoner transcend his or her problematic behaviors. Of course, implicit in this notion is the requirement that staff treat prisoners with respect at all times, and take their problems and their pains seriously.[18]

A lot of attention needs to be paid to the traumas of a prisoner's life—those that occurred prior to incarceration and those that occur inside prison. Given the omnipresence of trauma in prisoners' lives, education about and treatment for PTSD needs to be readily available. The harshness of prison life needs to be ameliorated, and more intensive efforts need to be made to prevent sexual assault and other forms of violence in the prisons.

While "malingering" does occur in prison, staff need to understand its roots in the severe deprivations prisoners experience. Before questioning whether a prisoner is really hearing bona fide voices, or is really intent on committing suicide, staff need to ask themselves what has driven the prisoner to the point of contemplating his or her own demise, or what pain is causing him or her to exaggerate symptoms. In other words, to the extent malingering is an issue, it is a symptom that requires attention.

Attention to antisocial personality disorder and psychopathy can be useful in helping shape individualized therapeutic interventions. But to the extent the diagnosis of an "Axis II Disorder" or psychopathy leads clinicians to give up on helping a dysfunctional prisoner, that diagnosis needs to be downplayed while a more effective intervention is sought. In other words, we need to stop blaming the victim's innate "badness" for failed interventions, and we need to try harder.

Mental health treatment services need to be expanded significantly. We must work on finding places other than jails and prisons for individuals suffering from serious mental illness, but in the meanwhile those who find their way into the prisons need adequate care. They must not be consigned to isolation in punitive segregation units, rather they require comprehensive treatment in settings that maximize their safety and their motivation to comply with treatment.

When recidivism rates rise, and when a growing number of parolees are "violated" and returned to prison, instead of blaming the prisoners for their incorrigibility, we need to interpret the trend as a failure of our prisons to "correct," and we need to seek better ways to manage the prisons, and better interventions to help prisoners learn what they need to learn in order to succeed as members of the community after they are released.

Of course, what I am outlining here in very abstract terms is what has been tried, and proven effective, for example in the groundbreaking work of Hans Toch with "disturbed/disruptive" prisoners,[19] and at Grendon Prison in the United Kingdom.[20] The ingredients of humane prisons must include staff's constantly expressed respect for prisoners and their predicament; constant stress on communication between staff and their wards as well as among staff and among prisoners; skilled interventions by security staff as well as vocational trainers, teachers, and medical and mental health clinicians; and, very important, a kind of perseverance and resilience that permits staff and prisoners to rebound from the inevitable mishaps and failures along the way to ending the madness and building a truly corrective prison system.

---

1. Erving Goffman (1962) *Asylums: Essays on the Social Situation of Mental Patients and Other Inmates.* Aldine, Chicago. Thomas J. Scheff (1966) *Being Mentally Ill.* Aldine, Chicago.

2. Terry A. Kupers (1999) *Prison Madness: The Mental Health Crisis Behind Bars and What We Must Do About It.* Jossey-Bass/Wiley, San Francisco.

3. Paul B. Paulus, Garvin McCain, and Verne C. Cox (1978) Death Rates, Psychiatric Commitments, Blood Pressure, and Perceived Crowding as a Function of Institutional Crowding. *Environmental Psychology and Nonverbal Behavior*, 3, 107–117. Terence P. Thornberry and Jack E. Call (1983) Constitutional Challenges to Prison Overcrowding: The Scientific Evidence of Harmful Effects. *Hastings Law Journal*, 35, 313–53.

4. David Garland (2001) *The Culture of Control: Crime and Social Order in Contemporary Society.* University of Chicago Press, Chicago.

5. Christopher J. Mumola (1997) *Substance Abuse and Treatment, State and Federal Prisoners, 1997.* Bureau of Justice Statistics Special Report, U.S. Department of Justice, NCJ 172871, Washington, DC.

6. Robert Martinson (1974) What Works? Questions and Answers about Prison Reform. *Public Interest*, 3, 5, 22–54.

7. Robert Martinson (1979) New Findings, New Views: A Note of Caution Regarding Sentencing Reform. *Hofstra Law Review*, 7, 2, 243–58.

8. Joseph T. Hallinan (2001) *Going Up the River: Travels in a Prison Nation.* Random House, New York.

9. Paula M. Ditton (1999) Mental Health and Treatment of Inmates and Probationers. *Bureau of Justice Statistics Special Report.* U.S. Department of Justice, Washington, DC.

10. Terry A. Kupers (2005) Posttraumatic Stress Disorder (PTSD) in Prisoners, in *Managing Special Populations in Jails and Prisons,* (ed. Stan Stojkovic) Civic Research Institute, Kingston, New Jersey.

11. Norman Holt and Donald Miller (1976) Explorations in Inmate–Family Relationships. Research Report No. 46, California Department of Corrections, Sacramento, California.

12. Human Rights Watch (2001) No Escape: Male Rape in U.S. Prisons. Human Rights Watch, New York.

13. Human Rights Watch (1996) All Too Familiar: Sexual Abuse of Women in U.S. State Prisons. Human Rights Watch, New York.

14. King, 1999.

15. Stuart Grassian and Nancy Friedman (1986) Effects of Sensory Deprivation in Psychiatric Seclusion and Solitary Confinement. *International Journal of Law and Psychiatry*, 8, 49–65. Sheilagh Hodgins and Gilles Cote (1991) The Mental Health of Penitentiary Inmates in Isolation. *Canadian Journal of Criminology*, 175–82.

16. Chad S. Briggs, Jody L. Sundt, and Thomas C. Castellano (2003) The Effect of Supermaximum Security Prisons on Aggregate Levels of Institutional Violence. *Criminology*, 41, 4, 301–336.

17. Christina Maslach and Michael P. Leiter (1997) *The Truth About Burnout:*

How Organizations Cause Personal Stress and What to Do About It. Jossey-Bass, San Francisco.

18. James Gilligan (2001) *Preventing Violence.* Thames & Hudson, London.

19. Hans Toch and Kenneth Adams (2002) *Acting Out: Maladaptive Behavior in Confinement.*

20. David Jones (Ed.) (2004) *Working with Dangerous People.* Radcliffe Medical Press, Oxford. Mark Morris (2004) *Dangerous and Severe – Process, Programme and Person: Grendon's Work.* Jessica Kingsley, London.

Solitary Confinement
and the Law

Laura Rovner

Laura Rovner is the Ronald V. Yegge Clinical Director and an associate professor at the Civil Rights Clinic of the University of Denver's Sturm College of Law. She and her students have represented clients in several groundbreaking Constitutional challenges to conditions of confinement in both state and federal supermax prisons. Her twenty-year career as an attorney, advocate, and legal scholar has focused on disability rights as well as the rights of the incarcerated. In the following piece, she provides a detailed review of how courts have addressed the issue of solitary confinement in the nation's prisons.

ALMOST AS SOON AS IT BECAME WIDESPREAD, THE PRACTICE OF SOLItary confinement in the United States faced legal challenges. As far back as 1890, the U.S. Supreme Court recognized the significant harms solitary confinement causes and nearly declared it unconstitutional. In *In re Medley*, the Court struck down on *ex post facto* grounds a statute that required death-sentenced prisoners to be held in solitary confinement prior to their executions.[1] Writing for the majority, Justice Samuel Miller, who was a physician as well as a lawyer, emphasized:

[E]xperience demonstrated that there were serious objections to it. A considerable number of the prisoners fell, after even a short confinement, into a semi-fatuous condition, from which it was next to impossible to arouse them, and others became violently insane; others, still, committed suicide; while those who stood the ordeal better were not generally reformed, and in most cases did not recover sufficient mental activity to be of any subsequent service to the community. It became evident that some changes must be made in the system . . . and it is within the memory of many persons interested in prison discipline that some thirty or forty years ago the whole subject attracted the general public attention, and its main feature of solitary confinement was found to be too severe.[2]

Given this unequivocal condemnation of solitary confinement by the nation's highest court, the resurgence in the use of penal isolation over the next century—and the judiciary's countenancing of it—was unexpected to say the least. Most historians and sociologists trace the unprecedented use of solitary confinement in the United States to a confluence of events that began in the 1970s, when incarceration rates across the country began to rise dramatically as a result of changes in sentencing, probation, and parole policy.[3] At the same time, there was a shift away from a more rehabilitation-based philosophy of corrections to a belief that "nothing works."[4] As a result, prison systems dramatically reduced or eliminated treatment programs, moving instead to a correctional philosophy of "incapacitate and punish."[5] During this same period, the deinstitutionalization movement also was unfolding, resulting in the transfer of thousands of people with mental illness out of state psychiatric institutions and into the community, where a lack of services and supports ultimately led to many of them simply being confined in prison instead.[6]

These events in the aggregate produced extraordinary overcrowding in the nation's prisons, and with it, unsurprisingly, an increase in prison violence. The need for prison systems to curb this violence coupled with the shift in correctional philosophy meant that the late 1980s and early 1990s saw an unprecedented growth in the number of supermax cells in the United States. Believing that "criminals were harder"[7] and unable to be rehabilitated, the only thing left to do in the minds of many correctional administrators was to isolate prisoners from one another—as completely as possible for as long as possible.[8]

During this period, the federal courts also were undergoing a shift in philosophy. Having finally abandoned the "hands off" doctrine that effectively precluded judicial review of virtually all prison conditions until the 1960s, the courts became inundated with prisoner lawsuits shortly thereafter.[9] In the ensuing decades, the Supreme Court—particularly during the Rehnquist era—has significantly scaled back judicial scrutiny of prison conditions, with the Court giving correctional officials considerable (sometimes complete) deference to decide what restrictions should be placed on people in prison.[10]

Solitary Confinement and the Constitution

I. Eighth Amendment

The Eighth Amendment to the U.S. Constitution prohibits the infliction of "cruel and unusual punishments." In determining whether any given form of punishment is "cruel and unusual," the Supreme Court, following a 1976 decision in *Gregg v. Georgia*, interprets the Amendment "in a flexible and dynamic manner."[11] This was interpreted by the court in a 1981 ruling in *Rhodes v. Chapman* to mean that "[n]o static 'test' can exist by which courts determine whether conditions of confinement are cruel and unusual, for the Eighth Amendment 'must draw its meaning from the evolving standards of decency that mark the progress of a maturing society.'"[12]

To prevail on an Eighth Amendment claim that a prison condition is cruel and unusual in light of these rulings, people in prison must satisfy a two-pronged test with objective and subjective components. The objective prong requires prisoners to demonstrate that the challenged condition is sufficiently serious to merit review, either because it deprives them of a "basic human need" or because the condition presents a "substantial risk of serious harm."[13] The subjective prong requires showing that prison officials acted with "deliberate indifference" in imposing or maintaining the condition despite knowing about the harm or risk of harm.

With respect to the objective prong, people who have brought Eighth Amendment challenges to long-term isolation have asserted that solitary confinement deprives them of several basic human needs, including normal human contact and social interaction, environmental and sensory stimulation, mental and physical health, exercise, sleep, nutrition, meaningful activity, and safety.[14] They also assert that these deprivations cause them serious physical and psychological harm and that they are at substantial risk of future harm if the isolation continues.[15] With respect to the subjective prong, the prisoner is required to demonstrate that prison officials knew about the harm or risk of future harm to him as a result of long-term isolation and recklessly disregarded it.[16]

So far, most of the federal courts to consider whether the use of long-term solitary confinement violates the Eighth Amendment have held that it does not, except in situations where the person is a juvenile or has a preexisting mental illness. Those exceptions are grounded in the idea that youth and mental illness make people more vulnerable to the harmful effects of solitary confinement.

For example, in the leading case of *Madrid v. Gomez*, brought on behalf of mentally ill prisoners held in solitary confinement in California prisons, the court likened the placement of a person with mental illness in solitary confinement to "putting an asthmatic in a place with little air to breathe."[17] For that reason, the court held that confining those men in supermax conditions could not "be squared with evolving standards of humanity or decency" because the risk of exacerbating their mental illness was so grave—"so shocking and indecent—[that it] simply has no place in civilized society."[18]

In that same case, however, the court held that confining men who were not mentally ill in identical conditions was not a violation of the Eighth Amendment. The court explained that "while the conditions in the SHU may press the outer bounds of what most humans can psychologically tolerate, the record does not satisfactorily demonstrate that there is a sufficiently high risk to all inmates of incurring a serious mental illness from exposure to conditions in the SHU to find that the conditions constitute a *per se* deprivation of a basic necessity of life."[19]

The *Madrid* case was decided in 1995, but the court's distinction between prisoners who have mental illnesses and those who do not with respect to Eighth Amendment protections has largely been followed by other courts in the ensuing twenty years. One of the most striking examples of this is *Silverstein v. Bureau of Prisons*, in which the U.S. Court of Appeals for the Tenth Circuit held that Thomas Silverstein's *thirty-year* confinement in extreme isolation did not constitute cruel and unusual punishment.[20] Despite recognizing that the conditions in which Mr. Silverstein was confined were the most isolating in the entire federal prison system and that his three decades of solitary confinement was unprecedented, the court nevertheless held that his conditions did not violate the Eighth Amendment. The Silverstein case brings into sharp focus some of the issues about the way Eighth Amendment jurisprudence has evolved, particularly with respect to solitary confinement.

Most of the court's rationale for holding that thirty years of solitary confinement did not violate the Eighth Amendment was based on security concerns: Mr. Silverstein was convicted of three murders while in custody, one of which was of a correctional officer in 1983. Although thirty-one years had passed since the murders and Mr. Silverstein had clear conduct ever since (and was in his sixties), the court nevertheless deferred completely to prison officials' claim that no lessening of his isolation was possible without threatening institutional safety. Indeed, the court's deference to prison officials was so absolute that it denied Mr. Silverstein a trial in which the court could have considered evidence that there were ways to ease his isolation without jeopardizing security. The beginning and end of the court's inquiry into the penological issues raised by correctional officials can be summed up by its statement that "the opinion of a prison administrator on how to maintain internal security carries great weight and the courts should not substitute their judgment for that of officials."[21]

For those concerned about the Eighth Amendment, the court's approach to analyzing security issues is troubling for two reasons. First, the Eighth Amendment's two-pronged test does not expressly contemplate the role of the prison's "legitimate penological interest."[22] This has resulted in courts varying considerably in their analysis of whether, how, and how much they should consider an asserted penological interest in determining whether the Eighth Amendment has been violated.

The second separate issue concerns how much deference courts should give to that asserted interest. The Supreme Court has affirmed that the limits imposed on prisoners' other constitutional rights do not apply to claims of "cruel and unusual punishment" because doing so would thwart that clause's entire purpose: protecting those who are incarcerated.[23] The Court has explained that "[t]he full protections of the eighth amendment most certainly remain in force [in prison]."[24] Accordingly, the Court has held that affording "deference to the findings of state prison officials in the context of the eighth amendment would reduce that provision to a nullity in precisely the context where it is most necessary."[25]

Despite this, the tenth circuit court in the *Silverstein* case—and other courts that have considered the constitutionality of solitary confinement under the Eighth Amendment—have given enormous deference to the judgments of prison administrators and staff—even to the extent of profoundly minimizing or even ignoring evidence that conflicts with those judgments. The result has not only produced judicial decisions sanctioning the use of prolonged solitary confinement, it has also perverted Eighth Amendment jurisprudence more broadly.[26]

In addition to the deference the *Silverstein* court gave to the prison's asserted penological interest in continuing to hold Mr. Silverstein in solitary confinement into a fourth decade, the court also relied on the fact that Mr. Silverstein had not been diagnosed with a serious mental illness prior to his being held in isolation. Further, the court found that the mental health issues he developed during his time in solitary—including anxiety disorder, cognitive impairment, hopelessness, inability to concentrate, memory loss, and depression—were "minor mental health symptoms" and therefore his thirty years of isolation was not "sufficiently serious so as to deprive him of the minimal civilized measure of life's necessities."[27]

Mental harm has always been more difficult to prove than physical injury.[28] But in the case of solitary confinement, an established and growing worldwide consensus exists that long-term isolation produces a constellation of mental harms—a consensus born of the fact that these same types of harms are found and reported over and over again in people who have spent long periods of time in solitary.

This consensus matters for Eighth Amendment purposes because contemporary values—the aforementioned "evolving standards of decency"—necessarily shape the inquiry about whether a given prison condition is constitutional.[29] In other contexts where the federal courts have considered whether a particular form of punishment violates the Eighth Amendment (for example, execution of people with intellectual disabilities), those courts have looked to national and international authorities[30] to determine society's evolving views about what punishments are cruel and unusual. In particular, the Supreme Court has found legislation enacted by the country's state legislatures to be "the clearest and most reliable objective evidence of contemporary values."[31] Precisely because the Eighth Amendment's meaning is governed by evolving standards of decency, a court may find that a punishment is unconstitutional even if other courts have previously held that same punishment to pass constitutional muster.[32]

For that reason, the groundswell of condemnation of prolonged solitary confinement that has emerged in recent years is particularly significant with respect to Eighth Amendment claims. Since 2011, the UN Special Rapporteur on Torture has declared that the use of solitary confinement for more than fifteen days constitutes torture. The Senate Judiciary Committee has held two hearings investigating the use of solitary confinement in our nation's prisons. Various state correctional systems have dramatically reduced their use of solitary confinement and some have eliminated it for prisoners with mental illness and juveniles. Denunciations of solitary confinement have come from a broad array of medical and mental health organizations, human rights groups, religious entities (including the pope), and even correctional administrators.[33] The Justice Department has issued rulings finding state correctional systems in violation of the Eighth Amendment as well as disability discrimination statutes because of their confinement of mentally ill individuals in long-term isolation.

The increasing societal condemnation of solitary confinement comes amidst more and more research demonstrating the effects of isolation on the human brain, reports documenting increased rates of suicide and self-harm among people held in prolonged isolation, massive hunger strikes by California prisoners held for decades in solitary confinement and reports from NGOs and human rights organizations documenting the harm isolation causes, as well as its disproportionate use with people of color.

This overwhelming body of scientific evidence, professional opinion, international human rights law, and reduction in the use of segregation through state legislative initiatives supports the notion that evolving standards of decency can no longer hold with the use of long-term solitary confinement. Given the Supreme Court's admonition that the "basic concept underlying the Eighth Amendment" is "nothing less than the dignity of man,"[34] it is my hope—and also my prediction—that in the not-too-distant future, the judiciary will no longer countenance indefinite isolated confinement, finding instead that such conditions are indeed cruel and unusual.

II. Due Process

Another constitutional provision implicated by the use of long-term solitary confinement is the Due Process Clause of the Fifth and

Fourteenth Amendments, which prohibits the government from depriving a person of life, liberty, or property without due process of law. Unlike the Eighth Amendment, the Due Process Clause does not prohibit the government from imposing any particular prison condition, even if it is harsh or atypical. Rather, due process safeguards are intended to ensure that people are not caused to suffer deprivations in error or without reason.

For the past thirty years, courts have sought to define when the Due Process Clause applies to prisoners placed into solitary confinement, for either punitive or administrative reasons. In 1995, the Supreme Court decided *Sandin v. Conner*, in which the Court held that people in prison retain a protected "liberty interest" only when conditions cause an "atypical and significant hardship" compared to the "ordinary incidents of prison life."[35] The challenged condition in *Sandin* was a thirty-day period of isolation imposed as a disciplinary sanction for a prison infraction.

The Sandin Court considered both the severity of the conditions at issue and the duration that the prisoner was subject to them, comparing the restrictions to those found in other prisons within the Hawaii system. Regarding the severity of conditions, the Court determined that they were similar to those imposed upon other prisoners, even those in general population units during lockdowns. The Court also looked at the duration of the conditions and found that thirty days was insufficient to be atypical or to "work a major disruption in [Mr. Sandin's] environment."[36] Thus the Court held that due process was not required.[37]

Ten years later, in *Wilkinson v. Austin*, the Supreme Court examined placement in Ohio's supermax facility (OSP) and held that unlike the conditions in *Sandin*, confinement in OSP did give rise to a protected liberty interest.[38] The conditions at OSP were typical of administrative segregation or supermax prisons, which had become common by 2005. The Court noted the need to determine "the baseline from which to measure what is atypical and significant in any particular prison system."[39] Yet it declined to adopt a particular baseline. Rather, the Court determined that the conditions at OSP were an atypical and significant hardship when considered under "any plausible baseline."[40]

In holding that the conditions created a liberty interest, the *Wilkinson* court highlighted several factors related to the severity and duration of the restrictions at OSP.[41] First, conditions at OSP were more restrictive than any other form of incarceration in Ohio. Second, OSP imposed "especially severe limitations on all human contact."[42] Third, unlike the thirty-day placement in *Sandin*, the duration of placement at OSP was indefinite and reviewed only annually. Finally, placement at OSP disqualified an otherwise eligible prisoner for parole consideration. Even though "any of these conditions standing alone might not be sufficient to create a liberty interest," the Court held that "taken together," these conditions imposed an atypical and significant hardship such that process was due to those incarcerated at OSP.[43]

In the ten years since the Supreme Court decided *Wilkinson*, the lower courts have continued to wrestle with the question of what baseline to use in determining whether a prisoner's confinement in isolation is sufficiently atypical and significant so as to create a liberty interest. While there is no single test employed by all of the circuit courts of appeal, most of them consider the severity of the restrictions, the duration of isolated confinement, and the indefiniteness of that confinement.[44]

Although the central feature of solitary confinement is social deprivation, prison isolation units typically also impose a group of attendant deprivations such as a lack of institutional programming, denial of outdoor exercise, restrictions on phone calls and visits, and strict limits on books or magazines. Some individuals in segregation units or supermax prisons do not have access to natural light, spending weeks, months, or even years in windowless concrete cells. In the aggregate, these conditions may give rise to a liberty interest if a prisoner is subjected to them for a long enough period of time.

If a prisoner is able to establish a protected liberty interest in his conditions, courts then must judge the adequacy of the existing procedural safeguards used by prisons in placing or retaining the person in solitary confinement. The Supreme Court found that because a prisoner's liberty has been curtailed "by definition," "the procedural protections to which [they are] entitled are more limited than in cases where the right at stake is the right to be free from confinement at all."[45] With that caveat, the *Wilkinson* court identified that people held in the Ohio supermax must: 1) receive notice of the factual basis for their placements; 2) be given an opportunity to object and be heard before the decision is made; 3) be provided a statement of the reasons for the decision; 4) receive an appeal, or multiple levels of review; and 5) continue to receive periodic and meaningful reviews assessing the ongoing basis for the placement.[46] The requirement of periodic reviews is especially important to ensure that segregation is not a "pretext for indefinite confinement."[47]

Of course, these procedural protections—which are already considerably less robust than those guaranteed to non-prisoners—are only as good as the genuineness with which they are applied. While placement in many supermax prisons and segregation units used to be more of a behavior management tool—prisoners "earned their way in and earned their way out" through their conduct—correctional systems have increasingly put prisoners in these units for status-based reasons such as gang affiliation (actual or perceived), being labeled a "terrorist,"[48] or being under a death sentence.[49] In these situations, the due process requirement of periodic review is meaningless because the outcome of that review is predetermined: It is difficult if not impossible for people in prison to change the situation giving rise to their placement in segregation, so what is there to review? Nor does the process provide them with "a guide for future behavior"[50] since their behavior may be entirely irrelevant to their placement and retention in segregation.

In sum, the procedural Due Process Clause, while not toothless, cannot be said to provide significant constitutional protection against long-term isolation. Even when courts at the circuit level have found a liberty interest in solitary confinement, the relief those victories confer is the limited due process available in correctional settings.[51]

A judicial determination that a set of conditions constitutes "an atypical and significant hardship" may nonetheless have independent value in the sense that it signals to prisoners, correctional administrators, and the public that those conditions are troubling enough to warrant constitutional scrutiny. Further, because the Eighth Amendment prohibits consideration of conditions in the aggregate, instead insisting on a showing of a deprivation of a single, identifiable human need, the Due Process Clause is really the only constitutional vehicle for courts to consider the range of individual deprivations and conditions that comprise long-term or indefinite isolation.

Solitary Confinement as Disability Discrimination

In addition to the constitution, certain federal statutes also may have a bearing on the use of supermax confinement for some people in prison. The Americans with Disabilities Act (ADA) and § 504 of the Rehabilitation Act (RA), for example, prohibit state and federal prisons from discriminating against people with physical and mental disabilities.

Qualifying disabilities are physical or mental impairments that substantially limit one or more major life activities, such as learning, concentrating, thinking, and communicating, as well as the operation of neurological and brain functions (among others).[52] Significantly, several circuit courts of appeal have determined that an impairment that substantially limits a person's ability to interact with others qualifies as a disability.[53]

People with disabilities—especially mental disabilities—are disproportionately held in solitary confinement in American prisons. In particular, correctional administrators often house prisoners with mental disabilities in segregation, and assert that doing so is necessary either for their own protection or because prison officials believe they are too violent to be housed with other prisoners in the general population.

By confining individuals with disabilities in solitary confinement, however, the prison not only isolates them from other prisoners, but also imposes on them the group of other restrictions typically associated with segregation, including access to reading material, educational and vocational programming, religious services, telephone calls and visits, outdoor exercise, etc.—in short, "most of the things we know are beneficial to prisoners." To the extent that a person is placed in segregation because of a disability, the prison's decision to withhold these programs, services, and activities may constitute an act of discrimination under the disability rights statutes.

Under the ADA and RA, the denial of equal access to services for behavior resulting from a disability constitutes discrimination regardless of the specific intent motivating the denial. Discrimination is defined to include "[d]eny[ing] a qualified individual with a disability the opportunity to participate in or benefit from the aid, benefit, or service" or affording a disabled person "an opportunity to participate in or benefit from the aid, benefit, or service that is not equal to that afforded others."[54] Additionally, the antidiscrimination mandate of the disability rights statutes requires public entities to make "reasonable modifications in policies, practices, or procedures when the modifications are necessary to avoid discrimination on the basis of disability."[55]

For that reason, in certain situations—typically involving individuals with physical disabilities placed in solitary confinement—courts have ruled that a prison's denial of equal services constitutes discrimination on the basis of disability and issued remedial orders to the prison.[56]

Some of these courts have parsed the various conditions that comprise segregation, and held that the only permitted deprivations are those that prison officials can demonstrate are necessary and "fundamental" to the prison's goals. For example, one court of appeals determined that although segregation of disabled people was shown to serve legitimate safety goals, there was no basis to deny the prisoners access to educational and other programming.[57] Courts have found such denials to constitute additional "punishment" that is not justified and have ordered prisons to modify the programs to make them accessible to prisoners with disabilities.[58]

The disability rights laws provide a more nuanced approach to addressing the collection of conditions comprising solitary confinement, requiring prison officials to justify the need for each deprivation of a service or benefit in order to continue the denial. In this sense, the disability discrimination approach can be viewed as useful guidance for the direction that courts might move in the Eighth Amendment arena.

The law governing solitary confinement is complex and, in most instances, tilts heavily in favor of prison administrators. Since the 1960s, when confronted with legal challenges to long-term isolation, the federal courts have been loath to interfere with the judgment of correctional officials, deferring to them almost universally and uncritically when they assert safety and security justifications.[59] That said, the law is evolving, and solitary confinement appears to be one of those areas in which the law follows societal attitudes, rather than the other way around. The significant progress being made toward the reduction and condemnation of prison isolation by state legislatures, correctional systems, and international human rights bodies will, I hope, result in a comparable shift in American law.

---

1. 134 U.S. 160 (1890).

2. Ibid. at 168.

3. See, for example, Sharon Shalev, *Supermax: Controlling Risk through Solitary Confinement* 28–29 (2009).

4. Robert Martinson, "What Works? Questions and Answers about Prison Reform." *The Public Interest* 35 (Spring): 22–54 (1974).

5. Lecture, Craig Haney, Yale Law School Liman Program, 2010.

6. Ibid.

7. See generally, National Research Council of the National Academies,

The Growth of Incarceration in the United States: Exploring Causes and Consequences, 320–33 (Jeremy Travis, Bruce Western & Steve Redburn, Eds.).

8. One commentator describes this evolution of the proliferation of super-max confinement incisively: "Seemingly powerless to combat the rampant violence and pervasive idleness that often accompanies incarceration, the warehouse prison-type operates without the pretense that it does anything other than store and recycle offenders." James E. Robertson, *The Rehnquist Court and the "Turner-ization" of Prisoners' Rights*, 10 N.Y. City L. Rev. 97, 125 (2006).

9. Between 1970 and 1996, the volume of prisoner lawsuits instituted in federal courts increased more than 400 percent. Jim Thomas, *Prisoner Litigation: The Paradox of the Jailhouse Lawyer*, 61 (1988).

10. See, for example, *Overton v. Bazzetta*, 539 U.S. 126, 132 (2003) ("We must accord substantial deference to the professional judgment of prison administrators, who bear a significant responsibility for defining the legitimate goals of a corrections system and for determining the most appropriate means to accomplish them.")

11. *Gregg v. Georgia*, 428 U.S. 153, 171 (1976).

12. *Rhodes v. Chapman*, 452 U.S. 337, 346 (1981) (quoting *Trop v. Dulles*, 356 U.S. 86, 101).

13. See *Farmer v. Brennan*, 511 U.S. 831, 832–33 (1994); *Helling v. McKinney*, 509 U.S. 25, 33 (1993).

14. See, for example, *Ashker v. Brown*, 09-cv-05796-CW (N.D.CA), 2AC para 180. Ibid. at para's 179–82; *see also Silverstein v. BOP*, Madrid, Ruiz. Arguably, all of these human needs could be viewed as elements/subcategories of the basic human need of safety. Importantly, the Supreme Court has held that to prove the objective prong of an Eighth Amendment violation, a prisoner must demonstrate the "deprivation of a single, identifiable human need." "[O]verall conditions," the Court held, are too "amorphous" to constitute an Eighth Amendment violation. *Wilson v. Seiter*, 501 U.S. 294, 304–5 (1991).

15. Ibid., citing *Helling*, 509 U.S. at 33–34.

16. See *Farmer*, 511 U.S. at 838 (holding that "prison official cannot be found liable under the Eighth Amendment for denying an inmate humane conditions of confinement unless the official knows of and disregards an excessive risk to inmate health or safety").

17. *Madrid v. Gomez*, 889 F. Supp. 1146, [PIN] (N.D. Cal. 1995). Other courts also have held that placement of prisoners with mental illness in prolonged solitary confinement violates the Eighth Amendment. See, for example, *Jones'El v. Berge*, 164 F. Supp. 2d 1096 (W.D. Wis. 2001) (placing seriously mentally ill prisoners in Wisconsin supermax violates the Eighth Amendment); *Austin v. Wilkinson*, No. 4:01-CV-071, Doc. 134 at *27 (N.D. Ohio Nov. 21, 2001) (order granting preliminary injunction) (noting that the defendants offered little opposition to a preliminary injunction prohibiting the placement of seriously mentally ill prisoners at the Ohio supermax); *Ruiz v. Johnson*, 37 F. Supp. 2d 855, 915 (S.D.

Tex. 1999) (finding that prison conditions can pose too great a threat to the psychological health of mentally ill inmates, violating the Eighth Amendment).

18. *Madrid* at 1266.

19. *Madrid* at 1267.

20. *Silverstein v. Bureau of Prisons,* 559 Fed.Appx. 739, 745 (10th Cir. 2014).

21. *Silverstein,* 559 Fed.Appx. at 754, quoting *Whitley v. Albers,* 475 U.S. 12 (1986).

22. For a more in-depth discussion of this issue, see Brittany Glidden, *Necessary Suffering?: Weighing Government and Prisoner Interests in Determining What Is Cruel and Unusual,* 50 Am. Crim. L. Rev. (2013).

23. *Johnson v. California,* 543 U.S. 499, 511 (2005) ("[T]he integrity of the criminal justice system depends on full compliance with the Eighth Amendment").

24. Ibid., quoting *Spain v. Procunier,* 600 F.2d 189, 193–94 (9th Cir. 1979).

25. Ibid.

26. An especially troubling basis for this deference is sometimes found in courts' invocation of separation of powers principles. In such cases, courts recite that prison administration is uniquely the province of the executive branch and that separation of powers concerns counsel judicial restraint. While this argument is not without merit, taken too far it represents abdication of the judicial role. See, for example, *Brown v. Plata,* 131 S.Ct. 1910, 1928–29 (2011) ("courts may not allow constitutional violations to continue simply because a remedy would involve intrusion into the realm of prison administration").

27. Ibid. at 40.

28. This principle has been codified in the Prison Litigation Reform Act (PLRA), which provides that "[n]o Federal civil action may be brought by a prisoner confined in a jail, prison, or other correctional facility, for mental or emotional injury suffered while in custody without a prior showing of physical injury." Prison Litigation Reform Act of 1995, Pub. L. No. 104-134, § 803(d), 110 Stat. 1321 (1996), codified at 42 U.S.C. § 1997e(e).

29. *Rhodes v. Chapman,* 452 U.S. 337, 346 (1981) (quoting *Trop v. Dulles,* 356 U.S. 86, 101 [1958]).

30. See, for example, *Roper v. Simmons,* 543 U.S. 551, 575 (2005) ("[A]t least from the time of the Court's decision in *Trop,* the Court has referred to the law of other countries and to international authorities as instructive for its interpretation of the Eighth Amendment's prohibition of 'cruel and unusual punishments.'").

31. *Penry v. Lynaugh,* 492 U.S. 302, 331 (1989).

32. Compare *Penry v. Lynaugh,* 492 U.S. 302 (1989) (holding the Eighth Amendment does not categorically prohibit the execution of people with intellectual disabilities) with *Atkins v. Virginia,* 536 U.S. 304 (2002) (finding the Eighth Amendment categorically prohibits execution of people with intellectual disabilities).

33. Some of these organizations include the American Psychiatric Association, Physicians for Human Rights, the National Alliance for the Mentally Ill, and the National Religious Campaign Against Torture.

34. *Hope v. Pelzer*, 536 U.S. 730, 739 (2002) (citation and quotations omitted).

35. Ibid.

36. Ibid. at 486.

37. Ibid. at 485–86.

38. 545 U.S. at 223–24.

39. Ibid. at 223.

40. Ibid.

41. 545 U.S. at 223–24.

42. Ibid. at 224.

43. Ibid. at 223–24.

44. See, for example, *Harden-Bey v. Rutter*, 524 F.3d 789, 793 (6th Cir. 2008) ("Consistent with [*Wilkinson* and *Sandin*] most (if not all) of our sister circuits have considered the nature of the more-restrictive confinement and its duration in determining whether it imposes an 'atypical and significant hardship.'") (citing cases) (emphasis in original); *Iqbal v. Hasty*, 490 F.3d 143, 161 (2d Cir. 2007) (finding that "[r]elevant [*Sandin*] factors include both the conditions of segregation and its duration," and further holding segregation for 305 days is "sufficiently atypical to require procedural due process protection."); *Serrano v. Francis*, 345 F.3d 1071, 1078 (9th Cir. 2003) (citing duration and degree of the restraint imposed as relevant factors to an inquiry into whether a prison hardship is atypical and significant); *Shoats v. Horn*, 213 F.3d 140, 144 (3rd Cir. 2000) ("[W]e have no difficulty concluding that eight years in administrative custody, with no prospect of immediate release in the near future, is 'atypical' in relation to the ordinary incidents of prison life. . . ."); *Estate of DiMarco v. Wyoming Dep't of Corr., Div. of Prisons*, 473 F.3d 1334, 1342 (10th Cir. 2007) (finding that the explanation for segregation, the severity of restrictions, the effect on duration of confinement, and the indeterminateness of placement are all factors relevant to *Sandin* analysis); *Skinner v. Cunningham*, 430 F.3d 483, 487 (1st Cir. 2005) (finding a legitimate penological interest in isolating a prisoner for forty days just after he murdered another prisoner, and observing that the six-week duration was not excessive); *Perkins v. Kansas Dep't of Corr.*, 165 F.3d 803, 809 (10th Cir. 1999) (remanding case for consideration of both the duration and the nature of a prisoner's confinement where the prisoner had been confined in segregation for at least two years, and citing *Sandin*); and *Hatch v. District of Columbia*, 184 F.3d 846, 858 (D.C. Cir. 1999) (reversing a grant of summary judgment and remanding the case for evaluation of the nature and duration of a seven-month-long administrative segregation, also citing *Sandin*).

45. *Wilkinson*, 545 U.S. at 225.

46. Ibid. at 226. The court also held, however, that prisoners in OSP were not

entitled to present adverse witnesses, reasoning that any right to confront adverse witnesses was outweighed by the state's interests in order and control. The prisoners' receipt of a short statement of reasons for confinement was, according to the court, enough to buffer against "arbitrary decision making." Ibid.

47. *Hewitt v. Helms*, 459 U.S. 460, 477 n.9 (1983).

48. See, for example, *Rezaq v. Nalley*, 677 F.3d 1001 (10th Cir. 2012), *Al Owhali v. Holder*, 687 F.3d 1236 (10th Cir. 2012).

49. The latter may be changing; recently, a Virginia federal district court struck down the automatic, permanent confinement of death row prisoners in isolation as violating the Due Process Clause. *Prieto v. Clarke*, [CITE] [comp: carry query to 1st pass—we're need this citation info] The case is currently on appeal before the U.S. Court of Appeals for the Fourth Circuit.

50. *Wilkinson*, 545 U.S. at 226.

51. A prisoner who prevails on a procedural due process challenge may also be able to recover damages against individual prison officials, but the additional set of legal hurdles that a prisoner-plaintiff must clear in order to obtain damages is a daunting task.

52. 42 U.S.C. § 12102(1) & (2). A person also meets the definition if he has a record of such an impairment or is regarded as having such an impairment.

53. See, for example, *Jacques v. DiMarzio, Inc.*, 386 F.3d 192, 202 (2d Cir. 2004). Although each individual prisoner's disability will vary, many people in administrative segregation may qualify as disabled within the meaning of the disability rights statutes because their mental illnesses significantly impair their ability to interact with others. Indeed, the inability to interact with others, which often results from mental illness, is the main reason that many people are placed in solitary confinement.

54. 28 C.F.R. § 35.130(b)(1)(iii).

55. 28 C.F.R. § 35.130(b)(7).

56. See, for example, *Pierce v. County of Orange*, 526 F.3d 1190, 1220-22 (9th Cir. 2008); *Love v. Westville Corr. Ctr.*, 103 F.3d 558, 560 (7th Cir. 1996).

57. *Love*, 103 F.3d at 560.

58. *Pierce*, 526 F.3d at 1221–22.

59. Indeed, the High Court of Ireland denied the United States' request to extradite a man to face trial in the U.S. on terrorism-related charges based in part on the Court's finding that if convicted and sent to the federal supermax, "[i]t is therefore clear that there is no meaningful judicial review of the conditions of detention and the necessity for same in the U.S.A. . . ." Observing that "the judicial review has to meet certain minimal levels which amount to an independent judicial authority reviewing the merits of and reasons for a prolonged measure of solitary confinement," the court held that "[t]he level of scrutiny by the U.S. courts does not, on the evidence presented by the U.S. authorities, reach that minimal standard." *Attorney General v. Damache*, [2015] IEHC 339, High Court of Ireland, (Donnelly, J.), at ¶ 11.11.18 (May 21, 2015).

Torture of a Student

JEANNE THEOHARIS

*Jeanne Theoharis is Distinguished Professor of Political Science at Brook-
lyn College of the City University of New York. She is the author of numerous books and articles on the civil rights movement, the politics of race
and education, social welfare, and civil rights in post-9/11 America. Her
most recent book is the award-winning biography* The Rebellious Life
of Mrs. Rosa Parks. *When one of her own students was imprisoned on
terrorism-related charges, Theoharis became a leading thinker and activist
around the issue of the treatment of Muslim Americans in the U.S. justice
system, including their frequent incarceration in solitary confinement, both
pretrial and post-conviction.*

JULIE OTSUKA'S SUBLIME NOVEL ON JAPANESE INTERNMENT, *When the
Emperor Was Divine*, devotes nearly a fourth of the story to the trip to
the internment camp.[1] As the families are taken from San Francisco to
the Topaz camp in Utah, the scene grows bleak, more forgotten and
forbidding, if also beautiful outside the train window. The children
peer out the glass looking for wild horses, a spectral freedom.

The two-hour drive south from Denver to the federal supermax
prison in Florence, Colorado, has a similar feel. The mountains loom.

The desert appears. This expanse of land and sky serves as a poignant rebuke to the horror of what happens out here. This is the land of prisons.

I have traveled to this deserted place—this place for the "worst of the worst"—because a former student, Syed Fahad Hashmi, is imprisoned here. I have followed his case and the extensive rights abridgement that he, a U.S. citizen charged with material support to terrorism, encountered in the federal system.

Opened in 1994 as a behavioral management unit where prisoners earned their way in by bad behavior, the U.S. Penitentiary Administrative Maximum, or ADX, houses what the federal government deems its most dangerous prisoners. However, since 9/11, a conviction on any sort of terrorism charge can land a person here.

ADX walls itself off from public scrutiny. Since opening two decades ago, the prison has allowed only a single visit by human rights groups. Two UN special rapporteurs on torture have requested to visit and been denied. Before 9/11, some journalistic access was granted—but from 2002 to 2007, according to a FOIA request, every press request to visit ADX was denied. In 2007, ADX permitted a one-time monitored media event. The author of a 2015 *New York Times* feature on ADX entitled "Inside America's Toughest Federal Prison" actually hadn't been allowed inside at all.[2]

Hunger strikes and hundreds of force feedings have recently taken place at ADX—but they are kept well away from prying human rights eyes or the news media. Few pictures are publicly available of the inside of ADX, as most photos of the cells, hallways, and exercise spaces are governed by protective orders. With little access for journalists or human rights groups over the past decade, the wall of silence is formidable.

Prison rules at ADX stipulate that people must have a preexisting relationship with a prisoner to visit, so that precludes most researchers and human rights experts. But because Fahad was my student, I am allowed to visit.

The visiting room at ADX is eerie, a visiting room without visitors; the expense to come to this remote place (along with its various rules limiting who is allowed to come) makes visits rare. These are non-contact visits—made through thick Plexiglas by talking on the phone. I am permitted no pencil or paper. Locked into a phone-booth-sized cubicle, Fahad sits on a concrete lump; I curl up on the other side of the window in a plastic chair. We have five hours. The calls are taped and there is a camera over our heads recording it all. Periodically, he gets uncomfortable on the concrete and so we both stand. While the sparkle in his eyes that I remember from class has dimmed, he smiles at me repeatedly and is profusely grateful for the visit.

An outspoken Muslim activist, Fahad had been a student in my senior seminar on civil rights at Brooklyn College in 2002. In and out of class, Fahad loved to debate—and believed with a good argument, he could win people over to his cause. Politically active and religiously devout, he held controversial political beliefs. Deeply critical of U.S. foreign policy and the treatment of Muslims at home, his utopia was an Islamic state. In 2002, *TIME Magazine* and *CNN* quoted him at a student meeting praising John Walker Lindh and calling the United States a terrorist.

Graduating from Brooklyn College in 2003, he went to England and got his master's in international relations at London Metropolitan University. In June 2006, he was arrested at London's Heathrow Airport on a U.S. warrant on charges of material support to Al Qaeda. His arrest was blasted across the top of the evening news: *homegrown terrorist, Al Qaeda quartermaster, military gear to the enemy.*

Despite its scary outlines, the news of his case didn't sit right with me. Upon closer examination, his undergraduate political beliefs and activities were a key part of the government's case and initial surveillance of him.³ The charges against him stemmed from allowing a friend, Junaid Babar, to use his cell phone and to stay for two weeks in his London student apartment with luggage containing raincoats, ponchos, and waterproof socks (the "military gear") that Babar later allegedly took to an Al Qaeda leader in Pakistan. Subsequently picked up, Babar became a cooperating witness for the government in numerous terrorism cases in exchange for a reduced sentence, and is now a free man. Fahad, a U.S. citizen fearing the treatment he would receive in U.S. courts and prisons, fought his extradition for eleven months but lost. In May 2007, he was returned to the United States and placed at the Metropolitan Correctional Center (MCC) in lower Manhattan.

A U.S. citizen, Fahad spent three years in solitary confinement before trial at MCC, just miles from where he grew up and where his family lived in Flushing, Queens. One day before trial and one day after the judge granted the government's request for an anonymous jury with extra security, Fahad took a government plea bargain of one count of conspiracy to provide material support. He had knowingly let Babar and his luggage stay in his apartment. Fahad was sentenced to fifteen years and transferred to ADX to begin serving his sentence.

I had been allowed no contact with him for the first four years of his case because the federal government had additionally placed Fahad under Special Administrative Measures (SAMs), which restrict an inmate's communication with the outside world, even before trial. In November 2011, the federal government did not renew those measures. This meant we could correspond. And then I visited.

Barack Obama was elected in 2008 promising to right the course of civil liberties that had gone astray after 9/11. But this is a story of continuing inhumanity and pretrial torture under the law. While attention has focused on abuses at Guantánamo, Abu Ghraib, and other CIA black site prisons, the prosecution and treatment of terror suspects in federal courts and prisons within the United States—and the coercive use of prolonged pretrial isolation and sensory deprivation— have garnered little public investigation.[4] The use of prolonged solitary confinement is a practice the international community deems torture, but its legality in the United States legitimates its use and obscures its horrors.

The terror that struck me going into ADX lasted for days. I was working on a law review essay that used Fahad's case to examine rights protection in the federal system post-9/11. Would this be used against him? Me? Those recently removed SAMs could be reinstituted. Now, as I write this chapter—with the government's fetish for secrecy, capacious definitions of national security, and persecution of whistleblowers—I am filled with worry for his safety and my own and have not shown this essay to him nor consulted with him on it. But to choose to be silent about these inhumane conditions because of this chilling climate carries more far-reaching consequences.

We spent the first visit talking about the conditions he faced those three years at MCC awaiting trial. Located in lower Manhattan and run by the Federal Bureau of Prisons, MCC houses about 750 people facing charges brought by the Southern District of New York. Conditions of confinement at the facility vary significantly depending on the prisoner, and are extreme in their severity for Muslims facing terrorism charges. Former Guantánamo prisoner Ahmed Ghailani was quoted in the *New York Times* as saying that MCC was worse than what he left at Guantánamo.[5] Defense lawyers for other terror suspects at Guantánamo and MCC have affirmed this.[6] The prolonged isola-

tion and sensory deprivation is especially pernicious pretrial, as the inhumanity carries a double blow, degrading a person's health *and* ability
to participate effectively in his own defense.

Fahad Hashmi's incarceration began in solitary confinement in the
Special Housing Unit on the ninth floor. He was permitted only indoor recreation—although a couple times in the first five months, he
was allowed to exercise alone in the prison's exercise kennels on the
roof. Three times a week, he was taken from his solitary cell for a
shower and clean clothes. He was given access to a radio and newspapers, and his whole family could visit him at once.

Five months later, without reason, his conditions worsened. His
conduct while incarcerated both at MCC and in the United Kingdom
(where he had been held in general population at Britain's notorious
Belmarsh Prison) had been without complaint. But Fahad was unwilling to cooperate with the government.

First, he was moved to the more-restrictive 10 South unit of MCC.
The isolation there is relentless. With a shower in the cell, prisoners on
10 South never leave their cell, except for one-hour-a-day recreation,
when granted, in a solitary indoor cage. They took his radio and there
was no television. In the nearly three years he spent in the unit, 10
South held almost exclusively Muslims.

A month after his arrival on 10 South, at the end of October 2007,
the attorney general ordered Fahad Hashmi put under Special Administrative Measures. SAMs are prisoner-specific confinement and
communication rules, imposed by the attorney general but carried out
by the Federal Bureau of Prisons (BOP) if "there is a substantial risk
that a prisoner's communications or contacts with persons could result
in death or serious bodily injury to persons, or substantial damage to
property that would entail the risk of death or serious bodily injury to
persons." A prisoner's SAM spells out in intricate detail the nature of
the isolation and restrictions, including how many pages of paper he
can use to write a letter to his family or what part of the newspaper
he is allowed to have and after what sort of delay. It does not have to
provide reasons for those particular restrictions.

SAMs were introduced in 1996 for people with a demonstrated
reach outside of prison, whose word could inspire violence. The legal
standard was established in *U.S. v. Felipe*, when the Second Circuit
upheld extraordinarily restrictive conditions of confinement imposed
on a leader of the Latin Kings who had a documented history of directing murderous conspiracies from prison. After 9/11, however, the

standards for the application and renewal of SAMs were relaxed considerably. No longer needing to prove reach, an alleged connection to Al Qaeda or other foreign terrorism organization became grounds for applying SAMs.

In later court documents, the government cited as the grounds for Fahad's SAMs: (1) his former membership in an "Islamic fundamentalist organization [ALM] whose members promote the overthrow of Western society" [a group the United States did not designate a terrorist organization]; (2) the fact that he had allowed the cooperating witness to store luggage in his apartment and use his cell phone; and (3) his alleged statements on arrest. So Fahad had been placed under these extraordinary measures for conduct not yet proven by the very entity that was also opposing counsel in the case. Further, part of the justification for his SAMs was *not* dangerous communication with the outside world but angry comments he made to the arresting officers as they threw him to the ground at Heathrow Airport.

Under his SAMs, which remained in effect for the two-and-a-half-year duration of his pretrial detention and through the first fifteen months of his incarceration at ADX, Fahad was allowed no contact with anyone other than his lawyer, his parents, and later his brother. Even talking to other prisoners through the walls could draw punishment. Cells in 10 South are electronically monitored inside and out, which means prisoners shower and use the toilet within view of the camera, and any attempt to talk through the walls is recorded.

Except for one cell, windows in 10 South cells are frosted and let in little natural light. Two and a half years of never going outside and almost no direct sunlight—all *before* any conviction.

MCC is not a modern facility. Lawyers attest the prison is dirty and rundown. Weeks would sometimes go by without a change of clothes or cell-cleaning supplies. The shower in the cell had no curtain, making regular cell cleaning essential to ward off dampness and mold. The unclean nature of the cell was particularly significant for Muslim prisoners who, five times a day, use the floor to pray. The temperature in the cells was under-regulated, making it dreadfully hot in the summer and unbearably cold in the winter, so extreme it was difficult to think. Prisoners report sleeping in layers of clothes to try to keep warm. A light always remained on.[7]

Fahad's SAMs stipulated that he was forbidden any contact—directly or through his attorneys—with the news media. He could read newspapers, but only limited portions approved by his jailers—and not until thirty days after publication. (All references to anything in the Muslim world would be ripped out of his paper.) The lack of news was devastating—to be without news in our modern world is almost to exist outside of time. He was not allowed to write letters to any other civilians except his immediate family.

In many ways, the appearance of redress rather than the possibility of actual remedy underlies the treatment of Muslims facing terrorism charges in the federal system. The existence of pretrial hearings and administrative remedies has led numerous commentators, liberals and conservatives alike (although for very different reasons), to set up a dangerous binary between the unfairness of Guantánamo and the fairness of the federal system. Rights are protected and the federal system is open, most claim, and excesses can be corrected through this legal process. Upon examination, however, the process itself becomes a mechanism to justify and legitimate rights denials. And protesting does little good, except to render a person a troublemaker.

Never one to accept injustice, Fahad protested to the guards, wrote letters to prison officials, and began filing numerous administrative remedies to challenge these conditions. In the legal context, filing an administrative remedy with the appropriate agency is a necessary precursor to bringing a court case. And Fahad—highly educated and feisty—seemed well suited to avail himself of this process for redress, filing numerous administrative remedies on his conditions. All were met with bureaucratic acknowledgment but no substantive remediation. The form's design trivializes the inhumanity documented on it. To have to write in a small third-of-a-page space that your cell is not fit for human habitation effectively diminishes the power of the complaint.

Highlighted throughout many of the remedies Fahad filed was the discrepancy he observed between the treatment Muslims in 10 South and other people held at MCC received. Repeated in the government's response was that this unequal treatment was legitimate based on the (unproven) terrorism charge.

The public can hear about the specifics of his treatment and the unsuccessful remedies he filed only because Fahad is no longer under SAMs. Years after these pretrial injustices occurred and years after they became clear to his lawyer and parents, the particulars of his treatment can now be made known. This reveals another insidious aspect of SAMs: they muzzle everyone around the prisoner—keeping inhumane situations under wraps. Under SAMs, lawyers and immediate family members allowed contact with the inmate are legally *forbidden* to speak about any communication they have had. Put another way, during Fahad's four years under SAMs, no member of the public except for his attorneys and three family members—not a reporter, researcher, or UN expert—was able to communicate with him in any form, even by sending a letter. The few people allowed to communicate with him were also forbidden, under threat of criminal sanction, from speaking to the public about anything he told them.

This creates a wall of silence around the abuses being committed in real time. Indeed, lawyers and family members risk prosecution if they provide any detail from conversations or quotes from the detainee. By way of comparison, part of how the American public came to know what Chelsea Manning was experiencing in the brig or the extent of the hunger strike at Guantánamo was that lawyers and other advocates could reveal certain contents of their conversation with these prisoners to the American public and challenge the government's claims.[8] For people under SAMs this is simply not the case.

The fear of prosecution lurks over every family member, advocate, lawyer, and researcher I know working with prisoners under SAMS.[9] Fahad's parents, who were allowed to visit him sporadically during his time at MCC, were forbidden by the government from saying anything publicly about what they heard from Fahad of his conditions and declining health. Forbidden to say the ways their son was being harmed. Forbidden from talking publicly of the specifics of this legalized torture.

These conditions of prolonged isolation are designed to induce acquiescence.[10] Because the government holds control over the defendant's conditions and the courts have been loath to intervene, the SAMs rig the contest, weakening a person's ability to participate in his own defense. The number of plea bargains in the Justice Department's roster following years of prolonged pretrial solitary confinement suggests the "success" of these practices.

Fahad's defense team challenged the SAMs' application shortly after he was put under them. The judge denied their motion. Following more than a year of SAMs, his defense went back to court in 2009 (just a day after President Obama's executive order ending torture) and made a second challenge to the SAMs. Citing extensive research on the health impacts of prolonged solitary confinement and the impact these conditions imposed on Fahad's ability to participate in his defense, the defense requested a set of modest changes. The judge was unmoved, stating for the record that the measures were "administrative not punitive" and therefore constitutional.

The court's unwillingness to put any limits on the government's treatment of terrorism suspects pretrial was not particular to Fahad's case. Oussama Kassir (held at MCC for eighteen months pretrial) and Muhammad Warsame (held in Minnesota for five and a half years pretrial), both placed under SAMs during the same period, also filed challenges to their SAMs which were heard by different judges. In all three cases, there was no previous criminal conduct or any proven reach outside of prison. Still, the court was unwilling to intervene. The government's claims of national security trumped all.

As the isolation mounted, Fahad's ability to concentrate diminished. Not a large man to begin with, Fahad began losing weight. In court hearings, he seemed less able to concentrate—although his lawyers were tight-lipped, fearing that if they said too much, they could be disciplined. Nine months into the SAMs, Fahad received his first disciplinary infraction for "unauthorized gestures" for doing martial arts in his cell.

Then he was punished for his conduct when he yelled at Eric Holder during the attorney general's visit to the prison. As a result, in the last eight months before trial, because of these infractions, Fahad was not allowed a single family visit. He kept losing weight. His health declined. Finally a doctor put him on Ensure. He was malnourished and dehydrated. After three years of isolation and in poor health, one day before trial and one day after the judge granted the government's request for an anonymous jury, Fahad accepted a government plea bargain of one count of conspiracy to provide material support.

While there has been little outcry within the United States in response to these conditions for people facing terrorism charges, the UN Special Rapporteur on Torture subsequently issued a public statement finding "no justification" for Fahad's prolonged pretrial detention: "[I]t appears that his harsh conditions of detention are related exclusively to the seriousness of the charges he faced. If that is so, then solitary confinement with its oppressive consequences on the psyche of the detainee is no more than a punitive measure that is unworthy of the United States as a civilized democracy."[11]

While public debate has focused on torture as a means, effective or not, to secure information, another application has largely escaped scrutiny. The use of prolonged pretrial solitary confinement helps create the landscape for convictions, because such conditions make it difficult for people to participate effectively in their own defense. And, as groups such as the Center for Constitutional Rights and the Brennan Center for Justice at NYU have noted, such treatment makes it much more likely that people will take a plea rather than risk a lifetime under such isolation. These pretrial conditions are coercive and strategic. In a War on Terror costing billions of dollars that requires evidence of the effectiveness of law enforcement, a record of arrest *and* conviction is paramount.

This pretrial treatment of Muslims follows a forty-year expansion of America's penal state, the skyrocketing use of solitary confinement, and the near-complete discretion granted to prison officials to do whatever they need to do in the name of "public safety" and "national security."[12] It also follows a long history of legalized torture in America. As a growing body of historians have shown, the Fugitive Slave Act, convict leasing, and legal lynching all used the law to validate doing harm to the black body.[13] All were justified as necessary, if unfortunate, treatment to maintain the order and security of the nation amidst unique dangers. All considered the nonwhite body as requiring special measures for discipline and control.

The appearance of a legitimate legal process—of trials and pleas, of pretrial motions and administrative remedies—also sanctions draconian post-conviction incarceration. And so a similar problem occurs with the ADX prison in Colorado as with the MCC jail in New York, as inhumane conditions are deemed necessary, and simultaneously kept from public view.

ADX houses 490 people at capacity. The most restrictive prison in the federal system, ADX was designed to limit prisoner communication. Every prisoner is kept in solitary confinement. ADX prisoners eat all meals alone inside their cells, within arm's length of their toilet. With a small window to the cement "yard," cells have no view of any nature.

Most discussion with guards, doctors, chaplains, or psychiatrists happen through the door. The only "contact" ADX prisoners have with other inmates is attempted shouting through the thick cell walls, doors, toilets, and vents. The only time prisoners are regularly allowed outside of their cells is for an hour of recreation in an indoor cell empty except for a pull-up bar, or an outdoor solitary cage known as a "dog run." Perhaps most significant for many Muslim prisoners such as Fahad, religious practice at ADX is severely limited. Religious services are shown on the closed-circuit television and group prayer—even the most important Friday communal prayer—is completely prohibited.

ADX sharply restricts not only information getting out about conditions there but also information coming in. To keep focused, through subscriptions paid for by his family, Fahad regularly read the *New York Times*, *The Nation*, and *The Economist*. In March 2012, Erica Goode's *New York Times* article "Fighting a Drawn-Out Battle against Solitary Confinement" was taken out of Fahad's paper by ADX officials.[14] In September 2013, I wrote an introduction to a series in *The Nation* on "America After 9/11" that talked about Fahad's case, again taking the risk of making his story public.[15] ADX censored the issue with my article; Fahad was not allowed to see an article that described his own imprisonment.

No federal prisoner has ever successfully challenged his placement in ADX through the administrative remedy program. Legal suits are routinely dismissed at summary judgment. As at Guantánamo and MCC, prisoners have used hunger strikes at ADX and have been subjected to long periods of force feedings, but the public has largely not heard about them in any timely manner because of the secrecy enveloping the prison.

To watch the effects of torture—to bear witness to someone fighting to maintain his equilibrium amidst a slow, persistent torment—is unbearable. For Fahad's family, knowing that this inhumanity was happening just miles from their home when Fahad was at MCC in New York, and being unable to stop it, or even to speak fully about it, was devastating. "My American dream became an American nightmare," his father, who had brought the family from Pakistan when Fahad was small, and all became U.S. citizens, flatly observed. Then Fahad was transferred to ADX. The isolation continued, and for the first six months of his incarceration there, his family did not receive a call or letter from him. His health continued to decline.

The inhumanity of isolation and sensory deprivation takes those aspects nearest and dearest to a person's personality and slowly contorts and corrodes them. To be alone in a concrete box for days, then weeks, then years, to be punished for speaking, to go for months without speaking to anyone but a prison official, is an unimaginable terror.

Slowly, a person shuts down. On my second visit, Fahad was no longer willing to talk about his treatment in prison. It was too difficult and he was not interested in being a supplicant.

Fahad and I have always had political and religious differences. A Salafi Muslim, his utopia was an Islamic state, and he tended to look at the world through the lens of what affected Muslims here and abroad. He left materials encouraging me to convert to Islam in my office mailbox, the only student ever to do this. Unfailingly polite and generous, as a student Fahad held strong beliefs and was an indefatigable debater but was respectful to me and other classmates. Having grown up in New York City, with a sparkle in his eye, he possessed a spunky willingness to challenge authority and the belief that the Bill of Rights protected him.

Solitary confinement has decimated that sparkle and made dialogue of the sort we used to have impossible. Years of sensory deprivation has, unsurprisingly, had the effect of distorting his expression and ways of relating to people. Many letters contain long political and religious diatribes and angry, offensive ramblings about feminism and African American history, homosexuality, global politics, and the situation of Jerusalem. In letters back and forth, and then again during my second visit, we argue. He grows angry when I stress kindness, but then he consistently expresses his gratitude for my work against injustice, for being his teacher and a "real Christian." As numerous researchers have documented, these changes are consistent with what happens to people kept in prolonged isolation.[16]

Worried about how solitary confinement was impairing his ability to concentrate, remember, and interact, Fahad tried to construct a regimen at ADX to control despair and anger: fasting regularly, praying religiously, and reading the Koran daily. He would pace for hours a day in a cell smaller than a New York bathroom: two steps one way, two steps back. He sometimes treated himself to a Snickers bar on Fridays to mark Jummah (the Muslim Sabbath), although the Muslim requirement is that Friday's prayer be with others.

He also took classes, which at ADX are actually television programs shown for one hour a week on the prison's internal TV system. After each class, prisoners are sent a ten-question quiz to fill out. There is no reading, no discussion, no correspondence with the teacher, no papers. Eight to twelve weeks in length, these classes focus on subjects such as: "How the Earth Works," "National Parks," and more recently (and horrifyingly) "The Rights of Man." and "Effective Communication Skills." The first class on the syllabus, "The Magic of Everyday Communication: The Complex Layers of Face-to-Face Talk," boggles the mind in its perverse cruelty for people enduring years of solitary confinement.

At the successful end of the course, the inmate gets a certificate. Fahad, who has a master's degree in international relations, sent me a couple of his—a poignant reminder that the façade is all that must be provided, not actual education that proceeds toward a degree but a taunting mirage. Taking these classes counts toward "good behavior," so prisoners at ADX like Fahad dutifully watch their televisions and fill out their quizzes.

In recent years, there has been repeated outcry regarding America's use of torture: Abu Ghraib, waterboarding, CIA black sites. But in our public imagination, torture is brutal, gruesome, and loud—extralegal and offshore.

Yet in lower Manhattan, in Florence, Colorado, and in penitentiaries across the country, torture resounds in isolation. It proceeds under the law, making it difficult to see and even more difficult to challenge.

Like the worst injustices in U.S. history—from slavery to the stripping of Native American land to segregation to Japanese internment—solitary confinement is horribly legal. The legality of the treatment, the rational "necessity" of these measures, soothed and silenced people then, as it does now. But that history provides a sober caution to the bulwark of "national security" we construct through the law today.

Much like contemporary federal counterterrorism practices, Japanese internment was cast as nonracial and necessary for national security by the government and the courts.[17] The treatment of Japanese Americans, which we now regard with chagrined horror, hardly raised an eyebrow with journalists or most Americans during WWII. In her novel, Julie Otsuka quietly noted the neighbors' acquiescence as the family left for the internment camp. "They had all seen us leave, at the beginning of the war, had peered out through their curtains as we walked down the street with our enormous overstuffed suitcases. But none of them came out."[18]

In June 2014, after spending seven years—a quarter of his life—in solitary confinement, Fahad Hashmi was transferred to the Communication Management Unit in Terre Haute, Indiana. He is serving a fifteen-year sentence and is set to be released in July 2019. He is no longer in solitary confinement.

---

1. Julie Otsuka, *When the Emperor Was Divine* (New York: Anchor, 2003).

2. Mark Binelli, "Inside America's Toughest Federal Prison," *New York Times* (March 26, 2015).

3. For a longer treatment of his case and the extensive rights issues involved, see Laura Rovner and Jeanne Theoharis, "Preferring Order to Justice," *American University Law Review* (2012). For the broader context of surveillance and targeting of Muslim communities in New York and Muslim students in particular, see Matt Appuzzo and Adam Goldman, *Enemies Within: Inside the NYPD's Secret Spying Unit and bin Laden's Final Plot against* America (New York: Touchstone, 2013) and Chris Hawley and Matt Appuzzo, "NYPD Infiltration of Colleges Raises Privacy Fears," AP (October 11, 2011).

4. One exception is Columbia Law School Human Rights Institute and Human Rights Watch, "Illusion of Justice: Human Rights Abuses in U.S. Terrorism Exceptions" (2014). For broader numbers and patterns of government overreach and entrapment, see Trevor Aaronson, *The Terror Factory: Inside the FBI's Manufactured War on Terrorism* (New York: Ig Publishing, 2013).

5. Benjamin Weiser, "Report Shows Detainees Insight into Legal Process," *New York Times* (September 26, 2010).

6. For discussion of MCC 10 South, see Columbia Law School Human Rights Institute and Human Rights Watch, "Illusion of Justice: Human Rights Abuses in U.S. Terrorism Exceptions" (2014), 112–21.

7. Columbia Law School, "Illusion of Justice."

8. For broader discussion of Manning's case and conditions, see Chase Madar, *The Passion of Bradley Manning: The Story Behind the Wikileaks Whistleblower* (New York: Verso, 2013).

9. The reality of punishment for violating SAMs was concretized in the government's prosecution of longtime criminal defense lawyer Lynne Stewart, charged with violating the conditions of Sheikh Abdul-Rahman's SAMs, and the appellate court's order to lengthen her sentence.

10. Owen Fiss, "The War Against Terrorism and the Rule of Law," *Oxford Journal of Legal Studies* (summer 2006), 237.

11. See expert submission to the House of Lords: http://data.parliament .uk/writtenevidence/committeeevidence.svc/evidencedocument/extradition -law-committee/extradition-law/written/12515.html.

12. On mass incarceration and the development of the American penal state, see Ruth Wilson Gilmore, *Golden Gulag: Prisons, Surplus, Crisis and Opposition in Globalizing California* (Berkeley: University of California, 2007); Angela Davis, *Are Prisons Obsolete?* (Open Media: Seven Stories Press, 2003).

13. On slavery, see Craig Wilder, *Ebony and Ivy: Race, Slavery, and the Troubled History of American Universities* (London: Bloomsbury, 2013) and Paul Finkleman et al., *Slavery and the Law* (New York: Rowman and Littlefield, 2001). On convict leasing and the development of the Jim Crow South, see Robert Blackmun, *Slavery by Another Name* (New York: Anchor, 2009) and Robert Perkinson, *Texas Tough: The Rise of America's Prison Empire* (New York: Picador, 2010). On the criminalization of blackness and the Jim Crow North, see Khalil Gibran Muhammad, *Condemnation of Blackness: Race, Crime, and the Making of Modern Urban America* (Cambridge: Harvard University Press, 2010). On lynching, see Equal Justice Initiative, "Lynching in America: Confronting the Legacy of Racial Terror" (2015).

14. Erica Goode, "Fighting a Drawn-Out Battle against Solitary Confinement," *New York Times* (March 30, 2012).

15. Jeanne Theoharis, "Guantánamo in New York City," *The Nation* print edition (October 14, 2013).

16. See Stuart Grassian, "Psychiatric Effects of Solitary Confinement," *Journal of Law and Policy*, 22; Craig Haney, "Counting Casualties in the War on Prisoners," *University of San Francisco Law Review*, 43:1, (Summer 2008); Craig Haney, "A Culture of Harm: Taming the Dynamics of Cruelty in Supermax Prisons," *Criminal Justice and Behavior*, 35, (2008), Expert Report of Dr. Craig Haney, *Silverstein v. Bureau of Prisons*, 07-cv-2471-PAB-KMT (April 13, 2009).

17. See *U.S. v. Hirabayashi* (1943) and *U.S. v. Korematsu* (1944). See discussion in Peter Irons, *A People's History of the Supreme Court* (New York: Penguin, 2006).

18. Otsuka, *When the Emperor Was Divine*, 115.

The California SHU and the End of the World

Lisa Guenther

Lisa Guenther is an associate professor of philosophy at Vanderbilt University in Nashville, and also teaches at Riverbend Maximum Security Institution, including on the state's death row. She is the author of Solitary Confinement: Social Death and Its Afterlives. *Viewing solitary confinement through the lens of philosophy and ethics, Guenther writes of the impact it has on all members of society to subject their fellow human beings and compatriots to what can be called "civil death" or "social death" in isolated prison cells.*

WHAT DOES IT MEAN TO SHARE THE WORLD WITH MILLIONS OF PEOPLE in cages? How does the brute fact of those cages affect the meaning of the world, and of sharing, even for those of us not incarcerated? And at what point does the practice of caging threaten to destroy the very world that it claims to protect?

Philosopher Hannah Arendt reflected on the possibility of a world-destroying violence. In the wake of the Holocaust, and in the midst of the Cold War, she wrote:

> When a people loses its political freedom, it loses its political

reality, even if it should succeed in surviving physically.

What perishes in this case is not a world resulting from production, but one of action and speech created by human relationships. . . . This entire truly human world, which in a narrower sense forms the political realm, can indeed be destroyed by brute force.[1]

Arendt calls this violence "total war." It's a form of violence that is directed not only toward physical bodies but also toward voices, relationships, and the possibility of meaningful action. Total war is an attack on the political realm; it casts some people "outside the common world" by making it almost impossible for them to speak and be heard in public. As such, it collapses the space of mutual appearance that political life presupposes.[2]

There are many ways to destroy the world, not all of which involve an obvious display of brute force. We witnessed such an attack on our common world, and on the promise of politics itself, in the California Department of Corrections' response to the prison hunger strike that took place from July 8 to September 5, 2013.[3]

For decades, California has been a leader in mass incarceration and punitive isolation. By the end of 2010, more than one hundred forty thousand people were behind bars in California and a total of three hundred thousand people were under correctional supervision; that's almost 1 percent of the total state population.[4] Since 2011, California has been in violation of a Supreme Court order to address its prison overcrowding crisis,[5] which has produced conditions so intolerable that they violate the Eighth Amendment ban on cruel and unusual punishment—a notoriously difficult standard to prove in court, as Colin Dayan and others have shown.[6]

In addition to mass incarceration and unconstitutional prison conditions, California isolates close to eleven thousand prisoners for up to twenty-four hours a day in Security Housing Units (SHUs) or Administrative Segregation (Ad-Seg).[7] Among these, three thousand prisoners are isolated indefinitely as a result of being "validated" as gang members.

While the practice of solitary confinement is routinely justified as a necessary tool for prison management, there is a growing consensus among researchers, policy makers, and even some prison officials that extreme isolation does not reduce violence in prison or in the community. Furthermore, solitary confinement is itself a form of violence against the relational structure of being-in-the-world: namely, the interdependence of human beings on each other and on a shared context for meaning. Extreme isolation not only blocks the prisoner's access to other people, it also exploits his or her capacity for social relationships and for the thought, emotion, perception, and action that sociality implies. To put it bluntly, solitary confinement would be no big deal if we were not thinking, feeling creatures who rely on our relationships for a meaningful sense of ourselves. But we are, and we do. By exiling the prisoner from a worldly context within which these capacities could be exercised meaningfully, solitary confinement turns the prisoner's agency and intelligence into a source of suffering rather than strength. As such, the social and sensory isolation of solitary amounts to a living death sentence.[8]

In these pages, I want to reflect on the impact of extreme isolation on the status of the prisoner, not just as a relational being but also as someone who speaks, listens, and—ideally, at least—is heard by others who listen and respond in a meaningful way. This is what it means to share a world: not just the cohabitation of planet Earth, but a sharing of meaning with others, and the creation of a social context for individual experience in language and in our material culture.

Hannah Arendt's account of the world as the space where words and deeds come together to create the sense of reality provides a framework for understanding the violence of excluding a group of people from the shared world and blocking the effectiveness of their words and deeds.

In *The Origins of Totalitarianism*, she reflects on the status of those who have been deprived of their citizenship, and therefore deprived of a meaningful political framework for enforcing their claim to basic human rights, writing, "The fundamental deprivation of human rights is manifested first and above all in the deprivation of a place in the world which makes opinions significant and actions effective."[9]

Without this "place in the world," the stateless person is deprived not just of the right to freedom of expression but also of the right to a voice, the right to exist in a community of others as a person of meaningful words and deeds. The stateless are not just positioned "outside the pale of the law," they are cast out of the common world and condemned to a civil death.

Arendt contrasts the stateless person's loss of "the right to have rights" with the convicted criminal's loss of the right to freedom.[10] From her perspective, the convicted criminal is in a better position than the stateless person because at least he is recognized as a legal subject with a specific (albeit limited) place in the common world.

But Arendt's analysis reaches a limit in the age of mass incarceration, the hyper-incarceration of people of color, widespread felon disenfranchisement, and the indefinite isolation of "Security Threat Groups." When does the convicted criminal cease to be a subject of law and a member of the common world? At what point does the (non)position of the prisoner converge with that of the stateless person, or the "enemy combatant," or the "illegal alien," or any of the other euphemisms we have invented for civil death in the twenty-first century?

"Erring on the Side of Life"

There was a moment in the 2013 California prison hunger strikes when the California Department of Corrections and Rehabilitation (CDCR) declared "total war" against prisoners, even while framing its intervention as an act of life-preserving care.

On August 19, 2013, U.S. District Court Judge Thelton E. Henderson ruled that prisoners on hunger strike in California may be force fed, even if they had signed an advance directive to refuse medical resuscitation. Joyce Hayhoe, a spokesperson for California Correctional Health Care Services, commented on the decision: "It's better to err on the side of life."[11] She cited claims made by the CDCR—and refuted by the Hunger Strike Mediation Team—that some prisoners have been coerced into signing Do Not Resuscitate (DNR) orders by prison gang members.[12]

These claims formed part of the CDCR's broader public relations campaign to discredit the strike action by representing it as a "gang power play." But given the way that gang validation and debriefing policies function as mechanisms of social and civil death within the CDCR, this strategic appeal to gang violence amounts to a criminalization of both the collective resistance and the collective *existence* of people behind bars.[13]

These administrative mechanisms of social and civil death in California prisons were both intensified and obscured by Judge Henderson's "refeeding" order.[14] While the hunger strike ended before any prisoners were actually force fed, the very fact that this law passed constitutes an act of world-destroying state violence, couched in the language of care and protection. The order states the importance of balancing a need for "institutional safety and security" with a respect for "inmate-patient autonomy over their person and the receipt of medical treatment."[15]

> Medical staff are concerned that [the current refeeding policy] does not provide sufficient guidance with respect to when clinicians may refeed in the face of *possible, but uncertain*, coerced participation in the strike or coerced execution of "do not resuscitate" directives.[16]

Here, as in official CDCR documents, the prison administration represents itself as a provider of care, security, and other life-supporting services to an inmate-patient clientele, while absolving itself from any meaningful sense of responsibility for the survival and well-being of hunger strikers. In effect, it gives these protesters two options: consent to be force fed, or consent to die.[17]

But Judge Henderson's refeeding order goes even further; it removes the latter option, mobilizing the language of respect for "inmate-patient autonomy" and a concern for the possible (but uncertain) "coercion" of prisoners as an alibi for *disrespecting* the autonomy of prisoners and *coercing* them to be fed against their will.

And not just against their will. The refeeding order also undermines the meaning and efficacy of their words in a document that, if it were signed by anyone else, would have a legally binding status. In this sense, it perpetuates the civil death of prisoners and intensifies the de facto "status crime" of existing as a validated gang member and daring to resist, even at the cost of your health and even your life.

The refeeding order recognizes three basic conditions under which a hunger striker's DNR directive could be rendered invalid:

> For purposes of this order, a previously executed "do not resuscitate" directive will not be considered valid if a) the CME [chief medical examiner], reasonably and in good faith, determines it was the result of coercion or otherwise not the product of the hunger striker's free will when executed; b) a court has determined the directive is invalid as a matter of law; or c) the hunger striker, or an attorney-in-fact for the hunger striker acting pursuant to a properly executed power of attorney, revokes such directive.[18]

While the second two conditions seem reasonable enough, the first introduces what we could call a "subjective component" into the evaluation of the validity of DNR directives. The chief medical examiner is granted the authority to revoke a prisoner's signed directive if he determines, "reasonably and in good faith," that it was not the product of the prisoner's "free will." How he manages to discern the true contents of this will, we will never know; we would have to slice through the metaphysical paradox of a free will whose self-knowledge and self-expression depends on the reasonable judgment of another to "validate" it.

But this is not about truth, it's about power. Or rather, it's about the power to determine the truth. This refeeding order grants the chief medical examiner (at least the possibility of) a reasonable mind, while the hunger striker is both granted and denied a "free will" to make his own autonomous decisions.

And that's not all. The refeeding order continues:

> In addition, in view of the risk that inmates may be or have been coerced into participating in the hunger strike, for purposes of this order a "do not resuscitate" directive executed by a participant in the hunger strike *at or near the beginning of or during the strike* will be deemed not valid.[19]

In other words, the only way a prisoner could issue a DNR directive that would *not* be undermined by this clause is by signing that directive long before the current hunger strike began, or after it has ended. Anyone who signs such a directive *"at or near the beginning of or during the strike* will be deemed not valid." No matter that copies of advance directive and POLST forms were distributed to hunger strikers *three weeks after* the strike action began, as part of the CDCR's former hunger strike policy![20] If a prisoner had not made up his mind to sign an advance directive well in advance of any actual hunger strike, his decision will be rendered invalid, nominally for the sake of respecting his autonomous will and protecting him from the coercive power of gang members (even if he, too, has been "validated" as a gang member).

In this way, the "free will" of the hunger striker is not just *subordinated* to the "reasonable" mind of the CME; any semblance of a will, free or conditioned, is canceled out by the very fact of participating in the strike action. To put this differently: if you dare to exercise your will in a way the CDCR does not approve—even if it causes no harm to anyone but yourself—your will, your capacity to express that will, and your right to have the legal expression of your will respected by others will be invalidated.

Again, this is more than disrespect for the prisoners' individual autonomy; it is criminalization of the hunger strikers' resistance and existence, a disqualification of their mind, their will, and their capacity for meaningful speech.

Judge Henderson's authorization of the refeeding order compounds the civil death of prisoners, even as it claims to "protect" them from the harm of biological death. It not only compromises their autonomy as individuals, it also—and more importantly—undermines their capacity to enter into a binding legal agreement, to make their words speak and be heard in a document that carries legal and social weight. It withdraws their legal competence to speak for themselves, regardless of their mental or physical health.

This was not the first time Judge Henderson has issued a legal decision that perpetuates the social and civil death of prisoners, even while invoking a rhetorical respect for human dignity. In *Madrid v. Gomez* (1995), Henderson ruled that:

> Conditions in the SHU may well hover on the edge of what is humanly tolerable for those with normal resilience, particularly when endured for extended periods of time. They do not, however, violate exacting Eighth Amendment standards, except for the specific population subgroups identified in this opinion [i.e., for the mentally ill].[21]

The "population subgroups" Henderson identified as deserving of protection from cruel and unusual punishment were 1) prisoners who are already mentally ill, and 2) prisoners who are at "unreasonably high risk" of becoming mentally ill if held in SHU conditions (at 1267). By limiting Eighth Amendment protection to those already suffering from mental illness or recognizably on the verge of it, Henderson created a loophole into which virtually every prisoner could fall.

In brief: If you are already mentally ill or "unreasonably" close to mental illness (whatever that means, and however it is measured), you are protected from conditions that would exacerbate your condition. You are recognized as a human being, with an intrinsic dignity that no civilized nation would dare to violate. But if you are not (yet) mentally ill—if you display "normal resilience" to barely tolerable conditions—then you may be confined in a situation that is acknowledged by psychiatrists such as Craig Haney and Stuart Grassian to *produce* mental illness. In other words: Unless you can obtain a diagnosis of mental illness, you may be subject to conditions that typically produce mental illness.

Colin Dayan develops a brilliant analysis of *Madrid v. Gomez* and other cases in *The Story of Cruel and Unusual* and *The Law Is a White Dog*. She has also commented on the new refeeding order in an article for Al Jazeera America.[22] In an interview with Jill Stauffer for *The Believer*, Dayan warns: "We have invented a new form of death" in spaces of indefinite detention and extreme isolation like the SHU and Guantánamo Bay.[23]

But we have also invented a new form of life: a life that is allowed neither to flourish nor to pass away; a life both dangerous enough to be locked down twenty-three hours a day, and fragile enough to warrant care and protection as an inmate-patient, even when he has explicitly refused such care. The speaking-being of such a life is invalidated in advance, condemned to both a (social and civil) death and an irremissible biological life under the protection and control of the state.

This is a classic case of what French philosopher Michel Foucault calls biopower: the power to make live and let die. The CDCR reserves the right to "make" prisoners live, even if they have refused nourishment and signed a legal document requesting not to be fed, even after they have lost consciousness and are no longer able to speak.

But it goes even further: the CDCR *would not even let the hunger strikers die*, at least not on their own terms, as expressed by their own will, both in a legal document and in a collective effort to reclaim some meaning for words like *freedom* and *self-determination*.

This is a particularly intense form of biopower. It is the power to make live and *not* to let die; the power to issue a (social and civil) death sentence under the cover of care, protection, and respect for the autonomy of the individual's "free will."

A system that neither lets you live nor lets you die is not "erring on the side of life." It is deploying life as an instrument and alibi for death. And it is undermining the very foundation of law in a respect for the binding word of another. As President Obama said of the hunger strikers at Guantánamo, "I don't want these individuals to die."[24] But there is no rule of law without a respect for the other's binding word.

In effect, the refeeding order authorized by Henderson transfers the silence of "brain death" and biological death into the living, breathing, resistant life of hunger strikers by undermining the power of their words to bind the actions of others, to make a claim on the institution of the prison and the courts, and to exercise even the minimal social power to let themselves die.

Force feeding prisoners—whether at Guantánamo Bay or in the California prison system—does not err on the side of life. It errs *against* life, and against the social relations that make life meaningful and, quite frankly, bearable.

Political life is grounded in the possibility of conversation, on the exchange of meaningful words. And you can't talk with a tube shoved down your throat.

---

1. Hannah Arendt, *The Promise of Politics*, ed. Jerome Kohn (New York: Schocken, 2005), 161–62.

2. Hannah Arendt, *Origins of Totalitarianism* (New York: Harcourt, Brace, Jovanovich, 1973), 302.

3. Prisoner Hunger Strike Solidarity (2011), http://prisonerhungerstrike solidarity.wordpress.com/. Accessed on August 5, 2013.

4. California Department of Corrections and Rehabilitation. http://www .cdcr.ca.gov/Reports_Research/Offender_Information_Services_Branch/ Annual/CalPris/CALPRISd2010.pdf. Accessed on August 5, 2013.

5. http://www.nytimes.com/2011/05/24/us/24scotus.html?hp. Accessed on August 6, 2013.

6. Colin Dayan, *The Story of Cruel & Unusual* (Boston: MIT Press, 2007).

7. http://solitarywatch.com/faq/. Accessed on August 15, 2013.

8. http://opinionator.blogs.nytimes.com/2012/08/26/the-living-death-of -solitary-confinement/. Accessed on August 7, 2013.

9. Arendt, *Origins of Totalitarianism*, 296.

10. Ibid., 296.

11. http://www.reuters.com/article/2013/08/20/us-usa-california -hungerstrike-idUSBRE97I0ZV20130820. Accessed on August 10, 2013.

12. http://prisonerhungerstrikesolidarity.wordpress.com/2013/08/21/day -45-statement-from-the-mediation-team/. Accessed on August 6, 2013.

13. For an argument in support of this claim, see Lisa Guenther, "Social Death and the Criminalization of Resistance in the California Prison Hunger Strikes" (August 2, 2013), Truthout, http://truth-out.org/opinion/item/17948-social

-death-and-the-criminalization-of-resistance-in-the-california-prison-hunger
-strikes. Accessed on August 2, 2013.

14. http://www.scribd.com/doc/161727249/Order-Granting-Joint
-Request-Authorizing-Refeeding. Accessed on August 2, 2013.

15. Ibid., 2.

16. Ibid., 2, emphasis added.

17. http://www.nytimes.com/2013/04/15/opinion/hunger-striking-at
-guantanamo-bay.html?_r=0. Accessed on August 12, 2013.

18. Refeeding Order, http://www.scribd.com/doc/161727249/Order-Gra
nting-Joint-Request-Authorizing-Refeeding, 4.

19. Ibid., 4, emphasis added.

20. CCHCS Mass Hunger Strike, Fasting, & Refeeding Care Guide, 3, http://
www.cphcs.ca.gov/docs/careguides/MassHungerStrikeCareGuide2012-10-4
.pdf. Accessed on August 10, 2013.

21. *Madrid v. Gomez.* 889 F.Supp. 1146 (N.D. Cal. 1995), at 1280.

22. http://america.aljazeera.com/articles/2013/8/21/fear-and-hunger
-inpelicanbay.html. Accessed on August 22, 2013.

23. http://www.believermag.com/issues/201302/?read=interview_dayan.
Accessed on August 20, 2013.

24. http://www.nytimes.com/2013/05/01/opinion/president-obama-and
-the-hunger-strike-at-guantanamo.html?_r=0. Accessed on August 13, 2013.

Afterword: Exposing Torture

Juan E. Méndez

I WANTED TO BECOME A LAWYER FROM THE AGE OF FIFTEEN. I LIKED THE idea of defending workers and springing people from jail. I guess it was always political, but by the time I started practicing law in the early 1970s, the situation in Argentina under the military dictatorship was so bad, it couldn't be anything but political.

It started with death threats. First they painted RIP—in Spanish it's QEPD—on the building I worked in. Then my name started showing up on walls all over town: "Death to Juan Méndez." It became obvious that the town where I lived, Mar del Plata, was too small for someone doing this kind of work. At first the threats came from thugs or armed groups. It was when the police got involved that I knew I had to leave.

So I moved to Buenos Aires when I was about thirty years old. A small group of us worked together, filling habeas corpus writs, submitting petitions. Most importantly, we tried to find out where people were taken to be tortured. We hoped we could stop it. Then, in 1975, I was arrested myself.

In the first two or three days I was moved to at least three different locations. They needed to shift me around because if a judge found them and broke into a place like that, a lot of people would have been in trouble. My father came to the first location and was chased away at gunpoint. So they were careful to move me around. Unfortunately, though, they had plenty of places to go.

What I endured was a combination of physical and psychological torture. The psychological made the physical much worse. They used the *picana*, the electric prod, on me and told me, "We have your children; we're going to do this to them next." I really had no way of knowing whether it was true. The threats I could withstand, but combined with violence . . . There was a moment when I almost faltered and started giving them names. Almost.

They picked me up before there was really a policy of "disappearance." There were just a few isolated cases, mostly the really well-known lawyers, a little older than me. A few had already been killed; some were in exile. But at this point that was still rare. Later, during what came to be called the "Dirty War" in Argentina, tens of thousands would be abducted, imprisoned, and killed.

They tried to charge me with car theft and possession of weapons, but when the owner of the car didn't even recognize me, the judge decided to clear me. Then, the government immediately stepped in and put me under administrative detention. This also become common in those years: no trial, no charges, they just held people indefinitely.

When we arrived at the prison, they took us straight to solitary—for two or perhaps three weeks. The cells were spare—no window, just an opaque piece of glass, a hole in the ground for your toilet, and a slab for your bed. That's it. No reading materials, just your clothes, and the food was delivered through a slot in the door. They were always spying on us, trying to break us down. That was the purpose of isolation.

I knew about an organization called Amnesty International, so the first time my family was able to visit I suggested they write them. I became the first Prisoner of Conscience from Argentina that Amnesty adopted after the coup. After eighteen months of detention, the majority in general population, I was suddenly released. My wife and children were waiting in the United States, so that was the logical place to go—and there I hoped I would have the opportunity to speak out for the others. A year after I was arrested a good friend of mine was burned to death in his car by a right-wing group. Another friend was disappeared, and never reappeared. So I felt responsible for the others. I'd had so many lucky breaks.

After forty years of working on human rights, I was appointed to the position of United Nations Special Rapporteur on Torture and Other Cruel, Inhuman or Degrading Treatment or Punishment in 2010. I'm now on my second (and last) three-year term. The special rapporteur's mandate calls for me to transmit urgent appeals to states with regard to individuals reportedly at risk of torture, to undertake fact-finding country visits, and to submit annual reports to the Human Rights Council and the General Assembly.

The issue of solitary confinement came to me early in this position, when I received complaints about Bradley (later, Chelsea) Manning. I started looking into her case, and it seemed to me incredibly cruel to make someone who had not even been charged spend so much time alone—first in Iraq and then at Quantico. Although the Pentagon never called her condition solitary confinement, it did agree to the general features: twenty-two to twenty-three hours a day alone, one hour of exercise alone in a larger cell. The Pentagon called it "prevention of harm watch." But when I asked, "Are you saying he's suicidal?" the response was, "We can't tell you that." The other rationale I was given for her isolation was the severity of her crime—which in and of itself is a violation. We all have the right to the presumption of innocence.

Precisely because as special rapporteur I have such a large mandate—exposing torture wherever it may take place—the most I can do is select areas where I think I will have an impact. The case of solitary confinement is interesting because when I wrote my report on solitary confinement in 2011 I had no idea it would have such resonance. My report stated unequivocally that twenty-two or twenty-three hours a day alone in a prison cell for more than fifteen days at a time can cause permanent, lasting psychological damage and can constitute torture. It was surprising, and encouraging, how quickly people picked it up, and how far they've been able to take it.

Prior to my report, international law had been largely silent on the issue, in terms of what constitutes solitary confinement, when these conditions can be considered "cruel, inhuman and degrading treatment," and when they are in fact torture. In human rights we talk about hard and soft law—a treaty, for example, is hard law; it's binding for the signatory countries. My report is the softest of soft law, just recommendations really, but it can be authoritative if there's enough pressure behind it.

Whether solitary confinement is considered torture is partially an issue of intent. "Cruel, inhuman and degrading treatment" can be the result of pure negligence; for example, conditions of overcrowding. Yet if you *deliberately* subject a prisoner or captive to extreme pain and suffering, even if your *reasons* are considered good or valid—to discipline, for example, or solve a crime—the fact that the decision was made intentionally is what makes it torture.

In my opinion, indefinite isolation is *always* torture, and there's also a question of degree. The science we have shows that the mind starts working differently after fifteen days in solitary, so my report specifies that any period over fifteen days should be subject to stringent review. If a prisoner has books, the ability to write and receive letters, television, and family visits—then maybe the period can be extended to thirty days maximum, but only when that is absolutely necessary. It has to be counted in days, maybe weeks, but never months and definitely not years.

The public generally associates torture with physical violence; they sometimes have a hard time accepting that there are equally brutal forms of mental torture. It's interesting though—back in the 1940s and 1950s, when stories came out about communist regimes holding prisoners in isolation for very long periods of time, we had no problem calling that torture.

Different people will react differently to the same conditions. For juveniles and the mentally ill, I've recommended a complete ban on isolation. But the essential thing is that when you subject someone to these conditions, you don't know how he or she is going to react. One person may be more or less okay; the next may have permanent mental damage. The state is not allowed to speculate. If there's a chance that someone may suffer irreversible effects, then the state is responsible.

Another huge problem we have is that the information we have access to is very limited and anecdotal. The public has a right to know how many people are in solitary in this country, for how long, and the reasons they've been put there. The best estimate we have is that there are eighty thousand people in isolation in U.S. prisons on any given day, but no one knows that for sure. It could be fewer, and it could be far more.

I think it is safe to say that the United States uses solitary confinement more extensively than any other country, for longer periods, and with fewer guarantees. Over the past thirty years, there's been huge overcrowding in U.S. prisons due to the explosion of the incarcerated population. This has resulted in more violence in prisons, and we've seen solitary confinement mushroom. In cases like California, we know that they have sent prisoners to solitary based on their "association" with gangs. Up until the recently announced reform, California uses isolation more than any other state in terms of sheer numbers. Even recognizing that the state has a responsibility to deal with prison violence and with gang affiliation doesn't suspend our long-revered principles of due process and presumption of innocence. When people go to prison they don't surrender all their rights.

In the federal system, solitary is used extensively in counterterrorism cases. If somebody is extradited from Europe, for example, they will likely spend three years in isolation before even being tried. In those cases solitary is used to try and break their will, force them to accept a plea with perhaps a twenty-year sentence. Using isolation as a way of extracting confession is clearly prohibited in the Convention Against Torture, to which the United States is a signatory. The United States was voted into the Human Rights Council—a position that carries with it an obligation to cooperate.

The United States is a very isolationist country. There is a sense that U.S. sovereignty demands not accepting the decisions of any courts over its own. The United States may come back to pushing for good human rights practices around the world, but first it's going to have to change its own practices. Other countries look to the United States for how it does things, and how we in the United States build and run our prisons is no exception to that. That is why reforming prisons is so urgent, and the most urgent issue is solitary confinement, because in a real way the whole system relies on it. I think it would be ideal if we could litigate by attacking the practice of solitary as a whole, but the reality is that the chances of getting movement on a global or even national basis is close to nil. And so we're stuck with chipping away at different aspects, state by state, lawsuit by lawsuit, and hopefully slowly shrinking the problem.

It's interesting that we're completing this anthology at this very important moment. Just two weeks ago as of this writing President Obama announced a general call for prison reform, specifically denounced the use of solitary confinement, and called for a nationwide review. The review will be conducted by the Department of Justice and I'm assuming it will be a serious one. What they must do is gather all the data we need to properly inform the public as to how many people are in solitary confinement in the United States, for what reasons, for what length of time, and the damage it's done to these many individuals. This has the possibility of leading to serious reform, at least within the federal prison system; which could, in turn, compel other states to follow suit.

The recent statement by Supreme Court Justice Kennedy is also very encouraging. He called for a review of the constitutionality of solitary confinement. Kennedy is inclined to apply international law standards within the United States, which is a very good indication of how he might rule in a case. So sooner or later the Supreme Court is going to have to deal with this issue.

Now, I'm not saying the fight is over—not at all. Whether or not this results in serious change depends entirely on all of us, those of us who have been pushing so hard for so long. At this point, we have no idea what the proposed limits will be. My hope, of course, is that the reforms will be comprehensive; that they will limit disciplinary solitary confinement to fifteen days at a time; abolish indefinite solitary confinement; and ban even a single day for children, people with mental disabilities (even those acquired while in prison), and pregnant women.

It's not going to be easy. The system has maintained this practice for many years in the shadows and there are powerful actors who don't want to see this change happen. In my case, the indefinite nature of my detention was difficult because at my lowest moments I feared the worst. There are many, many prisoners in that same position in the United States today. There was always hope, for me, that the end could be right around the corner. That pressure from the outside would force the Argentinian government to show a better face to the world. I believe that the same pressure is showing results here. I do think this could be a turning point; it's up to us.

Acknowledgments

WE TRIED AS MUCH AS POSSIBLE NOT TO WRITE THIS BOOK IN ISOLATION. Many people have contributed in many ways.

Sarah thanks Nora Dye, Sakura Saunders, Aaron Juchau, Kelly Winter, Marie Morley, and Jennifer Doan for transcribing letters and interviews with prisoners. Thanks to Jonathan Simon of University of California, Berkeley, for providing office space and to Shirin Azadi, Azadeh Zohrabi, Dorsey Nunn, Dolores Canales, Francisco Cacique, and others for helping with logistics and accommodation during prison visits. Thanks to Bonnie Kerness, Carol Stickman, Penny Schoner, Carol Travis, Bernadette Rabuy, and Olga Tomchin for introducing me to some of the writers inside prison who contributed to this anthology. Thanks to Jackie Sumell and Angad Bhalla for access to recordings of and letters from the late Herman Wallace.

Jean and Jim thank all the supporters of Solitary Watch who make possible our contact with people in prison, from which many of the pieces in this book are drawn. Special thanks to Bill Murray, Neil Getnick, Ralph Nader, Caroline Ramsay-Merriam, Gordon Roddick, Jon Utley, and Bill Zabel for your steadfast and generous support. Thanks also to the Flom Family Foundation and the Puffin Foundation, along with hundreds of individual donors, for supporting our Lifelines to Solitary project, which helps us reach out to people in isolation.

We all wish to thank The New Press and Diane Wachtell for your faith in our project, and Jed Bickman for being everything we could want in an editor. Special thanks to Molly Crabapple for the powerful cover drawing. Most of all, our gratitude to all of the contributors: this is your book.

About the Editors

Jean Casella is a co-director of Solitary Watch, a web-based watchdog project, and a Soros Justice Fellow. She is the editor of two previous anthologies and lives in Brooklyn, New York.

James Ridgeway has been an investigative journalist for more than fifty years and is the author of seventeen previous books. He is a co-director of Solitary Watch and a Soros Justice Fellow. He lives in Washington, D.C.

Sarah Shourd, a journalist and playwright, was held as a political hostage by the Iranian government, including 410 days in solitary, an experience she chronicled in *A Sliver of Light: Three Americans Imprisoned in Iran*. She lives in Oakland, California.

About Solitary Watch

Founded in 2009 in response to what was then a largely invisible domestic human rights crisis, **Solitary Watch** is a national watchdog group that investigates, reports on, and disseminates information on the use of solitary confinement in U.S. prisons and jails. Its mission is to provide the public—as well as attorneys, scholars, corrections officials, policy makers, educators, advocates, and currently and formerly incarcerated people and their families—with the first centralized source for background research, unfolding news, and original investigative reporting on solitary confinement.

To learn more about solitary confinement, and about current campaigns to end or limit its use, visit www.solitarywatch.org.